Word as Action

RACINE, RHETORIC, AND THEATRICAL LANGUAGE

MICHAEL HAWCROFT

CLARENDON PRESS · OXFORD

1992

Oxford University Press, Walton Street, Oxford OX2 6DP
Oxford New York Toronto
Delhi Bombay Calcutta Madras Karachi
Petaling Jaya Singapore Hong Kong Tokyo
Nairobi Dar es Salaam Cape Town
Melbourne Auckland
and associated companies in
Berlin Ibadan

Oxford is a trade mark of Oxford University Press

Published in the United States
by Oxford University Press, New York

British Library Cataloguing in Publication Data
Data available

Library of Congress Cataloging-in-Publication Data
Hawcroft, Michael.
Word as action: Racine, rhetoric, and theatrical language/
Michael Hawcroft.
(Oxford modern languages and literature monographs)
Includes bibliographical references and index.
1. Racine, Jean, 1639–1699—Technique.   2. Rhetoric—1500–1800.
3. Tragedy.   I. Title.   II. Series.
PQ1909.H38 1992   842'.4—dc20   91-26152
ISBN 0-19-815185-3

Typeset by Best-set Typesetter Ltd., Hong Kong
Printed and bound in Great Britain by
Biddles Ltd., Guildford and King's Lynn

FOR MY PARENTS

Les actions sont l'âme de la tragédie, où l'on ne doit parler qu'en agissant et pour agir.

(Pierre Corneille)

The orator stands armed for battle, ever ready for the fray, and his eloquence will no more fail him in the courts than speech will fail him in domestic affairs and in the daily concerns of his life.

(Quintilian)

Acknowledgements

In preparing this book I have contracted many debts, which I gratefully acknowledge. The Department of Education and Science, St Cross College, and the University of Oxford gave financial support. The publishers of *The Modern Language Review* have granted permission to re-use in Chapter 6 some material which first appeared in an article of mine in that periodical. Brendan Biggs and Christopher Zealley offered practical help with word processors and proof-reading. Christopher J. Smith scrutinized and corrected my translations from Latin. Denys Potts, as the original supervisor of the thesis on which this book is based, Richard Parish, and Valerie Worth all took an encouraging interest in my work and made helpful suggestions. Latterly Ian Maclean has been a most generous and painstaking reader, saving me from errors and significantly improving the presentation of what follows. My greatest debt however is to David Maskell, who supervised my thesis during its later stages. His willingness to discuss my work in detail and at length over many years has set an example of scholarly selflessness for which I am enormously grateful. The book's inadequacies are to be laid at my own door: I did not always take the advice which was so generously given.

Keble College   M.N.H.
Oxford
1990

Contents

Note

EDITIONS

Unless it is otherwise stated, the following editions have been used: for Racine's plays and prefaces, the *Théâtre complet* by J. Morel and A. Viala; for Racine's other writings, the *Œuvres complètes* by R. Picard; for Pierre Corneille's plays, the *Œuvres complètes* by G. Couton; and for Corneille's critical writings, his *Writings on the Theatre*, edited by H. T. Barnwell. For publishing details about these editions and for details about the editions of other dramatists used, see the Bibliography.

LINE REFERENCES

Line references to plays are given as the number of the line or lines without the abbreviations 'l.' and 'll.'.

ORTHOGRAPHY AND PUNCTUATION

I have maintained the orthography and punctuation of all the works from which I quote. Inconsistencies in seventeenth-century spelling and punctuation have therefore not been removed.

TRANSLATIONS

Quotations from French works are in the original language. Quotations from works written in Latin are given first in Latin and then in translation. The translations used are listed in the Bibliography; if no translation is listed there, the translation is my own. Quotations from Greek works are given only in translation.

Abbreviations

The following abbreviations have been used for periodicals.

AJFS	*Australian Journal of French Studies*
DSS	*Dix-septième siècle*
FS	*French Studies*
IL	*L'Information littéraire*
JR	*Jeunesse de Racine*
MLR	*Modern Language Review*
PFSCL	*Papers in French Seventeenth-Century Literature*
RHLF	*Revue d'histoire littéraire de la France*
SCFS	*Seventeenth-Century French Studies*

Introduction

Je n'ai rien vu, mais j'ai entendu force paroles.

(Saint-Preux in *La Nouvelle Héloïse*, 230)

The eleven tragedies of Jean Racine have served as a testing-ground for the different approaches to the study of literature that have proliferated since 1945.[1] Among many examples are R. C. Knight's study of the relationship of Racine's plays to those of his ancient Greek predecessors,[2] L. Goldmann's Marxist analysis,[3] C. Mauron's psychoanalytical study,[4] R. Jasinski's attempt to find connections between Racine's life and his works,[5] and R. Barthes's structuralist analysis of the anthropology of Racine's tragic world.[6] More recent criticism includes thematic approaches like M. Delcroix's study of the sacred elements in the profane tragedies[7] and I. Heyndels's survey of tragic conflict in the plays,[8] as well as linguistically based approaches like N. C. Ekstein's narratological analysis of narrative passages in the plays.[9] Over the years the student of Racine has had to acquire a good many critical languages. Although these languages can contain radically different vocabularies, their users often seem to share similar preoccupations. One is the attempt to describe what is tragic in Racine's tragedies. Another is the aim of defining the poetic qualities of the plays. Both preoccupations can be seen skilfully interwoven in E. Vinaver's writings on Racine.[10]

It is not my aim to be preoccupied with either the tragic or the poetic qualities of Racine's plays, though the Conclusion will make some contribution to the discussion of the former. Nor do I

---

[1] See J. Racine, *Théâtre complet*, ed. J. Morel and A. Viala (Paris, 1980), 763.

[2] *Racine et la Grèce* (Paris, 1951).

[3] *Le Dieu caché* (Paris, 1959).

[4] *L'Inconscient dans l'œuvre et la vie de Racine* (Aix-en-Provence, 1957).

[5] *Vers le vrai Racine*, 2 vols. (Paris, 1958).

[6] *Sur Racine* (Paris, 1963).

[7] *Le Sacré dans les tragédies profanes de Racine* (Paris, 1970).

[8] *Le Conflit racinien* (Brussels, 1985).

[9] *Dramatic Narrative: Racine's 'Récits'* (New York, 1986).

[10] *Racine et la poésie tragique* (Paris, 1963); *L'Action poétique dans le théâtre de Racine* (Oxford, 1960); *Entretiens sur Racine* (Paris, 1984).

employ any of the critical languages mentioned above. Instead I adopt two other critical approaches which have been followed before, the rhetorical[11] and the theatrical,[12] and, by deploying them simultaneously, I hope to make new statements about Racinian rhetoric and theatricality which may to some extent modify currently held views about Racine's theatre.

Above all, I hope that the combination of the rhetorical and theatrical perspectives will provide some insight into the success of Racine's tragedies *on the stage*. Most of the studies mentioned give no heed to what should surely be a central concern of students of drama: namely, how does the dramatist seek to secure the attention of his audience for the duration of the performance? Unless a dramatist can do that, he cannot know success. J.-P. Sartre explains why: 'Le théâtre, étant une entreprise coûteuse et dont le rendement doit être immédiat, exige qu'une pièce réussisse sur l'heure ou qu'elle disparaisse . . . Un livre recrute peu à peu son public. Une pièce de théâtre est forcément "théâtrale", parce que l'auteur sait qu'il se fera applaudir ou siffler sur-le-champ.'[13] S. W. Dawson elaborates further:

It is characteristic of drama as of no other form of literature, that it makes an absolute and sustained demand on our attention . . . A play in performance demands our uninterrupted attention, not only for our own sakes, but for the sake of other members of the audience. Sitting in silence without conspicuous movement for as long as an hour and a half is a considerable achievement, possible for most of us only when our attention is entirely engrossed. It follows that the dramatist's primary responsibility is to seize and hold our attention.[14]

Racine knew that he had to write in such a way as to capture the interest of a theatre audience. His prefaces show him to be highly conscious of his spectators' desire to be entertained. On more than

---

[11] Most notably by P. France in *Racine's Rhetoric* (Oxford, 1965).

[12] Most notably by A. Capatti in *Teatro e 'imaginaire'* (Rome, 1975). H. T. Barnwell's scrutiny of plot-construction in *The Tragic Drama of Corneille and Racine* (Oxford, 1982) is an important contribution to one aspect of the plays' appeal in the theatre. Barnwell provides the basis for a theatrical reading of Corneille in '"They have their exits and their entrances": Stage and Speech in Corneille's Drama', *MLR* 81 (1986), 51–63.

[13] 'L'Auteur, l'œuvre et le public', in *Un théâtre de situations*, ed. M. Contat and M. Rybalka (Paris, 1973), 91–103 (p. 92).

[14] *Drama and the Dramatic* (London, 1970), 12.

one occasion he defends himself against the charges of his critics by referring to the reaction of the spectators in the theatre. He asks the critics of *Alexandre* what they have to complain about when he has been 'assez heureux pour faire une pièce qui les a peut-être attachés malgré eux depuis le commencement jusqu'à la fin' (p. 72). When the ending of *Britannicus* is attacked for extending beyond the news of the death of the hero, Racine observes that 'on l'écoute pourtant, et même avec autant d'attention qu'aucune fin de tragédie' (p. 255).[15] Despite the obvious need for the dramatist to be a master of theatrical technique, critical studies of Racine, with a few notable exceptions,[16] have tended either to ignore this aspect of his work or to take it for granted. Recently, however, D. Maskell has published a wide-ranging study of Racine's qualities as an *homme de théâtre*,[17] laying particular stress on the material and visual aspects of theatricality. The present work concentrates on the theatricality of discourse and, by focusing on the interaction of the rhetorical and the theatrical in the plays, highlights some of those features with which Racine sought to secure 'l'attachement de l'auditeur à l'action présente'.[18]

Gone, fortunately, are the days when rhetorical studies of writers had to be vigorously defended against the prejudices of the learned and not-so-learned, for whom rhetoric had associations of insincerity and bombast.[19] The pejorative associations still persist in popular usage. But over the last thirty or so years critics have seen in rhetoric, which was the basis of a normal education from classical times to the nineteenth century, an apparently comprehensive system and terminology suitable for the analysis of texts. What had for centuries been used primarily as a system for the

[15] See also the preface to *Bérénice* (p. 325).
[16] In addition to the studies by Capatti and Barnwell there are: G. Le Bidois, *De l'action dans la tragédie de Racine* (Paris, 1900); G. May, *Tragédie cornélienne, tragédie racinienne* (Urbana, Ill., 1948); and J. Scherer, *La Dramaturgie classique en France* (Paris, 1950).
[17] *Racine: A Theatrical Reading* (Oxford, 1991).
[18] The phrase is P. Corneille's. See *Writings on the Theatre*, ed. H. T. Barnwell (Oxford, 1965), 112.
[19] It is rhetoric in general, rather than rhetorical analysis, that B. Vickers defends in his recent *In Defence of Rhetoric* (Oxford, 1988). Moreover, most of this book is history and criticism, not apology in the narrow sense.

production of texts is now predominantly perceived as a method for analysing them.[20] Inevitably the critics' interest in rhetoric has itself generated numerous texts. On the history of rhetorical theory in Renaissance and early seventeenth-century France there is now M. Fumaroli's wide-ranging survey.[21] Meanwhile the works of many major and some minor French writers of the sixteenth and seventeenth centuries have been the object of rhetorical analysis. In addition to P. France's study of *Racine's Rhetoric*, there are notable studies of the rhetoric of, among others, Calvin,[22] Ronsard,[23] Montaigne,[24] Montchrestien,[25] early seventeenth-century preachers,[26] Corneille,[27] Pascal,[28] Descartes, Boileau, and Bossuet.[29]

Common to nearly all these studies is a predominant interest in just one part of rhetoric to the detriment of rhetoric as a whole. Rhetoric is the art of persuasion, or, as Aristotle puts it, 'the faculty of discovering the possible means of persuasion in reference to any subject whatever'.[30] This art is, by tradition, divided into a number of distinct skills, which are known as the five parts of rhetoric: (1) *inventio*, (2) *dispositio*, (3) *elocutio*, (4) *memoria*, and (5) *actio* or *pronuntiatio*. As rhetoric is an art designed in the first instance to help the persuasive speaker, the last two of these parts, *memoria* and *actio*, cover skills required specifically for the performance of a speech: remembering the words, adopting a suitable tone of voice, supplying appropriate bodily and facial

---

[20] On the evolution of the function of rhetoric see G. Genette, *Figures*, 3 vols. (Paris, 1966–72), ii. 23–42.

[21] *L'Âge de l'éloquence* (Geneva, 1980).

[22] F. M. Higman, *The Style of John Calvin in his French Polemical Treatises* (Oxford, 1967).

[23] A. L. Gordon, *Ronsard et la rhétorique* (Geneva, 1970).

[24] M. M. McGowan, *Montaigne's Deceits* (London, 1974).

[25] R. Griffiths, *The Dramatic Technique of Antoine de Montchrestien* (Oxford, 1970).

[26] P. Bayley, *French Pulpit Oratory 1598–1650* (Cambridge, 1980).

[27] S. Harwood, *Rhetoric in the Tragedies of Corneille* (New Orleans, 1977); H. Slamovitz, 'The Impact of Juridical Eloquence on the Dramaturgy of Corneille', Ph.D. thesis, Indiana Univ., 1984. See also items by Fumaroli, McFarlane, and Muratore in the Bibliography.

[28] P. Topliss, *The Rhetoric of Pascal* (Leicester, 1966).

[29] P. France, *Rhetoric and Truth in France* (Oxford, 1972) has sections on Descartes, Boileau, and Bossuet. On Bossuet there is also J. Truchet, *La Prédication de Bossuet*, 2 vols. (Paris, 1960).

[30] *The Art of Rhetoric*, 1355[b].

gestures. Consequently, these are parts of rhetoric which critics feel themselves unable to exploit for the analysis of the written word.[31] The first three parts, however, are concerned with the composition of the speech or written text and therefore have a more obvious claim to the attention of the critic. Yet only *elocutio*, which, in broad terms, deals with the choice of words and the appropriate way of arranging them, has stimulated the enthusiasm of critics. *Elocutio* has come to be seen as a framework for the discussion of a writer's style, and the emphasis laid upon *elocutio* in so many studies has brought about a situation in which the terms 'rhetoric' and '*elocutio*' are used almost synonymously. So R. W. Tobin claims that: 'Racine, indeed, utilizes the most noteworthy features of Greco-Latin rhetoric. Basically, they are periphrasis, apostrophe, metonymy, ellipsis, anaphora, enumeration, substitution of abstract for concrete, of plural for singular, the tropes, oxymoron and antithesis, and the frequently recurrent figure of interrogation.'[32] In assuming the tropes and figures, which belong to *elocutio*, to be the most noteworthy features of rhetoric, Tobin is representative of the 'constant tendency in modern times to regard rhetoric merely as the theory of stylistic ornament'.[33]

It may be that critics have become so fond of *elocutio* because, as E. R. Curtius suggests, of all the parts of rhetoric it is 'the most comprehensible to modern minds'.[34] The fact remains that rhetoric offers the orator not simply a means of cultivating a persuasive style, but a comprehensive package of tools for producing persuasive speeches. It follows that the critic ought to consider the usefulness for his own work of the first two parts of rhetoric. *Inventio* offers the orator a means of finding material for his speech, and more particularly a means of finding persuasive material, while *dispositio* suggests ways of structuring a speech so that its contents are effectively arranged.

---

[31] A. Grear in 'Rhetoric and the Art of the French Tragic Actor (1620–1750): The Place of *Pronuntiatio* in the Stage Tradition', Ph.D. thesis, Univ. of St Andrews, 1982, demonstrates the relevance for the 17th-cent. actor of the recommendations of contemporary rhetoricians in their discussion of *actio*. A special number of *Dix-septième siècle* (128 (1980)) contains articles on *actio*.

[32] *Racine and Seneca* (Chapel Hill, NC, 1971), 124.

[33] France, *Rhetoric and Truth*, 16.

[34] *European Literature and the Latin Middle Ages*, trans. W. R. Trask (London, 1953), 71.

Not all critics have entirely overlooked the possible help to them of *inventio* and *dispositio*. Some have given these parts momentary consideration before either rejecting them or making minimal use of them. So B. Vickers, the Shakespearean critic, in singling out *elocutio* as the most useful part of rhetoric for the dramatist (and hence for the critic?) has this to say on the other four parts:

Evidently the last two stages [*memoria* and *actio*] were relevant to the orator memorizing his speech and delivering it with appropriate gestures, but they were not much use to the dramatist, nor indeed were invention and disposition except in the generalized sense of the selection and ordering of plot-material. But since this material was the stuff of human life, the interaction between human beings, then the various rhetorical techniques for 'invention' and structure were of little relevance.[35]

In his study of *Racine's Rhetoric* P. France makes something of *inventio* and *dispositio*, but the analysis inspired by these two parts of rhetoric accounts for only a very small section of his substantial work (pp. 206–28). One of his conclusions is that 'it is above all the *elocutio* of rhetoric which is reflected in Racine's tragedies' (p. 240).

A major aim of this study is to explore the possibility of extending the analytical uses to which the critic might put the commonly neglected first two parts of rhetoric. The impetus for such an enterprise comes from the work of A. Kibédi-Varga.[36] In *Rhétorique et littérature* he notes the contrast between the popularity of *elocutio* and the general neglect of *inventio* and *dispositio*: 'leur leçon semble davantage oubliée' (p. 16). He sets about restoring the balance by giving a systematic exposition of the accounts of these two parts in the work of seventeenth- and eighteenth-century French rhetoricians writing in the vernacular. He closes his study

---

[35] 'Shakespeare's Use of Rhetoric', in K. Muir and S. Schoenbaum (eds.), *A New Companion to Shakespeare Studies* (Cambridge, 1970), 85. In his *In Defence of Rhetoric* Vickers criticizes contemporary work on rhetoric for contributing to the 'progressive atrophy of the discipline, not just from a primary to a secondary role—from oral to written communication—but to *elocutio* alone, now detached from its expressive and persuasive functions, and brought down finally to a handful of tropes' (p. 439). Vickers's own analyses in this book, however, still concern only *elocutio*.

[36] Especially *Rhétorique et littérature* (Paris, 1970). See also his articles listed in my Bibliography.

with an analysis of *inventio* and *dispositio* in several passages by authors ranging from Du Bellay to Chénier, and takes as one of his examples the scene from *Phèdre* in which Hippolyte asks Aricie to flee with him and become his wife (v. 1). Kibédi-Varga stresses the tentative nature of these analyses and throws open an invitation to future researchers (p. 127). 'Il va sans dire que les pages précédentes ne constituent que la première ébauche d'une étude des rapports entre ces deux formes d'expression [rhetoric and tragedy]. D'autres pièces restent à analyser et aussi d'autres aspects des relations possibles entre rhétorique et théâtre.'[37] The present book is a response to this challenge. It will extend the analysis of *inventio* and *dispositio* promoted by Kibédi-Varga over the whole corpus of Racine's tragedies and will explore the ways in which such a task can illuminate Racine's specifically theatrical art.

It is important that I stress the particular dramatic context in which my rhetorical analysis will operate. Other rhetorical analyses of drama are rarely situated in this same context. It is usual for critics to perceive the rhetoric being analysed to be that of the dramatist, which is aimed at the audience. The dramatist is seen to be analogous to the orator and the theatre audience is assumed to be ripe for persuasion. So P. France observes that most of his study of *Racine's Rhetoric* has dealt with 'the rhetoric used by Racine, working through his characters, to move and please his audience or his reader' (p. 205). In her book on Corneille's rhetoric S. Harwood reveals the same tendency (p. 23): 'Just as the orator appeals to the emotions in order to achieve his goal of persuasion and education, so does Corneille believe that the audience can be instigated to pursue the path of virtue through the arousal of their pity, their fear, and their admiration.'

Ultimately, of course, the communication taking place in the theatre is indeed between the dramatist and the audience, and there is no doubt that the dramatist conceived this as his primary aim. The spectators, however, do not perceive it in that way. While they sit watching the performance, they see themselves as privileged observers of communication between characters on

---

[37] J.-L. Backès's brilliant and highly idiosyncratic study, *Racine* (Paris, 1981), also invites more extensive rhetorical analysis of Racine's plays.

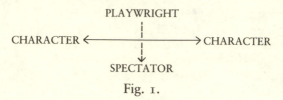

Fig. 1.

stage. P. France, acknowledging that rhetoric exists on this level of communication between characters as well as on that of communication between playwright and audience, writes that Racine 'has at times another rhetoric, that lent by him to his characters as they argue together, the rhetoric with which Hippolyte tries to convince Aricie of his love, Agrippine accuses Néron of ingratitude and Iphigénie pleads for her life' (p. 204). These two different perspectives on rhetoric at work in the theatre can be illustrated diagrammatically (see Fig. 1).[38] It is the rhetoric represented by the horizontal line, or the rhetoric on the 'stage axis', rather than that represented by the vertical line, the 'spectator axis', which is the object of my analysis.[39]

The distinction is important. Rhetorical analysis based on the spectator axis must necessarily focus on one issue: in the critic's opinion, is the playwright's rhetoric successful at persuading or moving the audience? Such a focus is fraught with danger not only because of the subjectivity involved (unless the critic can deploy the elusive evidence of actual performances), but also because of the difficulty of knowing just how the dramatist's rhetoric is supposed to be working on the spectators: it cannot work on them directly (hence the interrupted line in Fig. 1), but only through the multiple voices of the characters. By contrast, rhetorical analysis based on the stage axis is more feasible: one character uses rhetoric directly upon another. Moreover such an analysis is not limited by the single aim of having to speculate on the success of the rhetoric being used. The success of a character's rhetoric is made objectively plain by the dramatist. He may make the character's attempt at persuasion successful, unsuccessful, or partially successful, choosing whichever degree of success best suits his plot and seems

[38] The diagram is an adaptation of one used by C. Segre to illustrate types of communication in the theatre. See his article 'A Contribution to the Semiotics of the Theater', *Poetics Today*, 1 (1980), 46.

[39] 'Stage axis' and 'spectator axis' are terms used by N. C. Ekstein (*Dramatic Narrative* (New York, 1986), 9).

most likely to maintain the interest of the audience. My purpose, then, is to examine the rhetoric the characters use upon one another—to analyse, for example, how Hippolyte uses rhetoric to try and convince Aricie of his love—and, only then, to speculate about the effect that this stage-axis persuasion might have upon the spectator axis.

To consider how Racine makes his characters deploy their rhetoric is to face a vital aspect of his dramatic technique, to approach one of the most important ways in which he appeals for the attention of his audience. 'Je n'ai rien vu, mais j'ai entendu force paroles,' says Saint-Preux in *La Nouvelle Héloïse* (p. 230). He is reporting the half-remembered words of a spectator after a performance of a Greek tragedy (his source is Plutarch). He goes on to comment: 'Voilà ce qu'on peut dire en sortant des pièces françaises. Racine et Corneille, avec tout leur génie, ne sont que des parleurs' (p. 230). It has been usual to comment on the predominantly verbal nature of Racinian tragedy,[40] often to the exclusion of the visual dimension written into the plays by the dramatist. Yet if the verbal element has usually seemed more important than the visual element in Racine's plays, it is because, with the exception of pauses for the interval between acts, Racine's characters speak virtually non-stop from the beginning of the play to the end. Even moments of significant physical action are conveyed verbally.[41] So too is silence.[42]

The predominant importance of the verbal in these plays is clearly what the seventeenth-century commentator d'Aubignac had in mind when he suggested a concept of verbal action as a way of describing what happens on stage during plays like Racine's: 'Toute la Tragédie, dans la Representation, ne consiste qu'en Discours; c'est là tout l'ouvrage du Poëte, et à quoy prin-

---

[40] For instance, R. Parish describes Racine as 'a dramatist whose sole means of expression is necessarily verbal' in '"Un calme si funeste": Some Types of Silence in Racine', *FS* 34 (1980), 399.

[41] When guards dramatically surround Clytemnestre and prevent her from hastening off stage to rescue her daughter from the proposed sacrifice, the action is written into the text by the commentary of the indignant mother: 'Mais on se jette en foule au-devant de mes pas. | Perfides, contentez votre soif sanguinaire!' (*Iphigénie* 1664–5).

[42] To convey Pyrrhus's silence in *Andromaque* IV. 5, Hermione says: 'Vous ne répondez point?' (1375).

cipalement il employe les forces de son esprit . . . et s'il en réserve quelque chose à faire voir, ce n'est que pour en tirer occasion de faire parler ses Acteurs.'[43] D'Aubignac makes his point with memorable concision in the phrase '*Parler*, c'est *Agir*' (p. 282).

In Chapter 1 I consider what d'Aubignac means when he says that in tragedies of the period to speak is to act. I argue that a plausible interpretation is that the characters' words constitute actions in that, most often, they are performing acts of persuasion. According to the teaching of rhetoric, the orator wishing to persuade may use visual means, and Racine's characters certainly do make use of *actio*.[44] Yet most of the characters' energies seem to go into producing arguments and into structuring their presentation of them. It follows that their verbal action should lend itself to analysis according to rhetoricians' recommendations for *inventio* and *dispositio*. Neither of these parts of rhetoric is as well known as *elocutio*, so Chapter 1 also provides an account of those features of *inventio* and *dispositio* essential for an understanding of the ensuing analyses. I also suggest that there are in fact obvious links between persuasive activity and theatricality, often noted by rhetoricians, and known to Racine, as revealed in a survey of his extracts from Quintilian contained in a largely neglected manuscript.[45]

In the following chapters I examine the characters' *inventio* and *dispositio*. Each chapter focuses on a different dramatic setting in which persuasive activity can be observed. The most obvious setting for such activity is scenes of formal oratory: trial scenes, councils, and embassies. These are the kinds of oratory for which rhetoricians were principally offering advice and they are the subject of Chapter 2. Yet persuasion is of course not limited to formal oratory. Characters do not have to be ambassadors in order to draw on their persuasive resources. Accordingly, Chapters 3 and 4 examine scenes of informal oratory, first between two or more protagonists, then between a protagonist and a confidant. Chapters 5 and 6 turn, respectively, to monologues and narrations, where persuasion might be thought to be less important. I argue, however, that the persuasive element in Racine's monologues and

---

[43] *La Pratique du théâtre*, ed. P. Martino (Algiers, 1927), 283.
[44] The characters' visual means of persuasion are examined by D. Maskell in *Racine*.
[45] Bibliothèque Nationale: Fonds Français 12888.

narrations makes them part of the verbal action, which is one of the distinctive theatrical features of French tragedies of the period. In each analytical chapter some comparison is made with the plays of Racine's rivals, most notably those of Pierre Corneille, with a view to answering the question: does analysis of *inventio* and *dispositio* help the critic to pinpoint any specifically Racinian features of Racine's handling of verbal action? The overriding aim is to make a contribution to an understanding of how the tragedies of Racine, so often described as predominantly verbal, none the less work well in the theatre.

I

Verbal Action and Rhetorical Theory

> Aimer, souffrir, mourir, ce n'est jamais ici que parler...
> Voici peut-être la clef de la tragédie racinienne: parler, c'est
> faire.
>
> (R. Barthes, Sur Racine, 66)

In suggesting the key of Racinian tragedy to be speaking as doing,
R. Barthes seems to echo the seventeenth-century dramatic critic
d'Aubignac, who made the same point with the well-known for-
mulation '*Parler*, c'est *Agir*'.[1] What neither of these critics does,
however, is to say clearly what might be understood by the concept of speech as action, or, as I shall call it, verbal action. The
purpose of the present chapter is twofold: to offer an interpretation of the concept of verbal action, which I shall argue is implicit
in the writings of seventeenth-century theorists and dramatists;
and to describe the tools which I shall suggest are most useful for
an analysis of verbal action in Racinian tragedy, namely the precepts of the rhetoricians.

1. ACTION AND VERBAL ACTION

One reason for the lack of clarity in the phrase '*Parler*, c'est *Agir*'
is the wide range of meanings attached to the second verb's related
noun *action*. Perusal of seventeenth-century dictionaries, both
monolingual and bilingual (French–Latin), throws up a veritable
welter of meanings. The bilingual dictionaries of Nicot (1625),
Monet (1636), and Pomey (1687), along with the monolingual
works of Richelet (1680), Furetière (1690 and 1727), and the
Académie Française (1694), show an ever-widening range of connotations being recognized by the pioneering lexicographers.[2] The
core definitions of *action*, which all share, though with variations,
are:

---

[1] *La Pratique du théâtre*, ed. P. Martino (Algiers, 1927), 282.
[2] The dates given here are the dates of the edns. which I have consulted.

1. 'acte, fait, œuvre' (Académie Française),[3]
2. 'une demande et poursuite en justice' (Académie Française).

This second connotation always carries in its train a host of attendant legal terms (*action personnelle, action criminelle, action réelle, action pétitoire*). The bilingual dictionaries barely extend beyond the core definitions. Connotations proliferate, however, in the monolingual works and the list might continue thus:

3. 'maniere dont une cause agit, et par laquelle elle produit son effet' (Académie Française),
4. 'discours public, comme un Sermon, une Harangue, un plaidoyer' (Académie Française),
5. 'vertu, force d'agir' (Furetière, 1690 and 1727),
6. 'en Peinture . . . la posture & . . . la disposition du corps ou du visage, quand ils marquent quelque passion de l'ame' (Furetière, 1690 and 1727).

Three other connotations are treated in different ways by the various dictionaries. The dictionary of the Académie Française distinguishes all three connotations:

7. 'cette partie extérieure de l'Orateur, qui comprend le mouvement du corps, & les gestes' (Académie Française),
8. 'un geste . . . une contenance' (Académie Française),
9. 'la vehemence, la chaleur à dire, ou à faire quelque chose' (Académie Française).

These connotations are good indications of the slipperiness of words and meanings. Pomey recognizes 8 ('un geste'), though not specifically 7 (the orator's *actio*); but then 7 and 8 overlap a good deal, the more general 8 perhaps deriving from the more technical 7. For Furetière, who does not single out 8 at all, it is 7 and 9 that overlap: 'se dit plus particulierement des gestes, du mouvement du corps, & de l'ardeur avec laquelle on prononce, ou on fait quelque chose' (Furetière, 1690). This definition does not specifically mention rhetorical *actio*, but the illustrative examples make it clear that this is included in the definition: 'Le Faucheur a fait un joli traitté de l'Action de l'Orateur.' Furetière's dictionary is the only one to give the commercial connotation of the word *action*:

10. 'On appelle en Hollande *action*, une obligation sur les deux

---

[3] I give in parentheses the source from which I have taken the definitions.

Compagnies des Indes d'Orient, ou d'Occident' (Furetière, 1727).

And finally there is the aesthetic connotation, first noted by the Académie Française in relation to drama, then expanded in the later version of Furetière's dictionary:

11. 'l'intrigue, & . . . la representation d'une piece de theatre' (Furetière, 1727).

The examples he gives cover epic poetry as well as drama.

An adaptable, not to say promiscuous, term, *action* keeps such varied company as dramatists, painters, rhetoricians, lawyers, and businessmen. To focus on the life of the term in the dramatic context alone is to realize that the dictionaries hardly start to suggest its semantic complexity. Its life in the dramatic context certainly draws on connotation 11 (above), but also on some of the other senses.

There are three frequent connotations of the word in the dramatic context, one of which has occupied the attention of modern commentators of seventeenth-century French tragedy and dramatic theory almost to the exclusion of other connotations. This favoured connotation (11 above) is the one hinted at in the dictionary of the Académie Française: '[Action] se dit aussi en Poësie, du principal evenement qui fait le sujet d'une piece de theatre.' As an example of the word's use the dictionary offers: 'Cet Episode n'a point de rapport à la principale action.' It is this use of *action* which Corneille adopts when, in his second *Discours*, he mentions the death of Clytemnestra: 'Sophocle et Euripide l'ont traitée tous deux, mais chacun avec un nœud et un dénouement tout à fait différents l'un de l'autre; et c'est cette différence qui empêche que ce ne soit la même pièce, bien que ce soit le même sujet, dont ils ont conservé l'action principale' (*Writings*, 47). With this definition and this example of its use, *action* seems to refer to the main event in a play, which may or may not be represented on stage; to which all that happens in the play is subordinate; which the audience fully perceives only by the end of the play; but which must have occupied a central position in the dramatist's mind as he conceived the play. The action is, then, the subject of a play. It is tempting to suggest, in the light of this definition, that, when Racine says of *Britannicus* that 'ma tragédie n'est pas moins la disgrâce d'Agrippine que la mort de Britannicus' (p. 258), he is wrestling with a definition of the action of his play, in terms of its subject.[4] According to this view, action is readily distinguishable from plot which might be defined as a particular sequence of events, the particularity of the sequence constituting the plot. Thus, as Corneille suggests, two plays can have the same action, but a different *nœud* and a different *dénouement* ensure that they have different plots.

This major connotation of the word *action* is complicated by a number of factors. First, modern commentators are not all in agreement about the distinction between action and plot outlined above. H. T. Barnwell is careful to maintain the distinction.[5] But C. J. Gossip points out 'the confusion between the terms even in semi-technical discussion' and suggests that what is known as unity of action ought, strictly speaking, to be renamed unity of plot: a suggestion which illustrates the uncertainty of the meaning of the two words.[6]

A second complicating factor lies in the discussions of seventeenth-century commentators, who are not entirely consistent in their use of the word *action* in this sense. Corneille, for instance, when discussing the treatment of Clytemnestra by Sophocles and Euripides, seems to distinguish *nœud* and *dénouement* as elements of plot from *action*. But, in his third *Discours*, he makes a remark which obfuscates this neat distinction: 'Bien que l'action du poème dramatique doive avoir son unité, il y faut considérer deux parties: le nœud et le dénouement' (p. 66). What *were* elements of the plot now seem to have become elements of the action. Or does the word *action* now mean plot as well? Corneille further complicates

---

[4] It is probably this same kind of action that he has in mind in the first preface to *Britannicus* and the preface to *Bérénice* when he recommends 'une action simple' (pp. 256, 325). Speaking of Mithridate he says that it is 'sa mort, qui est l'action de ma tragédie' (p. 448).

[5] 'Action is not the same as plot, but is represented by plot. It has been suggested that the action of a play is something which takes place in the mind of the dramatist and that it must be "bodied forth" by a plot behind which the spectator in his turn discerns the action. The action in *Pompée* may be said to concern the downfall of mighty men whose almost superhuman will is subject to the frailties, pitfalls and chance occurrences which beset ordinary mortals' (Barnwell in the introduction to his edn. of Corneille's *Pompée* (Oxford, 1971), 10).

[6] *An Introduction to French Classical Tragedy* (London, 1981), 96. Gossip seems to echo Scherer, who suggests that action should be equated with plot and claims to owe this equation to Marmontel (see *La Dramaturgie classique en France* (Paris, 1950), 100–4). According to Scherer, 17th-cent. theory on action and plot lagged behind 17th-cent. practice.

discussion of the term by introducing a plural usage (pp. 62–3):

Ce mot d'unité d'action ne veut pas dire que la tragédie n'en doive faire qu'une sur le théâtre. Celle que le poète choisit pour son sujet doit avoir un commencement, un milieu et une fin; et ces trois parties non seulement sont autant d'actions qui aboutissent à la principale, mais en outre chacune d'elles en peut contenir plusieurs avec la même subordination. Il n'y doit avoir qu'une action complète, qui laisse l'esprit de l'auditeur dans le calme; mais elle ne peut le devenir que par plusieurs autres imparfaites, qui lui servent d'acheminements, et tiennent cet auditeur dans une agréable suspension.

By postulating many minor actions which together lead to the major action, Corneille contributes yet more to the confusion between plot and action, and forces the critic to face a central question: is dramatic action concrete or abstract? That is to say, is it *an* action, an event like the death of Britannicus, which brings to a head all that has gone before? Or is it *the* action, the subject of *Britannicus* considered globally as the decline of Agrippine's influence which leads to the death of Britannicus? Modern critics will offer their own views on these questions, but there can be no definitive answer with regard to the seventeenth century, because there was no terminological consistency between and within the writings of individual theorists and dramatists. Even in this one context the meaning of *action* is unstable.

There can be no doubt that action as the subject or major event in a play is the connotation of the word to which twentieth-century dramatic commentators attach most importance. But to read through Corneille's *Discours*, d'Aubignac's *Pratique*, and other writings on drama in the seventeenth century is to discover other connotations, two of which are quite distinct and more easily discussed than the first.

One connotation is *action* as the fifth part of rhetoric. This is the sense of the word as used by S. Chappuzeau when he argues that a play must be performed in order to have its full effect:

Le discours ne touche pas comme l'action, & les plus belles pensées d'une harangue n'ayant sur le papier que la moitié de leur force, elles reçoivent l'autre de la bouche de l'Orateur. Il en est de même du Poëme Dramatique, & il ne produit ses grands effets que sur le Théâtre par l'agrément que luy donne le Comédien.[7]

[7] *Le Théâtre français*, ed. G. Monval (Paris, 1876), 9.

Not unrelated to this, but not so narrowly rhetorical, is what might be called the popular connotation of action in drama. The modern audience might think of Shakespeare, of television drama, and of cinema, and suppose that action refers to movement of various kinds, to things being done visibly: from walking and playing games, to car-chases and committing murder. Action in the sense of physical activity which at any given moment might be the predominant focus of the audience's interest is common to all drama. The use of such activity in the tragedies of Racine and his contemporaries is generally thought to be comparatively sparing. Yet the word *action* in this sense is encountered in theoretical writings of the period. In the preface to his play *La Généreuse Allemande*, published in 1630, Antoine Mareschal draws attention to the physical action that he has incorporated into his play, suggesting that this is much more entertaining than long speeches. He asks if there is 'rien de si importun que ces rapports et ces longues narrations, qui feraient mourir d'ennui la plus ferme patience, qui nous surchargent la mémoire de paroles sans effets, nous ravissant par un tissu de longs discours tout le plaisir qu'on recevrait des actions? . . . La description m'importune, l'action me recrée.'[8] Mareschal is anticipating Victor Hugo, who, two centuries later, will criticize Racinian tragedy precisely for keeping the physical action in the wings.[9] Hugo is also anticipated by Corneille, who, like Mareschal, is proud to announce, in his preface to *Clitandre*, published in 1632, that he too wishes to offer his audience something to see, rather than merely long, boring speeches to be heard: 'J'ai mis les accidents mêmes sur la scène. Cette nouveauté pourra plaire à quelques-uns; et quiconque voudra bien peser l'avantage que l'action a sur ces longs et ennuyeux récits, ne trouvera pas étrange que j'ai mieux aimé divertir les yeux qu'importuner les oreilles.' (*Writings*, 174–5.) And indeed *Clitandre* provides a feast for the eyes as gruesome as anything to be found in *King Lear*.

It is the visual impact of drama that d'Aubignac stresses at the beginning of his chapter in the *Pratique* entitled 'Des Discours en général' (part iv, chapter 2): 'Ce poëme est nommé *Drama*, c'est à dire, *Action* et non pas *Récit* . . . le Lieu qui sert à ses Representa-

---

[8] Quoted by Scherer in *La Dramaturgie classique*, 242.
[9] *Préface de Cromwell* in *Théâtre complet*, ed. J. Thierry and J. Mélèze, 2 vols. (Pléiade edn.; [Paris], 1963–4), i, 432.

tions, est dit *Theatre*, et non pas *Auditoire*, c'est à dire, *un Lieu où on regarde ce qui s'y fait, et non pas où l'on Ecoute ce qui s'y dit*' (p. 282).[10] The sense of action as physical activity is closest to the ordinary, everyday sense, defined by the Académie Française as 'acte, fait, œuvre'. Yet this passage also recalls Aristotle's repeated emphasis in the *Poetics* on plays as dramatic rather than as narrative in nature and as showing people doing things (1448^a, 1449^b).

Action, in a dramatic context, might refer to the subject or plot of a play, to the performance skills of the actors and actresses, and to the physical activity of the characters. These are perhaps the three most obvious and distinct connotations of the word in this context, even though the first is rather fluid. Yet there are many other references to *action* in the writings of Corneille and d'Aubignac when none of these connotations is present and on these occasions the word *action* is used to refer to what I shall call verbal action in the plays, though theoretical writings of the period, and even less the dictionaries, do not spell out what verbal action is. Some more examples of the use of the word will help to suggest what this commonly implied but never defined sort of action might be.

In the *Pratique* (part iii, chapter 5) d'Aubignac discusses the question: how can the audience know when an act (that is, one of the five divisions of a play) has finished (pp. 220–2)? The obvious answer is that an act is over when the stage is left empty. But d'Aubignac acutely rejects this answer for two reasons. Unscrupulous actors might fail to observe an interval in order to complete the performance quickly, in which case the stage would not be left empty even though an act has ended. The stage might also be left empty even though an act has not come to an end, because the convention of *liaison des scènes* is not always correctly observed. D'Aubignac proposes a different answer to the question: 'J'estime que l'acte finit, non pas quand le Theatre est sans Acteur; mais quand il demeure sans Action' (p. 221). D'Aubignac gives an example of a tragedy in which a character remains on stage after the end of an act: 'L'Acteur demeure sur la Scène entierement incapable d'agir, comme l'Hecube d'Euripide qui tombe evanoüye

---

[10] Corneille also uses *action* in this sense in his *Discours*. For example, 'fait l'action' (*Writings*, 37, a translation of a phrase from Aristotle's *Poetics*) means 'kills'; and 'ces actions' (p. 47) means 'Medea's murder of her children and Atreus' roasting of those of Thyestes'.

d'affliction entre le premier et le second Acte.' There are also examples of Greek tragedies in which the actor remaining at the end of an act mingles with the chorus. About these two exceptional sorts of act-endings d'Aubignac comments: 'Or dans la premiere façon, l'Acteur qui restoit sur la Scène sans agir, quoy que visible, arrestoit le cours de l'Action Theatrale, et finissoit ainsi l'Acte: Et dans la seconde, l'acteur faisant partie du Chœur, donnoit à connoistre que l'Action du Theatre estoit cessé, et partant que l'Acte estoit finy.' For d'Aubignac an act ends when the theatrical action has stopped, and it might be deduced that the theatrical action is the purposeful interaction between characters or at least a purposeful monologue.

This notion of theatrical action is supported by, and expanded in, remarks made elsewhere in the *Pratique*. In the following quotation (from p. 90) d'Aubignac does not take account of the division of the play into acts, but the view of theatrical action to emerge seems largely the same as that implied in the quotation above:

Depuis l'ouverture du Theatre jusqu'à la closture de la Catastrophe, depuis que le premier Acteur a parû sur la Scéne, jusqu'à ce que le dernier en sorte, il faut que les principaux Personnages soient toujours agissants, et que le Theatre porte continuellement et sans interruption l'image de quelques desseins, attentes, passions, troubles, inquietudes et autres pareilles agitations, qui ne permettent pas aux Spectateurs de croire que l'action du Theatre ait cessé.

D'Aubignac here alludes to two connotations of the words *action*. One is action as the subject or plot. The spectators must not be allowed to think that this sort of action has been completed until the play is really at an end, or else they will lose interest and perhaps go home (p. 91). The other sense of *action* which is in play here and is evoked by the adjective 'agissants' is that sort of theatrical action which defines an act of a play. In an act, the characters must always be doing something, carrying out actions, and these actions, which are connected to the desires, passions, and personal interests of the characters, must be related to the overall action of the play in such a way that they prevent its being completed until the play ends.

But what sort of actions are these? One clue to an answer can be found in Corneille's first *Discours*, where he too uses the word *agissant* but says more about it than d'Aubignac: 'Les actions sont l'âme de la tragédie, où l'on ne doit parler qu'en agissant et pour agir' (p. 19). The actions of the characters are closely connected with speech. Corneille envisages dramatic speech to be dependent on action: characters in a play should not speak unless they are simultaneously carrying out an action. The converse, that characters should only carry out an action if they are also speaking, is not necessarily the case, because some of their actions are physical, not verbal. None the less, it would be, by and large, true to say that in tragedies of the period speech should normally be action and action will usually be speech.

This is still rather cryptic. For the suggestion is that it is possible to have speech which is not action and that such speech should be avoided by characters in plays. So what is the difference between speech which is action and speech which is not action?

Such a distinction might seem odd to those versed in Speech Act Theory as elaborated by twentieth-century philosophers and applied by some critics to the analysis of literary and dramatic texts.[11] To them any verbal utterance whatsoever constitutes a speech act and can be categorized as, for example, a command, a question, an assertion, a promise, which may or may not have a particular effect upon the hearer. Verbal action as envisaged by Corneille, however, must be distinct from the speech acts which all characters in all plays execute each time they speak. For Corneille not every speech act could be described as speech as action. Speech as action involves more than characters speaking interminably with little else to relieve their speeches. Corneille and d'Aubignac, in the phrase '*Parler, c'est Agir*', are commenting on a particular quality of characters' speech which makes it suitable for securing the attention of a theatre audience.[12]

[11] The two main philosophical works are: J. L. Austin, *How to Do Things with Words*, ed. J. O. Urmson and M. Sbisà (Oxford, 1975), and J. R. Searle, *Speech Acts* (Cambridge, 1969). For a useful summary of the application of the theory to the analysis of drama see K. Elam, *The Semiotics of Theatre and Drama* (London, 1980), 156–91. R. E. Goodkin in 'The Performed Letter, or, How Words Do Things in Racine', *PFSCL* 17 (1990), 85–102, uses some aspects of the theory to show how central to the tragic action of *Bérénice* and *Bajazet* is the performance of the speech act 'I love you'.

[12] The phrase '*Parler, c'est Agir*' has not received much analysis. P. France seems to assume that it is self-explanatory (*Racine's Rhetoric*, (Oxford, 1965), 31). M. L. Flowers assumes that it refers to narrations of off-stage events: 'since *bienséances* severely limited what actions could be represented on the stage, writers

It is, according to Corneille, active speech, speech related to and directed towards action, and the best way to understand what this means in practice is to look at some comments made by d'Aubignac and Racine about speech and action in specific plays. D'Aubignac precedes his statement that in tragedies to speak is to act with the explanation that 'les Discours qui s'y font, doivent estre comme des Actions de ceux qu'on y fait paroistre' (p. 282) and his idea of verbal action is then illustrated with three examples of speech as action:

Et de fait la Narration de la mort d'Hypolite chez Senéque, est l'Action d'un homme effrayé d'un Monstre qu'il a veû sortir de la Mer, et de la funeste avanture de ce Prince. Les plaintes d'Emilie de Monsieur Corneille, sont l'Action d'une Fille dont l'esprit, agité du désir de la vangeance et d'un grand Amour, s'emporte à des irrésolutions et des mouvemens si divers: Et quand Chimene parle à son Roy, c'est l'Action d'une Fille affligée qui demande Justice.

These three actions are in some ways very different from each other, and may well have been chosen by d'Aubignac to illustrate the three main sorts of verbal action used by dramatists: one is a narration of an off-stage death near the end of the play, another is a monologue opening a play, and the third is an attempt to influence a king at a mid-point in the play. But they all have certain basic elements in common. All three actions are speeches. Indeed *action* can, as the seventeenth-century dictionaries suggest, mean a public speech and d'Aubignac may well have this connotation in mind when he refers to 'l'Action d'un homme' and 'l'Action d'une Fille', with the expected formality of a public speech transposed into the theatrical context. On the other hand, d'Aubignac's use of the word clearly goes beyond the dictionary definition. For his examples are all speeches uttered by a character who has been

of serious drama regularly reverted to *récits*, to language, in order to bring before the audience in verbal form information about events essential to the plot. D'Aubignac defends this use of discourse as a substitute for action in his famous phrase: "*Parler*, c'est *Agir*"' (*Sentence Structure and Characterization in the Tragedies of Jean Racine* (Rutherford, NJ, 1979), 35). This is a narrow interpretation of the phrase; it takes no account of d'Aubignac's varied examples, and it perhaps misses the point by asserting that d'Aubignac is recommending speech as a substitute for action. N. C. Ekstein (*Dramatic Narrative* (New York, 1986), 22) is on the right lines when she glosses the phrase by quoting A. Ubersfeld's general view that in the theatre 'chaque protagoniste essaie de *faire faire quelque chose à un autre* (pour satisfaire à son propre désir)' (*Lire le théâtre* (Paris, 1978), 239).

moved to speak in order to have a certain effect on his or her listener, and for d'Aubignac it seems to be precisely this special dimension of motivation and intention that makes these speeches into actions. This is even the case for Émilie, who is speaking to herself in order to prompt herself to decide if Cinna's conspiracy against Auguste should go ahead. In all three examples the characters speak 'en agissant', in that their emotions are compelling them to have an effect on their real or notional interlocutor; and they speak 'pour agir', in that the effect which they wish to have is intended to contribute to the progression or completion of the one overall action of the play.

What these speeches have in common certainly stands out clearly when contrasted with a passage from Euripides' *The Phoenician Maidens* about which Racine, in his copy of the text, noted 'tout ceci n'est point de l'action'.[13] In Euripides' play, Polyneices has assembled a force to fight against his brother Eteocles, who will not hand over the throne to Polyneices, as had been agreed. Jocasta sends a messenger who persuades Polyneices to come and speak to his brother before taking up arms. But, before Polyneices arrives, Antigone and an old servant together survey the plain from the walls of Thebes and make leisurely remarks about Polyneices' forces, which they can see, though presumably the audience cannot. For example, Antigone asks (119–22):

> Who is he with the white helm-crest
> Who marcheth in front of their war-array,
> And a brazen buckler fencing his breast
> Highly his arm doth sway?

She goes on to ask more questions of the same nature. These are certainly speech acts: Antigone is asking questions. But Corneille would not call this speech as action. Nor does Racine think that this is action, and he may well be thinking of action in the sense of verbal action. For Antigone is not speaking 'en agissant' or 'pour agir'. Rather the dramatist is using Antigone to give a poetic and atmospheric description of some men of war. In themselves Antigone's questions have no urgency whatsoever.

At the same time as he gives his three examples of speech as action d'Aubignac specifically warns against speeches like that of

---

[13] *Œuvres complètes*, ii. 876.

Antigone, which do not constitute actions and which are therefore out of place in drama: 'Là *Parler*, c'est *Agir*, ce qu'on dit pour lors n'estant pas des Récits inventez par le Poëte pour faire monstre de son Eloquence' (p. 282). It is a warning which Corneille makes on more than one occasion: 'Ceux qu'il [le poète] fait parler ne sont pas des orateurs' (*Writings*, 19). And again: 'Ceux que le poète fait parler ne sont pas des poètes' (ibid.). Dramatists must not manipulate characters' speeches so as to display their own eloquence. Characters must only speak when plausibly moved to do so by their prejudices and emotions, and when speaking can help them to further their interests.

It is perhaps by veering towards this concept of speech as action that Corneille and d'Aubignac sought to respond to those earlier in the century (including Corneille himself) who criticized the inordinate amount of boring speech, and particularly narrations, to be found in some plays. The earlier answer seems to have been to rid plays of boring narrations by substituting physical action; the later answer is to substitute verbal action. Dramatic speech can be interesting, if it is made active.

Of d'Aubignac's three varied examples of verbal action (a narration, a monologue, and Chimène's plea), it is undoubtedly the third sort which dominates most of the tragedies of Corneille and all those of Racine. Long narrations are infrequent, as are monologues. But speeches in which a character tries to further his interests by engaging in debate with another character occur very frequently. In his *Dissertation sur Sophonisbe* d'Aubignac produces a splendid description of the theatrical potential of this predominant kind of verbal action. He regrets the decline in Corneille's talent, commenting that the utterances of the male characters in *Sophonisbe*

n'ont rien de ces belles contestations qu'il a mises tant de fois sur notre Théâtre, qui poussaient l'esprit de l'homme à bout, & où le dernier qui parloit sembloit avoir tant de raison, que l'on ne croyait pas qu'il fût possible de repartir, & où les réponses & les repliques excitoient de si grands applaudissemens, que l'on avoit toûjours le déplaisir d'en perdre une bonne partie, & qui contraignoient tout le monde de retourner plusieurs fois au même spectacle pour en recevoir toûjours quelque nouvelle satisfaction.[14]

[14] Granet, *Recueil de dissertations sur plusieurs tragédies de Corneille et de Racine* (Paris, 1739), i. 134–53 (pp. 143–4).

The verbal actions which d'Aubignac thinks are eminently suited to tragedy are nothing less than speeches of persuasion, the theatricality of which lies in the way in which spectators listen to different arguments in turn and wonder which will prevail, which party will win, and what course of action will be pursued as a result of the persuasion. Corneille too appreciates the theatricality of his own verbal action when he comments on the consultation scene in *Cinna* (p. 22): 'Auguste mande Cinna et Maxime. On n'en sait pas la cause; mais enfin il les mande, et cela suffit pour faire une surprise très agréable, de le voir délibérer s'il quittera l'empire ou non, avec deux hommes qui ont conspiré contre lui.' The ironical situation of course adds to the dramatic impact of the scene, but it is the verbal action that allows the irony to have its effect and this action is one of deliberation, or persuasion.

It is now possible to spell out what the predominant kind of verbal action envisaged by Corneille and d'Aubignac seems to be. Verbal action seems most often to be a persuasive action, that is to say a sequence of speeches delivered by characters who have particular interests, or motives, or compelling passions, and who wish to make their interests prevail over those of other characters by engaging in acts of persuasion and dissuasion (like Cinna and Maxime), and in acts of accusation and defence (like Chimène and Don Diègue). The phrase 'verbal action' can refer generically to this sort of activity distributed throughout a whole play; or to an instance of persuasive activity involving two or more interacting characters in a given scene; or, as in d'Aubignac's phrase 'l'Action d'une Fille', to a single persuasive act carried out by one character. All these acts of persuasion are precisely the sort of actions for the conduct of which rhetoricians from Aristotle to Bernard Lamy offered advice and recommendations. And it is their rhetorical treatises that d'Aubignac repeatedly urges the dramatist to read.[15]

What seems to be encouraged as a way of making a largely verbal drama theatrically interesting is the depiction of persuasive confrontations. That there really is such a link between the verbal actions of dramatic characters recommended by Corneille and d'Aubignac and persuasion as taught by rhetoricians can be seen not only in my reconstruction of what the theorists may mean by

[15] 'Je souhaiterois donc que les Poëtes se rendissent tres-sçavans en l'art de bien discourir, et qu'ils étudiassent à fond l'Eloquence' (*La Pratique*, 286). See also pp. 288, 304, 332.

verbal action; the link is also visible in the work of Nicolas Caussin (1583–1651), a Jesuit writer on rhetorical theory, but also the author of six published plays in Latin, no doubt intended for performance by schoolboys.[16] Each scene is preceded by a summary of its action. The verbs chosen by Caussin to describe the actions are revealing. Here are a few examples from his prose tragedy *Hermenegildus*:

[I. 1] HERMENEGILDVS   ERASISTRATVS.   HERMENEGILDVS GOIZVINTAE NOVERCÆ malis artibus, & Levigildi Patris armis vexatus, de suo negotio deliberat.

(Hermenigild and Erasistratus: Hermenigild, aggrieved by the evil wiles of Goisvintha his stepmother and by the weapons of his father Leovigild, deliberates about his business.)

[I. 2] ERASISTRATVS. Hermenegildi Comes dissuadet ne se paterno furori novercæ artibus instigato committat.

(Erasistratus, the friend of Hermenigild, dissuades him from exposing himself to the anger of his father provoked by the wiles of his stepmother.)

[I. 4] RECAREDVS FRATER HERMENEGILDI. Suadet reditum ad Patrem, et persuadet.

(Reccared, the brother of Hermenigild, counsels a return to his father and succeeds in persuading him.)

[IV. 2] HERMENEGILDVS causam dicit apud patrem in cilicio, & vinculis.

(Hermenigild pleads his case before his father, wearing a coat of goat's hair and in chains.)

'Deliberates' (*deliberat*), 'dissuades' (*dissuadet*), 'counsels' (*suadet*), 'persuading' (*persuadet*), 'pleads his case' (*causam dicit*) are all verbs which evoke deliberative or judicial oratory.

To speak is to act in seventeenth-century French dramatic theory and practice in that for much of the time characters are motivated to speak persuasively to achieve certain aims. They are therefore performing oratorical, or persuasive, actions. It should be noted that the word persuasion has a particular and a general sense. Persuasion is one of the four branches of the two main kinds of

---

[16] His rhetorical theory: *De Eloquentia Sacra et Humana*; his tragedies: *Tragoediae Sacrae*. Of the volume of tragedies M. Fumaroli says: 'cette œuvre de dramaturge est en consonance profonde avec le traité de rhétorique publiée l'année précédente' (*L'Age de l'éloquence* (Geneva, 1980), 284).

oratory: deliberative oratory is constituted of persuasion and dissuasion; and judicial oratory of accusation and defence. Yet persuasion is also used as a global term to cover all these four kinds of speaking.

The idea of persuasive action is unmistakably appropriate for one of d'Aubignac's examples of speech as action. Chimène's pleading with the king in Le Cid is an act of accusation against Don Rodrigue. It may not be obvious that his examples of narration and monologue are instances of persuasive action in the same way, despite certain similarities of motivation and intention. Chapters 5 and 6 will be devoted respectively to a discussion of the monologue and the narration with a view to suggesting that these too can sometimes be employed as persuasive actions. The other chapters will focus on the much larger body of text whose status as verbal action is conferred by the persistently persuasive behaviour of the characters.

If the verbal actions are principally persuasive actions which interest the audience with the deployment of conflicting arguments, it follows that a knowledge of rhetorical theory will be useful in attempting an analysis of these actions.

ii. SOME AFFINITIES BETWEEN RHETORIC AND DRAMA

In the early and middle part of the twentieth century, when rhetoric was a distinctly unfashionable discipline and needed constant apology, critics of drama who identified the presence of rhetoric in the plays which they were studying reacted in one of two ways. Either they intimated their sorrow at the collocation of the rhetorical and the dramatic, two apparently incompatible forms of expression; or they pointed out that the rhetorical could be enjoyed in addition to the dramatic. So B. Weinberg expresses unease at the rhetorical elements in Racine's Alexandre;[17] and P. France assures his readers that 'there is no doubt that in Racine as in Pierre Corneille we do get a good deal of undramatic, non-tragic pleasure out of the debating'.[18] The dramatists themselves would have been none too flattered by this assurance. For it is the use of

[17] He speaks of 'the hesitation between rhetoric and drama' (The Art of Jean Racine (Chicago, 1963), 65).
[18] Racine's Rhetoric, 238.

rhetoric in the service, not at the expense, of drama which lies at the heart of the verbal action which fills their plays. D'Aubignac clearly thought that the rhetorical behaviour of the characters should exercise a constant hold on the attention of the spectators.

Modern commentators should not be surprised at the combination of the rhetorical and the dramatic. For in the writings of the theorists and in the practice of orators throughout the ages the link between oratory and the stage has always been felt. Both the orator and the dramatist via his actors wish to move an audience. The actor can learn from the orator, as Grimarest suggests: 'Le Comédien doit se considérer comme un Orateur, qui prononce en public un discours fait pour toucher l'auditeur.'[19] But equally the orator can learn from the actor. In his speech *Pro Quinctio* (24. 77) Cicero mentions that the actor Roscius was in court advising him. Quintilian, in his exposition of rhetoric in the *Institutio Oratoria*, makes a whole range of explicit and implicit links between rhetoric and drama. In 1. 11 he aims to answer the question: what can the actor teach the orator? Later he relates an anecdote about the tragic dramatist Accius, who was apparently thought to be such a good supplier of arguments to his characters that he was asked why he did not become a barrister. Accius replied that in the courts his adversaries would probably say just what he did not want them to say; he preferred to stick to drama because he could control the dramatic effects obtainable by manipulating both argument and counter-argument (5. 13. 43). The same dramatic effects which aroused applause in the theatre were no less capable of arousing applause in the schools of the rhetoricians and in the forum. Quintilian is not altogether approving of this phenomenon. He distances himself from those speakers whose sole aim seems to be to make their audiences applaud and clamour (4. 2. 37) and he is equally sober in regretting the applause which pupils so readily accord each other when practising declamation and debate (2. 2. 9–13). Yet Quintilian is very much aware of the potent effect that an orator can have on his audience. Indeed he carefully shows how an orator can move his audience to tears by painting a picture of a captured town:

Sic et urbium captarum crescit miseratio. Sine dubio enim, qui dicit expugnatum esse civitatem, complectitur omnia quaecunque talis fortuna

---

[19] *La Vie de M. de Molière*, ed. G. Mongrédien ([Paris], 1955), 162.

recipit, sed in adfectus minus penetrat brevis hic velut nuntius. At si aperias haec, quae verbo uno inclusa erant, apparebunt effusae per domus ac templa flammae et ruentium tectorum fragor et ex diversis clamoribus unus quidam sonus, aliorum fuga incerta, alii extremo complexu suorum cohaerentes et infantium feminarumque ploratus et male usque in illum diem servati fato senes; tum illa profanorum sacrorumque direptio, efferentium praedas repetentiumque discursus et acti ante suum quisque praedonem catenati et conata retinere infantem suum mater et, sicubi maius lucrum est, pugna inter victores. (8. 3. 67–9.)

(So, too, we may move our hearers to tears by the picture of a captured town. For the mere statement that the town was stormed, while no doubt it embraces all that such a calamity involves, has all the curtness of a dispatch, and fails to penetrate to the emotions of the hearer. But if we expand all that the one word 'stormed' includes, we shall see the flames pouring from house and temple, and hear the clash of falling roofs and one confused clamour blent of many cries: we shall behold some in doubt whither to fly, others clinging to their nearest and dearest in one last embrace, while the wailing of women and children and the laments of old men that the cruelty of fate should have spared them to see that day will strike upon our ears. Then will come the pillage of treasure sacred and profane, the hurrying to and fro of the plunderers as they carry off their booty or return to seek for more, the prisoners driven each before his own inhuman captor, the mother struggling to keep her child, and the victors fighting over the richest of the spoil.)

It is the accumulation of horrible details of suffering which seems to ensure the tears of the orator's audience. Is not the same technique used by Andromaque when she evokes the fall of Troy and appeals directly for the pity of her confidant and, indirectly, for that of the spectators (*Andromaque* III. 8)?

Traditionally, then, the practice of rhetoric has been seen almost as if it were a dramatic event. It should not therefore be surprising that tragedies composed largely of words uttered in the context of persuasive confrontation should be considered dramatic, all the more so as the dramatists of seventeenth-century France were of course well versed in rhetoric. Much of their education at school consisted in rhetorical theory and practice, and when they left university they might well go on to use their rhetoric, as Pierre Corneille did, for one of its primary aims, pleading in the courts of law.[20] It is not my purpose to suggest a cause-and-effect relation-

---

[20] Some of the implications of Corneille's legal background for an appreciation of his drama have been explored by H. Slamovitz in his Ph.D. thesis 'The Impact of Juridical Eloquence on the Dramaturgy of Corneille' (Indiana Univ., 1984).

ship between the education of seventeenth-century dramatists and the sort of tragedies that they wrote. If the persuasive confrontations of the characters are obviously an important aspect of a playwright's dramatic technique, the critic is amply justified in pursuing a rhetorical analysis of the characters' speeches, regardless of the education of the dramatist.

III. RACINE'S RHETORIC

There must be some interest, however, in the knowledge that the persuasive techniques used constantly by dramatic characters are those in which the dramatists themselves were regularly rehearsed at school. This interest is especially acute in the case of Racine, for there is exceptional evidence of his knowledge of rhetoric. Much has been written about the place of rhetoric in seventeenth-century French education[21] and even about Racine's attitude to rhetoric.[22] P. France concludes (p. 49) that 'the results of [his] inquiry into Racine's views on rhetoric are slight. We know that he was convinced of its value, we have a vague picture of the sort of rhetoric he preferred at different periods, but there is no clear statement of opinion except in the preface to *Bérénice*.' But P. France did not take account of the best evidence which Racine has left of his interest in rhetoric. For not only are there books which testify to such an interest; there is also a rather neglected manuscript.

That Racine was intimately acquainted with the precepts of the rhetoricians there can be no doubt. He left two volumes of Cicero's rhetorical writings with his own marginal annotations. In volume i of Cicero's *Opera*, published in Lyons in 1540, Racine annotated the first two books of the *De Inventione*, the first book of the *De Oratore*, and the *Orator*. Most of the annotations can be found in Mesnard's edition of Racine's *Œuvres* (vi.

---

[21] For the most recent *mise au point* of rhetoric in schools in 17th- and 18th-cent. France see L. W. B. Brockliss, *French Higher Education in the Seventeenth and Eighteenth Centuries* (Oxford, 1987), 126–33. He also comments on theatrical performances in the school curriculum (pp. 163–74).

[22] On Racine's education see W. McC. Stewart, 'L'Éducation de Racine', *Cahiers de l'Association internationale des études françaises*, 3 (1953), 55–71. On his attitude to rhetoric see France, *Racine's Rhetoric*, ch. 2 'Racine and Rhetoric'. France comments on the education offered at Port-Royal, Racine's refs. to rhetoric in his prefaces, the variants of his plays as sources for his attitude to rhetoric, and on his rhetorical practice outside drama.

332–5) and in Picard's (ii. 975–8), and the volume itself is in the Bibliothèque Nationale (Rés. X. 2293). In another edition of Cicero's rhetorical writings, published in Lyons in 1546, Racine annotated the *De Oratore* again, and the *Brutus*. These annotations are in Mesnard (vi. 335) and in Picard (ii. 978–9), but there is no longer any trace of the volume itself, which, according to Mesnard (vi. 331–2), was sold in 1868. Racine's annotations are mostly very brief summaries of the contents of the treatises, but show him alive to all aspects of rhetoric, its history, and its theory.

The list of Racine's books compiled after his death reveals that he possessed a copy of Quintilian's *Institutio*, published in Lyons in 1665, a copy of Aristotle's *Opera*, in both Greek and Latin, published in Geneva in 1605, and a copy of Aristotle's *Rhetoric*, translated into French and published in Paris in 1654.[23]

Most instructive of all as to the state of Racine's rhetorical knowledge is the manuscript in which he copied out extracts from Quintilian's work, preserved at the Bibliothèque Nationale (fonds français 12,888). This manuscript contains the dramatist's extracts from Tacitus' *Annals* and *Histories* and then, on pp. 239–493, his extracts from Quintilian. On the cover of the manuscript are the following words, apparently in the hand of Louis Racine:[24] 'Extraits ecrits par Jean Racine des auteurs Latins qu'il lisoit à Port Royal en 1656. il avoit alors environ 15 ans.' Louis Racine may well have wished to make his father even more precocious than he was, for in 1656 the future dramatist was 16 or 17, not 15.

Of the extracts from Quintilian P. France says no more than that they are 'numerous'.[25] Neither Mesnard nor Picard thought them worth editing. The only study of them occurs in a most unlikely place, C. Fierville's edition of the first book of Quintilian's *Institutio*, published in 1890. With alterations to spelling and punctuation, Fierville reproduces Racine's extracts from the Epistle to Trypho and book 1 of the *Institutio* (pp. cli–clxi) and in a few pages of commentary (pp. xxxvii–xl) makes the claim that

---

[23] See R. Picard, *Nouveau Corpus Racinianum* (Paris, 1976), 446–51.

[24] It is C. Fierville who identifies the hand as that of Louis Racine. See his edn. of Quintilian, *De Institutione Oratoria liber primus*, pp. xxxviii–xl (p. xxxviii n. 5).

[25] *Racine's Rhetoric*, 37.

'ce travail personnel d'un jeune homme qui était alors un simple écolier, et qui devait être le grand Racine, mérite d'être tiré de l'oubli où il est resté' (p. xl). A century on, the extracts still lie forgotten.

To some extent the extracts reveal Racine as the diligent school-boy simply copying out examples of fine writing. He is particularly fond of extended similes. So, for instance, he notes down Quintilian's comparison of the relationship of rhetorician and pupil to that of birds and their young (2. 6. 7; pp. 274–5):[26]

Cui rei simile quidam facientes aves cernimus, quae teneris infirmisque fetibus cibos ore suo collatos partiuntur; at cum visi sunt adulti, paulum egredi nidis et circumvolare sedem illam praecedentes ipsae docent, tum expertas vires libero caelo suaeque ipsorum fiduciae permittunt.

(We may draw a lesson from the birds of the air, whom we see distributing the food which they have collected in their bills among their weak and helpless nestlings; but as soon as they are fledged, we see them teaching their young to leave the nest and fly round about it, themselves leading the way; finally, when they have proved their strength, they are given the freedom of the open sky and left to trust in themselves.)

In the margin of p. 274 he draws attention to this extract with the note 'comparison with bees' ('Comp. ab avibus'). Alternatively, he extracts *sententiae*, striking for their epigrammatic expression of an unusual thought:

Ex quo mihi inter virtutes grammatici habebitur aliqua nescire. (1. 8. 21; p. 258.)

(Consequently I shall count it a merit in a teacher of literature that there should be some things which he does not know.)

The extracts are not simply the notes of someone who wishes to remember the essential elements of rhetoric presented by Quintilian. Indeed the subject-matter of the extracts is almost as varied as Quintilian's own all-embracing and leisurely presentation of the art. Racine notes that the genuine student of rhetoric should not have mercenary ends (1. 12. 16–19); he takes note of how the teacher should behave in class (2. 1. 5–8); he copies a long

---

[26] Refs. are first to the text of Quintilian, then, by p. number, to Racine's MS. The Latin quotations are as given in the edn. and trans. of Quintilian by H. E. Butler (Loeb). Racine was using an edn. which does not tally entirely with that of Butler, but the variants are mostly insignificant.

passage on the need for the student's imagination to be developed before his critical faculties (2. 4. 3–7). From books 3, 4, and 5 he takes note of Quintilian's advice on the various parts of a speech and on the use of arguments. He takes down the etymology of *eloqui* (8, pr. 15), the definition of 'metaphor' (8. 6. 4), and some points from a technical analysis of rhythm (9. 4), from a critical analysis of Greek and Roman writers (10. 1), and from a discussion of the importance and methods of imitation (10. 2). He shows an interest in Quintilian's serious discussion of the morality of the orator (12. 2), but also copies down the rhetorician's casual reflexion that the memory works better after a good night's rest (11. 2. 43).

Quintilian's book is about the entire education, indeed lifestyle, of the orator, and Racine's extracts reflect the same broad interest. But there are inevitably some extracts which acquire a special significance in the light of the schoolboy's subsequent career.

At the beginning of book 10 Quintilian discourses at length on all the main Greek and Roman authors. He covers the range of genres: philosophy, history, forensic and political oratory, epic, love poetry, didactic poetry, satire, comedy, and tragedy. This is the part of the *Institutio* from which Racine makes his greatest concentration of extracts. He avidly notes down Quintilian's critical comments on all the well-known writers of antiquity, with the sole exception of the tragedians. This may well be due to the influence of his masters at Port-Royal, not favourably disposed towards the dramatic arts. Clearly, the 16-year-old youth was yet to develop a special interest in tragedy, and while he was consolidating his knowledge of rhetoric with this close reading of Quintilian the idea of rhetoric in the service of drama must have been far from his mind.

Or was it? Subconsciously the schoolboy must have been learning about the dramatic nature of rhetorical activity. For instance, two of the references to Quintilian made in the previous section of this chapter to illustrate this were noted down by Racine: the story of Accius (p. 343) and how to provoke pity for a captured town (p. 386). But there are many other extracts which imply that the young Racine was struck by Quintilian's strong suggestion of the dramatic nature of oratory, his suggestion that the orator should be able to grip an audience. The would-be orator should go along to trials to watch the clashes between experienced orators; he should then go home and practise speaking on both sides in the same or similar cases (10. 5. 19–20; p. 439). The spectacle of two opposing orators deploying the figures of speech can be as exciting as a sword-fight:

Ut in armorum certamine adversos ictus et rectas ac simplices manus cum videre, tum etiam cavere ac propulsare facile est, aversae tectaeque minus sunt observabiles, et aliud ostendisse quam petas artis est, sic oratio, quae astu caret, pondere modo et impulsu proeliatur; simulanti variantique conatus in latera atque in terga incurrere datur et arma avocare et velut nutu fallere. (9. 1. 20–1; p. 394.)

(Just as in sword-play it is easy to see, parry, and ward off direct blows and simple and straightforward thrusts, while side-strokes and feints are less easy to observe and the task of the skilful swordsman is to give the impression that his design is quite other than it actually is, even so the oratory in which there is no guile fights by sheer weight and impetus alone; on the other hand, the fighter who feints and varies his assault is able to attack flank or back as he will, to lure his opponent's weapons from their guard and to outwit him by a slight inclination of the body.)

Though in book 11 he ignores many of the comments on persuasive gestures which he will later write into the text of his plays, he takes copious notes about the need to train the voice and control its tone. In his final book Quintilian gives a thumbnail sketch of the orator, who should always be ready to do battle:

Non oppressum se ac deprehensum credet orator, cui disciplina et studium et exercitatio dederit vires etiam facilitatis; quem armatum semper ac velut in procinctu stantem non magis unquam in causis oratio quam in rebus cotidianis ac domesticis sermo deficiet, nec se unquam propter hoc oneri subtrahet, modo sit causae discendae tempus; nam cetera semper sciet. (12. 9. 20–1; p. 480.)

(The orator, on whom training, study and practice have conferred the gift of facility, will never regard himself as lost or taken at a hopeless disadvantage. He stands armed for battle, ever ready for the fray, and his eloquence will no more fail him in the courts than speech will fail him in domestic affairs and the daily concerns of his life: and he will never shirk his burden for fear of failing to find words, provided he has time to study his case: for all other knowledge will always be at his command.)

While this ever-ready orator is not like all Racine's characters, he is like a good many, and I shall argue that it is precisely in the depiction of such alert, if not always successful, orators that the dramatic success of Racine's verbal action lies.

Both Corneille and d'Aubignac criticize the more leisurely or poetic use of language by dramatic characters, on the grounds that this is not verbal action; it is not dramatically interesting. Quintilian makes much the same point about orators who use purple, but irrelevant, passages in their speeches and thereby lose sight of their persuasive goal. It is a point which Racine notes down on three occasions.[27]

In this schoolboy exercise Racine reveals an early awareness of persuasive and dramatically interesting speech. In the survey of rhetorical theory which follows, I shall sometimes illustrate points by drawing on Quintilian. Whenever these points were also noted by Racine, I shall give the page reference to his manuscript.

iv. RHETORICAL THEORY: *INVENTIO* AND *DISPOSITIO*

If verbal action is to do with persuasive discourse, it follows that characters' confrontations might be analysed with the tools of traditional rhetoric. Though the precepts of the rhetoricians were designed to help those who wanted to compose a speech, the same precepts have long been used by those wishing to analyse the speeches of others. It should be possible to analyse the use that characters make of at least four of the five parts of rhetoric: *inventio*, *dispositio*, *elocutio*, and *actio*. *Memoria*, the fourth part of rhetoric, is rather the job of the actor who has to learn his lines.[28] I have explained in the Introduction that I shall be concerned with analysing the *inventio* and *dispositio* of Racine's characters. With the exception of a few comments when *actio* is used in the passages that I analyse, this fifth part of rhetoric has been left aside because the rhetoricians, in general, offer comparatively fewer guide-lines for a systematic analysis of *actio* in dramatic texts than they do for the first three parts of rhetoric. I have also left aside *elocutio* on the grounds that P. France, in *Racine's Rhetoric*, has already paid a considerable amount of attention to

---

[27] 7. 1. 41, p. 367; 12. 9. 1–6, p. 480; and 12. 10. 48, pp. 485–6 (specifically on *sententiae*).

[28] *Actio* has an ambivalent role. The characters conceived by the dramatist can make use of *actio* in their attempts to persuade one another; but the actors may also use *actio* for clues about how best to deliver their lines. It is this latter aspect of *actio* which interests A. Grear in her Ph.D. thesis on 'Rhetoric and the Art of the French Tragic Actor', Univ. of St Andrews, 1982.

this part of rhetoric in Racine's plays, albeit in the context more of a stylistic, rather than a theatrical, study. As well as these negative reasons for focusing simply on *inventio* and *dispositio*, there are positive ones. Verbal action certainly interests the audience by concentrating their minds on the persuasive strategies of the characters, but it is above all their use and presentation of arguments that holds the spectators in suspense as to what the resulting course of action might be. It is particularly *what* characters have to say (*inventio* and, to some extent, *dispositio*) rather than their choice of words and construction of sentences (*elocutio*) that makes verbal action such an effective theatrical technique. And it is precisely their *inventio* and *dispositio* that have received little attention in the past. Indeed, whilst he acknowledges that 'the plays are barely interrupted verbal battles' and that 'persuasion is an element of the first importance' (p. 206), P. France is so predominantly concerned with *elocutio* that he does not really show how *inventio* and *dispositio* can be wielded to demonstrate the theatricality of the characters' speeches. He claims that *mores*, one of the three main parts of *inventio*, are 'hardly relevant to tragedy since its purpose is to show the judges without ostentation how good a man the orator is . . . But in Racine all the characters know each other too well for this to be useful' (p. 220). It will emerge from my analyses that, on the contrary, *mores* are very relevant to tragedy and that they are a particularly theatrical strategy, precisely because the characters do not always know each other well enough.

In order to follow my analyses a knowledge of *inventio* and *dispositio* and their related terminology is essential. Although the hordes of figures pertaining to *elocutio* are now well known by literary critics, the elements of the first two parts of rhetoric, to judge from the lack of frequency with which critics mention them, are poorly known. Yet they are easier to master than the figures of speech, because they are considerably fewer. What follows is a sketch of those parts of rhetorical theory which will be used to illuminate my analysis of the theatricality of Racine's verbal action. I shall use mostly Latin terminology for reasons of clarity: the English or French terms are often words which have many non-rhetorical connotations.

There are of course other accounts of *inventio* and *dispositio* to which the critic might turn for guidance. The two enormous volumes of H. Lausberg's *Handbuch der literarischen Rhetorik* are substantial and authoritative, but confusing in their welter of detail. R. A. Lanham's *A Handlist of Rhetorical Terms* is useful as a reference list, but has too little discussion and explanation of the terms and too great an emphasis on *elocutio*. The two short works by P. Dixon (*Rhetoric*) and O. Reboul (*La Rhétorique*) are interesting introductions to rhetoric in general, but say too little about the features of *inventio* and *dispositio*. There is the same problem with a number of critical works which, though they offer a summary of rhetorical theory, lay particular stress on *elocutio* because for their authors rhetorical analysis is principally a study of this third part of rhetoric.[29]

The best and clearest account of *inventio* and *dispositio* for reference purposes is to be found in A. Kibédi-Varga's *Rhétorique et littérature*. If I am not content simply to refer my reader to this work it is because his account is based on not only seventeenth- but also eighteenth-century rhetoricians, all writing in the vernacular. Moreover, when presenting the *loci*, an important part of *inventio*, he follows the particular plan of the eighteenth-century writer, Crevier. I have preferred to base my account on the tradition which prevailed until the latter half of the seventeenth century. I have used the main ancient texts: Aristotle's *Rhetoric*; the *Rhetorica ad Herennium*; Cicero's *De Inventione, Topica, De Oratore*, and *De Partitione Oratoria*;[30] and Quintilian's *Institutio Oratoria*. I have also used the extremely popular school textbook of the Jesuit Soarez, *De Arte Rhetorica*,[31] which was apparently read at Port-Royal.[32] I have drawn on the more substantial reference work by N. Caussin, his *De Rhetorica Sacra et Humana*, as well as on some of the first vernacular rhetorics: R. Bary, *La Rhétorique française*; Le Gras, *La Réthorique* [sic] *française*; and

---

[29] e.g. France, *Racine's Rhetoric*, pp. 17–18, and *Rhetoric and Truth in France* (Oxford, 1972), ch. 1; B. Vickers, *Classical Rhetoric in English Poetry* (London, 1970), ch. 3; S. Harwood, *Rhetoric in the Tragedies of Corneille* (New Orleans, 1977), ch. 1; and P. Bayley, *French Pulpit Oratory 1598–1650* (Cambridge, 1980), ch. 2. A notable exception is M. Joseph's *Shakespeare's Use of the Arts of Language* (New York, 1966), which gives examples of *inventio*, as well as *elocutio*, from the plays of Shakespeare and the rhetorics of his contemporaries.

[30] His other works on rhetoric (*De Optimo Genere Oratorum, Brutus*, and *Orator*) say little about *inventio* and *dispositio*.

[31] Bayley gives a good impression of what it is like to read through Soarez's manual (*French Pulpit Oratory*, 23–9).

[32] France, *Racine's Rhetoric*, 37.

B. Lamy, *L'Art de parler.*[33] Moreover, although it is not a rhetoric book and is indeed hostile in some ways to traditional rhetoric, *La Logique; ou l'art de penser* by A. Arnauld and P. Nicole of Port-Royal is useful in promoting an understanding of some of the issues involved in *inventio*.

I shall present a coherent account of *inventio* and *dispositio* based on these various rhetorics. In doing this I shall leave aside that popular pastime of nearly all rhetoricians, splitting hairs, and shall take only what I need to conduct my analysis of dramatic texts. This procedure is sanctioned by Quintilian and, indirectly, by Racine, who noted down this passage:

Nam [historias] receptas aut certe claris auctoribus memoratas exposuisse satis est. Persequi quidem, quid quis unquam vel contemptissimorum hominum dixerit, aut nimiae miseriae aut inanis iactantiae est et detinet atque obruit ingenia melius aliis vacatura. (1. 8. 18; p. 258.)

(For it is sufficient to set down the version [of the story] which is generally received or at any rate rests upon good authority. But to ferret out everything that has ever been said on the subject even by the most worthless of writers is a sign of tiresome pedantry or empty ostentation, and results in delaying and swamping the mind when it would be better employed on other themes.)

1. THE PARTS OF RHETORIC

Rhetoric is the art, oratory is the practice. The art traditionally has five parts, of which it is generally said that *inventio* is about finding things to say; *dispositio* is about putting what one has found into some sort of order; *elocutio* is about dressing up one's findings in effective language; *memoria* is about memorizing the finished product; and *actio* is about performing what one has learnt with the appropriate tone of voice and gestures. 'Trouver, disposer, orner, retenir, prononcer' is Racine's summary of the five parts in an annotation of Cicero's *De Oratore* (*Œuvres complètes*, ed. Picard, ii. 978).

These categories are less watertight than they might at first appear. For instance, there are three kinds of oratory and rhetoricians

---

[33] I have used the 2nd edn., publ. in 1676, which has a 'discours dans lequel on donne une idée de l'art de persuader', absent from the 1st edn. of 1675.

treat discussion of them sometimes as part of *inventio* and some-times not. For the sake of clarity I shall discuss the three kinds of oratory separately from *inventio*: the distinction between the three kinds is vital for an understanding of Racine's verbal action. There is a similar fuzziness about the category of *dispositio*. *Dispositio* as treated by some rhetoricians includes many precepts which are actually about finding things to say suitable for particular parts of a speech. This is no doubt why Quintilian is inclined to consider *dispositio* as an aspect of *inventio* (1. pr. 22). Nor is there any obvious answer to the question 'What precisely is the orator putting in order or arranging with the help of the principles of *dispositio*?' Modern commentators assume that *dispositio* con-cerns the main component parts of a speech. Yet it is equally concerned with the organization of material within these parts and even, according to some rhetoricians, with the arrangement of some of the material found in the various *loci* of *inventio* into a suitable argumentative form. I shall treat forms of argument as part of *inventio*.

2. THREE KINDS OF ORATORY

Rhetoric aims to provide instruction in writing and speaking for just about every sort of formal occasion. Theorists distinguish three kinds of discourse: judicial or forensic, deliberative, and demonstrative or epideictic. Quintilian stresses the well-nigh all-embracing nature of these three kinds:

Aristoteles tres faciendo partes orationis, iudicialem, deliberativam, dem-onstrativam, paene et ipse oratori subiecit omnia; nihil enim non in haec cadit. (2. 21. 23.)

(Aristotle himself also by his tripartite division of oratory, into forensic, deliberative, and demonstrative, practically brought everything into the orator's domain, since there is nothing that may not come up for treat-ment by any one of these three kinds of rhetoric.)

Judicial oratory has its *raison d'être*, as its name suggests, in the lawcourts. Judicial speeches are based upon things that have happened in the past; they are concerned with accusing and de-fending, and look forward to the decision of a judge or jury, which will reveal whether the prosecution or the defence has proved more persuasive.

Deliberative oratory is most suited to the political arena, but can be used in all situations in which the orator wishes to persuade others to adopt a particular course of action or simply to change their minds. It is concerned as much with dissuading as with persuading and looks towards a decision which will affect the future.

Unlike judicial and deliberative oratory, the demonstrative kind is not concerned with the practical issue of decision-making. It can be seen much more as discourse for display, in which the orator, not trying to cover up his rhetorical technique and focus the listener's mind on a decision to be taken, unashamedly seeks to make the listeners revel in his performance: for they have no decision to make as a consequence. Traditionally, demonstrative oratory involves praising or, much less frequently, blaming some-one. Speeches of welcome and funeral orations are both examples of demonstrative discourse. Persuasion is not generally regarded as being of the essence in demonstrative oratory. If there is persuasion, it is of a less urgent, more leisurely kind.

Quintilian usefully demonstrates the breadth of rhetoric and, at the same time, the danger of trying to define the three kinds of oratory too narrowly, when he asks

in quo genere versari videbimur, cum querimur, consolamur, mitigamus, concitamus, terremus, confirmamus, praecipimus, obscure dicta interpre-tamur, narramus, deprecamur, gratias agimus, gratulamur, obiurgamus, maledicimus, describimus, mandamus, renuntiamus, optamus, opinamur, plurima alia. (3. 4. 3.)

(on what kind of oratory are we to consider ourselves to be employed, when we complain, console, pacify, excite, terrify, encourage, instruct, explain obscurities, narrate, plead for mercy, thank, congratulate, reproach, abuse, describe, command, retract, express our desires and opinions, to mention no other of the many possibilities)

The three kinds of oratory are not as sharply delineated as standard definitions suggest. Dissuading a group of councillors from adopt-ing Plan X might include an accusation against the promoter of Plan X, who might, for example, be motivated exclusively by unacknowledged personal interests. This speech would integrate judicial into deliberative oratory. About this kind of activity Le

Gras says: 'Pour ce qui est de la maniere de mêler ensemble les trois Genres ou de les substituer l'un à l'autre à propos; c'est la partie la plus considérable & la plus difficile de l'Eloquence' (p. 10). Although some flexibility is clearly necessary in identifying the kind of oratory in any given text, the basic distinction remains useful:

JUDICIAL: accusation and defence
DELIBERATIVE: persuasion and dissuasion
DEMONSTRATIVE: praise and blame

Although it is not central to the rhetorical tradition, I shall suggest in Chapter 3 that a fourth kind, inquisitorial oratory, is also of help to the dramatic critic.

3. *INVENTIO*

While *inventio* may be broadly seen as concerned with offering suggestions about finding things to say, its first task is to provide the orator with an explanation of the framework of his speech. These explanations are known as *status* doctrine. They concern judicial oratory and invite the orator to fix precisely the question which he is going to answer in his pleading. This part of rhetorical theory is extremely technical, because closely related to aspects of Roman law. 'It is safe to say', opines M. L. Clarke, 'that the world would have been none the worse without the *status* doctrine.'[34] Racine the schoolboy chose to ignore the complexities of Quintilian's pages on the subject. *Status* doctrine is of no help in analysing dramatic texts.

(a) Finding Things to Say

'Finding things to say' is a rather general and vague definition of *inventio*. *Inventio* more specifically concerns finding the appropriate means with which to secure persuasion and there are three sources from which most means of persuasion may be drawn: *mores* (also known as *ethos* or *les mœurs*), *affectus* (*pathos* or *les passions*), and *probationes* (*logos* or *les preuves*).

[34] *Rhetoric at Rome* (London, 1953), 163.

(1) *MORES* AND *AFFECTUS*

The use which the orator makes of *mores* and *affectus* is one of many features which distinguish his task from that of the philosopher, who, in theory, has no use for either of these parts of *inventio*. *Mores* means 'character', either the character of the orator, or that of the person or persons on whose behalf he is speaking, or indeed the character of his opponent. The orator should introduce into his speech such details as will create a good impression of his own cause and a bad impression of the opposite cause. If he comes across to the audience as a good man, he is more likely to be believed. In particular, according to B. Lamy, he needs to show 'témoignages d'amitié', 'un zèle sincère', 'la modestie', 'la probité', 'la prudence', and 'la bienveillance' (p. 294).

Affectus, the passions, are more concerned with the listeners. Each kind of oratory has its own passions, which, if successfully aroused in the audience, should help the cause of victory: pity and indignation are especially appropriate for judicial oratory, fear and hope for deliberative, admiration and scorn for demonstrative. The orator needs to be equipped with a knowledge of the passions and many rhetoricians, most notably Aristotle (1388[b]–93[a]), provide an elementary guide to psychology in which the deep-seated interests of different social groups at different ages are described in some detail. This guide, however, is but a substitute for a precise knowledge of the specific people whom the orator has to face. Le Gras points out three steps which the orator must take to arouse effectively the passions of his audience (p. 78):

La premiere [est] d'envisager son sujet de tous costés pour reconnoistre ce qu'il y a de malin, d'odieux & de miserable, pour dire ensuitte ce qui luy semble de plus capable de toucher le Juge ou l'Auditeur. La seconde est d'exaggerer les choses au delà de ce qu'elles sont, en élevant ce qui est mediocre à tel point qu'il paroisse tres-grand, tres-atroce, tres-insupportable.

The third step is an aspect of *actio* and involves the orator's acting as if he himself were under the effect of the very passions which he is trying to arouse.

Le Gras tries to give some indications as to what sort of topics will arouse the required passions. To stimulate a kindly disposition in his audience the orator will turn to 'les choses plaisantes, agreables & dignes de loüange & de recommendation' (pp. 72–3); to churn up hatred and indignation, he should look to 'les vices, l'indignité, la turpitude, la lâcheté, l'infamie & les richesses mal acquises' (p. 73); fear will be provoked by the mention of 'les choses facheuses & dangereuses' (p. 75); pity and compassion by 'les malheurs, les afflictions, la pauvreté, les maladies, les blessures & toutes sortes de souffrances' (p. 76).

Despite these indications, it is clear that rhetoricians can do little more than suggest methods of approach for the orator who wishes to find things which will exploit the basic interests of his audience and stir their passions; the same might be said of rhetoricians' advice for *mores*. Once the orator has grasped the function of these two parts of *inventio*, he must examine the subject of his case and the character of those whom he is trying to persuade. This process will prompt him into finding things to say. Further help regarding *mores* and *affectus* is given in the *dispositio* section of most rhetorics.

(II) *PROBATIONES*

Important as *mores* and *affectus* are for the successful accomplishment of the orator's task, *probationes*, the proofs, normally account for a substantial part of his means of persuasion. The rhetoricians are never at a loss when it comes to formulating specific rules and advice for the orator in search of proofs. Their major distinction is between real proofs and artificial proofs, *probationes inartificiales* and *probationes artificiales*. This is a case when the Latin terms are much preferable to the English, for the English word 'proof' conjures up a philosophical demonstration of the truth. This is quite different from the orator's *probationes*.

Probationes Inartificiales

Anything which is not a product of the orator's own thought-processes, but which he can enlist to support his case, constitutes a *probatio inartificialis*. Among the possible types, according to Quintilian, are legal rulings, rumours, evidence extracted by torture, documents relevant to a case, oaths taken by those involved, and the testimony of witnesses (5. 1. 2). Caussin specifies further: history, fables, parables, adages, aphorisms, laws, scripture (pp. 184–97). To these might be added: omens, dreams, and the quotation or citation of any relevant authority. Some of these are likely to be more persuasive than others.

Though not always classified as *probationes inartificiales*, *signa* fulfil a comparable function. The signs in question might, in a judicial case, be blood-stained clothing, dangerous weapons, or screams (Quintilian, 5. 9. 1). Like other *probationes inartificiales*, *signa* may be available for the well-informed orator to employ if advantageous use can be made of them.

Probationes Artificiales

The *probationes artificiales* are the most infamous part of *inventio*. To discover suitable *probationes artificiales* the orator has to look within himself; he has to make a mental visit to some places, the *loci*, from which he will return with material constituting a *probatio artificialis*. If the orator's mind is blank on any given subject, his use of the *loci* should give him suggestions about what to say:

Qvod literae sunt apud Grammaticos, hoc apud Rhetores loci: ut enim ex literis verba, sic ex locis rationes & argumenta coalescunt... Quamobrem & adolescentibus diligenter inculcandi sunt, & in iis frequenter exercendi, ex quo ad omnem dicendi materiam reclusos invētionis fontes commodiùs, feliciúsque habeant. (Caussin, p. 198.)

(What letters are to grammarians, so the *loci* are to rhetoricians; for as words are formed by letters, so arguments and proofs grow out of *loci*... Therefore boys should undergo careful instruction in the *loci* and be given frequent practice in them so that the very founts of invention will be opened up to provide material for every oratorical function, and the young will then have a firmer, happier grasp of them.)

Clearly the *loci* were thought extremely useful. Every schoolboy was as well practised in the use of the *loci* as in the use of the figures.

The *loci*, twenty-eight according to Aristotle, sixteen according to Cicero and his followers, and seven according to the eighteenth-century rhetorician Crevier,[35] are meant to be used as a checklist so that the orator can be sure of not passing by any ideas which he

---

[35] See Kibédi-Varga, *Rhétorique et littérature*, 38.

could use to his advantage. Everybody uses figures of speech, but most people do not realize it; similarly everybody uses the *loci*. But Caussin, perhaps to encourage the reluctant pupil, suggests that those who have learnt the art of using the *loci* can speak and write more effectively than those who have not (p. 198). A visit to the *loci* will throw up many ideas. After considering all the possibilities, the orator will be able to use the best ideas for his purpose.

Use of the *loci* implies a mental strategy which, so long as the orator has some knowledge to start with, should lead to a variety of things to say on any subject. I propose to demonstrate the mechanism of each of the Ciceronian *loci*, which were the ones most commonly referred to in the seventeenth century. I shall illustrate the way in which the orator sets about consulting each *locus* by quoting extracts from Caussin, who supposes that he has to produce a piece of demonstrative oratory in praise of the lily and takes his reader on a tour of the *loci* to show how they can be of help. Caussin's illustration (pp. 199–201) has the advantage of being sustained, whereas most rhetoricians give only brief, isolated examples of each *locus*. Although his example is destined for demonstrative oratory, the principle of visiting the *loci* is the same for all three kinds of oratory. Caussin's example also reveals the fluid nature of the *loci*. Some *loci* yield remarkably similar material. Hence Crevier's reduction of the number to eight. It is, therefore, not always possible to say that certain material has come from a specific *locus*. Moreover, in visiting any one *locus* different individuals will produce different material, or *probationes*. For these individuals will approach the *locus* with varying frames of mind and varying amounts of knowledge.

Here, then, is a rapid tour of the *loci* and of their yield in praise of the lily.[36]

(1) *Definitio*: This requires the orator to define the term or idea about which he wishes to say something so as to give it the gloss that he desires. Caussin gives two examples of *definitio* (p. 199), the first *per synoniam*, the second *per descriptionem*:

Qvid est enim aliud lilium, quàm terræ ornamentum, plantarum gloria, oculus florum, pratorum gemma, pulchritudo radiis suauiter emicantibus

---

[36] For Cicero's list of 16 *loci* see *Topica*, 18. 71.

fulgurans ... Vtuntur enim oratores, vt docebo, maximè in exornatiuo genere, definitionibus.

(For what is a lily, if it is not the ornament of the earth, the glory of plànts, the delight of flowers, the jewel of the meadows, beauty radiant with its sweetly shining rays ... Orators, as I shall show, use *definitiones* most of all in demonstrative oratory.)

Videte ut est ex omni parte formosum. Num excelsa facies? num maiestate cinctum caput, cuius oneri vix collum sufficit? Num argenteorum foliorum striati ordines? Num paulatim in latitudinem se explicantes angustiæ? Num resupina per ambitum labella?

(See how it is beautiful in every respect. Does it not have a lofty appearance? a head ringed with majesty, and a neck which can barely support the burden? Does it not have fluted ranks of silvery leaves? does it not have slenderness opening out into breadth? and a curled lip around the edge?)

(2) *Partitio* or *partium enumeratio*: The orator divides his term, or idea, or subject into its constituent parts. This *locus* provides Caussin with much to say about the lily. He illustrates its many varieties (p. 199):

Quò mihi videtur etiam spectasse natura, quæ lilia in tot pulchritudinis genera diuisit, ut non vnum dumtaxat florem, sed omnes omnium eximios colores, & dignitatem videantur assequuta; si candida consideres, quid purius, aut amabilius? Si Persiana, quid speciosus? Caulis est illis ternum cubitorum, quem fusè ambiunt folia ex cæruleo virentia, mucronata, flores nutantes nolarum effigie, nigricant: radix bulbosa, fissa, minimè squammis loricata, albida, aversa parte sessilis, & plana, porrectis subtus obscurè flaventibus. Si Polyrrhisa, quid artificiosius? ... Si rubra, quid magis varium? ... Si cruenta, quibus flores rutilant, & bulbos nucleis stipatos proferunt, quid ardentius?

(Thus nature seems to me to have ensured that she divided lilies into so many types of beauty that they seem to have attained the status of not just one flower but the dignity and outstanding range of colours of all flowers; if you considered the white ones, what could be purer or more attractive? if the Persian variety, what more beautiful? Their stems are three feet long, and their leaves spread out from them, green from blue, and dagger-like, while the flowers, shiney-black, nod like bells; their root is bulbous, split, not at all scaly, with one part flattened, and smooth, with yellow lines deep inside. If the many-rooted variety, what greater a work of art? ... If the reds, what more varied? ... If the blood-red ones, whose flowers glow like fire and produce bulbs crammed with little kernels, what could be more blazing?)

Approaching *partium enumeratio* in a different frame of mind, another orator might have produced what Caussin says under *definitio per descriptionem*.

(3) *Notatio* or *etymologia*: The orator considers the etymology of a relevant term to find out if its original meaning can be of help in formulating an argument (p. 199):

Nec immeritò profectò Græci λείριον & καλλείριον; Latini, Iunonis rosam; Mauritani, Susen ab vrbe potentissima, nobilissimáque appellant. Hæc omnia sapiunt blandam pulchritudinis maiestatem, sed efficaciùs λείριον venustum, suauem, amabilem florem significat.

(Not without justice do the Greeks call it lily; the Romans the rose of Juno; and the Mauritanians Susa, after the most noble and powerful city. All these names recognize the attraction and majesty of its beauty, but 'lily' particulary signifies the charming, gentle, and likeable flower.)

(4) *Coniugata*: '*Coniugata* are things which come from words of the same type' (Soarez, p. 38). Soarez (p. 39) furnishes the well-known line of Terence as an example: *Homo sum, humani nihil a me alienum puto* ('I am a human being; therefore I think nothing human irrelevant to me'). Caussin (pp. 199–200):

Nihil mirum igitur, si quicquid delicato pulchritudinis flore suauiter enitescit, hoc à lilio liliatum dicimus: Sic orationem liliatam dicimus, *une oraison fleurdelisée*.

(No wonder then, if anything gleams sweetly with the delicate flower of beauty, that we call it 'lily-like', after the lily; so the French call a speech 'lily-like': *une oraison fleurdelisée*.)

The *locus coniugatorum* exploits words with the same root.

(5) *Genus* and (6) *Species*: To explore the *locus generis* the orator will consider how the term or idea in which he is interested relates to an identifiably larger group of which it is a member. The *locus speciei* invites a consideration of the particular qualities of the word or idea within that larger group. Caussin gives the following examples, first of *genus*, then of *species* (p. 200):

Omnes quidem flores singularis naturæ ridentis clementia, ad humani generis oblectationem, vniversi decus, variásque utilitates, profudit; quorum vsu non modò profana recreantur, sed sacra ipsa excoluntur: (& hic latus dicendi campus).

(The exceptional clemency of smiling nature pours forth all the flowers for the delight of the human race, the pride of the universe, and various useful ends; with their use not only profane things are refreshed, but sacred things too are honoured (there is plenty of opportunity for expansion here).)

Verùm peculiari quodam iure lilium sibi vendicat, quod simul aspexeris, statim tibi praestantissimi omnium floris veniet in mentem.

(But by its own peculiar right the lily, once you have looked at it, comes immediately to strike you as the most outstanding flower of them all.)

The *locus generis* leads to praise of the lily because it is a flower. The *locus speciei* singles it out from all other flowers for particular, or special, praise. Another orator, instead of taking flower as *genus* and lily as *species* might have assumed lily to be *genus* and its many varieties to be *species*. Caussin, however, exhausted this line of development when he exploited *partitio*.

(7) *Similitudo*: The orator searches out things or actions similar to those in which he is principally interested to discover if they can be used to persuasive effect. Caussin points out that, like a tapestry, the lily is an object of universal admiration (p. 200):

Quid nos magis exhilaret quàm aspectus pulcherrimorum aulæorum? quæ natura omnium architecta, & parens, vbique strauit in suis latifundiis, ut admiranda forma & speciosa varietate colorum, radicis, caulis, ramorum, foliorum, floris, nostros oculos pasceret, ac reficeret, spectaculo quidem ornatissimo, & instructissimo?

(What can delight us more than looking at the most beautiful tapestries? Those things which nature, the architect and parent of everything, has scattered everywhere among its estates in order to feed and refresh our eyes with its wonderful beauty and outstanding variety of colours, roots, stems, shoots, leaves, flowers, in short with a most decorative and carefully executed spectacle?)

(8) *Dissimilitudo* or *differentia*: The orator explores the difference between the object of his interest and some other relevant object, a difference which his audience has probably not perceived and which should cast an advantageous light on the orator's cause. This *locus* is particularly useful for refuting a point developed by an opponent on the basis of the *locus similitudinis*. Caussin's example (p. 200):

Habent quidem manufacta, plerúmque egregiam venustatem: Sed tantum à naturali pulchritudine differunt, quantum natura Dei illius præpotentis administra, mortalium manus, vim, industriámque superat. (Et hîc excurri latiùs potest, in differentia naturalis pulchritudinis, & manufactæ.)

(Even man-made things for the most part have an outstanding charm; but they differ as much from natural beauty as nature, the hand-maiden of that powerful God, excels the industry, strength, and hands of mortals (and here it is possible to expand on the difference between natural and manufactured beauty).)

(9) *Contraria*: In a word, opposites. The orator explores things diametrically opposed to the object of his interest (Caussin, p. 200):

Si igitur natura ita instigante, flores nigros, infaustos, malè olentes detestatur: qua amoris beneuolentia lilium amplectemur? quo nihil ad candorem amœnius, nihil ad prosperitatis significationem candidius, ad odorem etiam, quem suauissimum spirat; dulcius quicquam esse potest?

(If nature prompts us to dislike black and unlucky flowers, and those which have an unpleasant smell, with what benevolence and love shall we embrace the lily? than which nothing is more pleasant in brightness, nothing fairer as a sign of prosperity; what a sweet breath it has; what can be more delicious?)

(10) *Adiuncta*: '*Adiuncta* are those things which are associated with the subject; like place, time and circumstance' (Soarez, p. 47). This invites an exploration of the circumstances surrounding whatever the orator is interested in. Caussin quotes a Latin hexameter to remind the orator of the traditional series of questions he can ask when visiting this *locus* (p. 242):

Quis, quid, ubi, quibus auxiliis, cur, quomodo, quando.

(Who, what, where, by what means, why, how, when.)

Caussin recalls things which have an historical connection with the lily, like the adoption of the flower as the French royal insignia (p. 200):

Acedit ad cæteras lilij virtutes, quòd in Francorum sit insignibus: Idque non humano consilio, sed Angeli cœlitùs deferentis beneficio: quo nihil ad lilij laudem dici potest illustrius.

(Another of the lily's virtues is that it is part of the French insignia; and this is not due to any human design, but thanks to an angel from heaven: nothing more illustrious could be said in praise of the lily than this.)

Such connections cast the flower in a favourable light.

(11) *Consequentia* and (12) *Antecedentia*: Closely connected with *adiuncta*, these *loci* suggest a consideration of the circum-

stances which necessarily precede or follow any given event. Caussin explains (p. 244):

Consequentia verò ea dico quæ rem necessariò consequuntur. Antecedentia, quæ rem necessariò antecedunt: ut si homo est, animal est; si Sol ortus est, dies est.

(In fact I call *consequentia* those things which necessarily follow the subject, and *antecedentia* those things which necessarily precede it: for example, if he is a man, he is an animal; if the sun has risen, it is day.)

These brief examples concerning man and animals, sun and day, both raise the possibility of an overlap between these *loci* and those of *genus* and *species* in the first case and *causae* and *effecta* (explained below) in the second. Thinking of the lily as the royal insignia, Caussin comes up with two possible courses of development, first *ex consequentibus*, then *ex antecedentibus* (p. 200):

Vbicunque Regia Maiestas ius dictura sederit, ibi lilia: vbicumque lilia fulserint, hîc Regiæ maiestatis quosdam radios præsentire te dicas.

(Wherever the regal majesty shall sit to deliver justice, there are lilies; wherever lilies shall shine, there you will say that you felt some rays of regal majesty.)

(13) *Repugnantia*: Though not unconnected with *contraria* and *dissimilitudo*, the *locus repugnantium* can produce possibilities for *probatio* which differ from those of the other two places. Soarez explains (p. 44):

Repugnantia neq; certa lege, neque numero inter se dissident, qua ratione à contrarijs, atque dissimilibus discernuntur: Exempli gratia, amare, & odio habere contraria sunt, amare verò & nocere, & lædere ... repugnantia sunt.

(*Repugnantia* do not disagree among themselves quantitatively or by being exact opposites, and this distinguishes them from *contraria* and *dissimiltudines*: for example, to love and to hate are *contraria*, but to love and to hurt or to harm ... are *repugnantia*.)

Caussin's illustration (p. 200):

Nec minùs repugnat Regem venerari, & calcare lilia, quàm Caesares adorare, eorúmque statuas frangere, deterere laureas, honoris insignia reuellere.

(To venerate the king and to spurn the lily is just as much an example of *repugnantia* as to adore the Caesars and to break their statues, to tear down their laurels, and to destroy their honourable insignia.)

An element of *comparatio* (explained below) has crept into this example of *repugnantia*.

(14) *Causae* and (15) *Effecta*:

Causa est, quæ sua vi efficit id cuius est causa: ut vulnus mortis ... ignis ardor. (Soarez, p. 44.)

(*Causa* is something which, of its own strength, brings about that of which it is the cause: for example, a wound is the cause of death ... heat the cause of fire.)

Effecta sunt ea quæ sunt orta de causis. (Ibid. 46.)

(*Effecta* are those things which result from causes.)

Soarez was particularly impressed by the *locus causarum* (ibid.):

Ex his causarum generibus tanquam ex fonte, non modò in causis, sed in omni scribendi genere magna argumentorum suppetit copia. Licebit igitur diligenter eo cognito non modò Oratoribus, & Philosophis, quorum est proprius, sed Historicis etiam & Poëtis multa, & varia & copiosa ex eo facilè depromere.

(From this kind of *causae*, as if from a spring, a great quantity of proofs flows forth, not only in judicial oratory, but in every type of writing. Therefore, once this is thoroughly known, not only orators and philosophers, for whom this is quite appropriate, but also historians and poets will be able readily to produce many various and copious things as a result of this.)

I shall leave aside the many divisions and sub-divisions of these two *loci*.[37] They would add nothing to my analyses. Here is what Caussin extracts from these *loci*: first (pp. 200–1), speculation about the origins of the lily (*causae*) and then (p. 201) suggestions about its benefit to mankind (*effecta*):

Siue igitur, cùm esset paruus, & lactens Hercules, nouercæ Iunonis vberibus suppositus, argenteus mammarum humor cælestibus stillis depluens, tantum florem produxerit, siue natura pleniùs suæ munificentiæ velificata ediderit, nihil in plantis inuenio diuinius.

(Therefore, whether, when Hercules was small and unweaned and still suckling at the breast of his stepmother Juno, the silvery liquid of her breasts produced this fine flower, or whether nature produced it with

---

[37] Bary's inventive powers are particularly efficient when he treats these two *loci*. For an explanation of his categories see Kibédi-Varga, *Rhétorique et littérature*, 42–5.

more than usual generosity, I find nothing more heavenly among the plants.)

Neque tantùm ob speciosam illam maiestatem dico, qua præditum est, sed propter magnas & vberes, quas in hominum commoditatem deriuat, vtilitates. Quis enim nescit quod habet Pallad. lib. 2 de re rustica, oleum lirinum ad morborum remedia, perquam salutare semper extitisse?

(I speak not so much because of the beautiful majesty with which it is endowed, but on account of its great and fertile usefulness which it employs for the convenience of men. For who does not know what Palladius says in his *De re rustica* (II), that lily-oil has always been a most wholesome cure for illnesses?)

(16) *Comparatio minorum, parium,* and *maiorum*:   There are three ways in which the orator can draw comparisons. He can compare the object of his interest with something similar, something greater, or something less. It is difficult to distinguish *comparatio parium* from *similitudo*. Comparison can involve the use of *exempla*. Le Gras particularly commended *exempla* to the orator (p. 62): 'Ils servent à orner les Arguments [i.e. *probationes*], & leur donner de l'agrément, & à les rendre forts & convain-quans.' Bary includes the following among his examples:

Si les travaux sont égaux, le salaire doit estre égal. (*comparatio parium*, p. 55.)

A-t-il esté chaste dans les tentations de la Cour? il sera continent dans les horreurs de la solitude. (*comparatio maiorum*, p. 57.)

Si cet ignorant est sage, quelle sagesse ne doit point avoir le sçavant? (*comparatio minorum*, p. 58.)

A final extract from Caussin's thoughts on the lily (p. 201) illustrates *comparatio minorum*:

Quid igitur si calthis, ac violis & huiusmodi floribus tantum tribuimus, quid lilio deberi existimatis? quod ipsum constat longè omnium esse præstantissimum?

(If we pay such tribute to marigolds, violets, and such like flowers, what do you think is owed to lilies, which, it is generally agreed, are by far the most outstanding of all?)

Such are the sixteen *loci* and the use to be made of them. One further example from the modern introduction to rhetoric by O. Reboul shows clearly and simply the genuine help that the *loci* can give to someone who needs to produce discourse on a given subject:

Supposons qu'un étudiant ait à disserter sur la 'culture'; sans avoir rien lu, il pourra appliquer les lieux de Lamy. A quel genre appartient la culture: savoir, savoir-faire? Quelle est sa différence: connaissances scientifiques, littéraires, 'générales'? Son étymologie: rapports avec l'agriculture, le culte? Ses conjugués: cultivé, culturel, inculte, acculturation? Ses incompatibilités: souci du résultat immédiat, spécialisation, fanatisme? Ses effets: sur l'intelligence, la moralité, la créativité? Ses causes: quel type d'éducation garantit-il la culture? (*La Rhétorique* (Paris, 1984), 23.)

Defined by Quintilian (5. 10. 20) as 'sedes argumentorum, in quibus latent, ex quibus sunt petenda' (the secret places where arguments reside, and from which they must be drawn forth), the *loci* above have nothing to do with what is generally understood by the term commonplaces. Commonplaces are set topics of a precise and fixed nature, which the orator can prepare in advance and insert into almost any speech with minimal adaptation. Of this practice Quintilian says:

Quidem sententiarum gratia verbosissimos locos arcessunt, cum ex locis debeat nasci sententia. Ita sunt autem speciosa haec et utilia, si oriuntur ex causa; ceterum quamlibet pulchra elocutio, nisi ad victoriam tendit, utique supervacua, sed interim contraria est. (2. 4. 31–2; Racine copied, p. 271, 'quamlibet ... contraria est'.)

(Some speakers, for example, introduce the most long-winded commonplaces just for the sake of the sentiments they contain, whereas rightly the sentiments should spring from the context. Such disquisitions are at once ornamental and useful, only if they arise from the nature of the case. But the most finished eloquence, unless it tend to the winning of the case, is to say the least superfluous and may even defeat its own purpose.)

The commonplaces, then, should be used sparingly and only when they genuinely help the cause of persuasion. The poverty of an orator's client might, for instance, provoke a digression on the appalling plight of the poor. Unlike the *loci* defined above, which are flexible and lend themselves to many applications, commonplaces are necessarily rigid and therefore of little help to those who are not intending to make a career of praising towns or speaking for poverty-stricken defendants.

The *loci* have had their detractors, particularly in the second half of the seventeenth century (though they clearly weathered the storm well, as they survived into the nineteenth). There are two main objections to emerge from the criticisms of Lamy (pp. 290–1) and Arnauld and Nicole (pp. 232–4). First, the *loci* are unnecessary: nobody really uses them to find material for a speech or a piece of writing; people use their common sense. And secondly, if people do try to use the *loci*, the result is often irrelevant and poor material. This is not the place to revive the *querelle des lieux*. It must be said, however, that it is impossible to know to what extent a speaker or writer steeped in the rhetorical tradition has consciously drawn on the *loci*. The same might be said of the figures of speech. Even rhetoricians admit that the use of the *loci* should become automatic and that the orator should eventually no longer need to use them as a checklist every time he wants an idea (Quintilian, 5. 10. 122–3; p. 336). Even Arnauld and Nicole, while making their criticism, imply that the *loci* can be of use to those who want to analyse the discourse of others: 'Il est vrai que tous les argumens [i.e. *probationes*] qu'on fait sur chaque sujet, se peuvent rapporter à ces chefs & à ces termes generaux qu'on appelle Lieux; mais ce n'est point par cette methode qu'on les trouve' (p. 234). As for the second objection, it is surely only bad orators who use the *loci* badly.

The *loci* have nothing definitive about them. Some material could be said to have been drawn from more than one *locus*. This does not matter, as long as the perusal of the *loci* has been a productive process for the orator. Moreover (and this is an important point), the material provided by the *loci*, sometimes no more than suggestions for lines of development, can rarely be inserted *tel quel* into a speech. It will usually have to be arranged into a form of argument relevant to the point being made. In practice, of course, the orator should be thinking about this at the same time as he is consulting the *loci*. Material found in the *loci* will be used alongside *probationes inartificiales* and alongside material suggested by a consideration of *mores* and *affectus*.

The completely ignorant orator stands little chance of finding anything to say. The *loci* will help the speaker with the momentarily blank mind, but not the one with the empty mind. To succeed, says Lamy, 'il faudroit posséder toutes les connaissances & n'ignorer rien' (p. 280). The orator must acquaint himself thoroughly with the subject of his speech and all its ramifications, before he sets about composing it. Knowledge is the first step to successful *inventio* and without it the orator's attempts to give the appropriate impression of himself and his client (*mores*), to arouse the right passions in the audience (*affectus*), and to find material (*probationes*), will leave him groping about in the dark.

(b) Forming Arguments

The word *argumentum* has two connotations in the language of rhetoric. It can connote 'proof' or *probatio* (what has been found as a result of consulting a *locus*). It can also connote 'a reasoned argument', the rational form in which the *probatio* can, but need not necessarily, be expressed.

The orator's material will usually be so deployed as to make it further the cause of persuasion. There are two schemes according to which he can shape his arguments: *ratiocinatio* (syllogistic reasoning) and *inductio* (inductive reasoning). The arrangement of the available material into persuasive arguments can have a bearing on the macrostructure and the microstructure of the orator's discourse. It is, however, not essential that all the material be so arranged. Poets, for instance, and demonstrative orators often do not arrange material into these forms of argument.

A whole speech might be constructed around a syllogism. Arnauld and Nicole show how Cicero's *Pro Milone* can be reduced to a variation on a syllogism (p. 228). The syllogism is the basic form of *ratiocinatio*, deductive reasoning.[38] It has three parts: major premiss, minor premiss, conclusion. For example:

> Tout arbre est vivant
> Le chesne est arbre
> Le chesne est vivant.   (Bary, p. 15)

While this form of reasoning, which allows the user to infer truth from truth, may suit the philosopher, it is not often of service to the orator, who would soon bore his audience by presenting a string of syllogisms and who, anyway, has frequently to deal with statements which are at most probable and which, therefore, would not carry conviction if used in the sparse framework of the traditional syllogism.

---

[38] *Ratiocinatio* also has a more precise sense: the comparison of the *rationes* of similar laws. See Cicero, *De Inventione*, 2. 49. 148.

The orator is more likely to use a variation on the syllogism. There are the more complex variations: the sorites, the dilemma, the epicheireme;[39] but the favourite, and the one which recurs persistently in dramatic texts, is the enthymeme.

The enthymeme is a reduced form of the syllogism, explained by Arnauld and Nicole as follows (p. 227): 'Les enthymemes sont . . . la maniere ordinaire dont les hommes expriment leurs raisonne-mens en supprimant la proposition qu'ils jugent devoir être facile-ment suppléée; & cette proposition, est tantôt la majeure, tantôt la mineure, quelquefois la conclusion.' An example from Bary (p. 19):

> Tout risible est homme
> Donc Pierre est homme. (p. 19)

This, to be a proper syllogism, would need the minor premiss: 'Pierre est risible'. It is also possible to have an enthymeme with only one part.

Inductio and *exempla* are related forms of argument, which draw their substance from the *loci similitudinis* and *comparationis*. According to Bary (p. 15): 'L'induction est un argument, dans lequel on tire une conclusion universelle du dénombrement de plusieurs choses semblables.' He gives this example of *inductio* (p. 15): 'Le Feu est corps, l'Eau est corps, l'Air est corps. Donc tout Element est corps.' He explains *exemplum* thus (p. 16): 'L'exemple est un Argument, dans lequel on tire une conclusion singulière ou universelle d'une ou de plusieurs propositions.' This is followed by an example:

> Sylla qui estoit fort redoutable, envahit la Republique.
> Il est donc à craindre que Cesar qui est fort puissant ne s'en empare.

Sound arguments, or at least arguments which appear to be sound, help the orator's appeal to the intelligence of his audience. But he must not forget that his appeal to their passions and interests, and the need to keep them attentive, have important consequences for his style of reasoning. Soarez, p. 113:

> Diligentissime est curandum, ne syllogismorum & enthymematum turba conserta oratio sit.

---

[39] On these see Kibédi-Varga, *Rhétorique et littérature*, 63–6.

(Extreme care should be taken that the speech is not filled with a pile of enthymemes and syllogisms.)

The formation of reasoned arguments is far from being the orator's most important task.

4. *DISPOSITIO*

Just as, while he is perusing the *loci*, the orator might also be thinking of the argumentative framework in which he might place what he discovers there, so he should all along bear in mind the overall framework of his speech. Advice given for this second part of rhetoric covers three areas: the component parts of a speech, things which might be said in each of these parts, and the organization of the material within the parts. The second of these two areas is closely related to *inventio* and often suggests topics which today might be called commonplaces.

A speech has in theory four basic parts: an *exordium*, a *narratio*, a *confirmatio*, and a *peroratio*. Other minor parts are used less frequently: a *propositio* and a *divisio* (after the *exordium*), a *digressio* (after the *narratio*), and a *refutatio* (after the *confirmatio*).

(a) Exordium

The *exordium* represents the orator's first contact with his audience. Rhetoricians agree that in the *exordium* the orator's aim is threefold. Caussin, p. 313:

Tractatur exordium ad conciliandam beneuolentiam, attentionem, docilitatem.

(The *exordium* is used for producing goodwill, attention, and tractability.)

The orator secures goodwill by giving a favourable impression of himself and his party and perhaps also by flattering his audience. This is the part of the speech where *mores* are most in evidence. Next, the orator earns the attention of his audience by insisting upon the novelty and interest of his subject and by pointing out that he will treat it succinctly. Docility, or tractability, according to Le Gras, requires a good 'sommaire de la cause' (p. 102): this ensures that the audience knows where it is being led. Sometimes, however, there are inherent in the subject certain obstacles which prevent its being broached directly. In such cases, before the usual business of the *exordium* can be carried out, the orator needs first to follow the procedure for *insinuatio*, whereby 'l'on prend un certain détour, à la faveur duquel, on se glisse insensiblement dans les esprits des Auditeurs' (Le Gras, p. 104).

The *propositio*, announcing the subject of the speech, and the *divisio*, explaining the stages by which the subject is to be treated, are best seen as parts of the *exordium*. They make a contribution to ensuring the tractability of the audience.

Making preliminary contact with the listeners in the way suggested by this advice is essential in judicial oratory. It is less important, according to the theorists, in deliberative and demonstrative oratory, although it can still be of help.

(b) Narratio

The *narratio* is obligatory in judicial oratory, where events have to be related in such a way that the orator attaches to them his own interpretation. In deliberative oratory this part of the speech can be omitted if all parties are familiar with the issue being discussed. In demonstrative oratory the *narratio* can be the most substantial part of the speech.

What is a *narratio*? Most frequently, 'c'est une exposition propre à persuader d'une chose faite ou de la maniere dont elle a esté faite' (Le Gras, p. 112). It must be brief, clear, and plausible (Soarez, p. 90). Why so? 'La clarté que le Juge comprend: la bréveté qu'il se souvient; & la vray-semblance qu'il croit' (Le Gras, pp. 114–15). How does the orator make his *narratio* plausible? Le Gras has two suggestions: 'Ce qui contribue le plus à donner à la Narration la teinture du vray semblable, est de la rendre Morale' (p. 119); 'Les images et les descriptions servent merveilleusement à rendre les Narrations plus vraysemblables' (p. 120). In other words, the good *narratio* gives such details about the character of those involved as to make their actions seem credible, and the introduction of concrete details makes for greater conviction than generalities.

There are a number of ways of organizing the *narratio*. The orator can narrate the facts in chronological order, or in any order which seems advantageous. He can even have several *narrationes*, each followed by its own *confirmatio*.

The *narratio* can be followed by a *digressio* in which the orator expands upon some aspect of the *narratio* or makes a smooth transition from *narratio* to *confirmatio*. In general *digressiones* are to be avoided, though they can in theory be used at any point in a speech 'comme un second Exorde pour rendre le Juge favorable à écouter, pour l'appaiser, ou pour l'exciter' (Le Gras, pp. 130–1).

(c) Confirmatio

It is the *confirmatio*, also known as the *argumentatio*, which especially allows the orator to display the discoveries which he has made in the *loci*. Theoretical discussion focuses on how the arguments are to be deployed. All rhetoricians warn against using the best arguments first and finishing with the weakest. It is possible either to start with weaker ones and finish on strong ones, or to place good arguments at the beginning and end of this section and tuck away the weaker ones in the middle.

Although this is the part of the speech in which the *probationes* are used to appeal to the intelligence of the audience, care should be taken that it does not become too dry and tedious; there should be variety of presentation (Caussin, p. 113).

Either at the end of the *confirmatio* or in the course of it, it would be normal to attempt a *refutatio*. If the orator is speaking before his opponent, the *refutatio* aims to forestall the arguments which the latter is likely to venture. If he is speaking after his opponent, it is possible that the whole of his *confirmatio* would take on the character of a *refutatio*. These two parts of a speech are not always easily distinguished, because, as Le Gras points out, 'les argumens qui servent à destruire se puisent dans les mesmes sources, & sont revestus de la mesme forme que ceux qui servent à confirmer' (p. 149).

All this seems scant advice for such an important part of the speech. Kibédi-Varga asks pointedly if this could represent 'l'aveu involontaire que l'essence même de l'art de la persuasion échappe à toute règle'.[40]

---

[40] Ibid. 78.

(d) Peroratio

It is with the *peroratio* that the orator makes his last impression on the audience. There are two important features to this part of the speech: *enumeratio* and *amplificatio*. The former is a recapitulation of the main point of the *confirmatio*. The latter involves the arousal of passions. For just as *mores* are of special help in the *exordium* and *probationes* in the *confirmatio*, so the rightful home of *affectus* is the *peroratio*. As Lamy says (p. 334), this is the moment when the orator opens up all the emotional wounds that he has inflicted earlier in the speech; this is the moment when he makes the audience hate his opponent and feel pity for his own cause; this is the moment when the audience is filled with fears or hopes, with anger or despair.

The strategies recommended by the rhetoricians in their treatement of *inventio* and *dispositio* are ones which anyone wishing to write or speak persuasively might usefully adopt, and they can clearly be used in reverse by literary critics who wish to dissect the persuasive strategies of others.

Racine's characters constantly allude to the persuasive nature of their activities. They may discuss how they have set about a persuasive task, as Acomat does, telling Osmin how he persuaded Roxane to fall in love with Bajazet and to contemplate a conspiracy against the sultan:

> J'entretins la sultane, et cachant mon dessein,
> Lui montrai d'Amurat le retour incertain,
> Les murmures du camp, la fortune des armes;
> Je plaignis Bajazet, je lui vantai ses charmes.
> (*Bajazet* 135–9)

Or characters may anticipate rhetorical strategies which may be used in future confrontations. This is what Néron does when he describes to Narcisse his fear of facing his mother Agrippine:

> Mon amour inquiet déjà se l'imagine [Agrippine]
> Qui m'amène Octavie, et d'un œil enflammé
> Atteste les saints droits d'un nœud qu'elle a formé;
> Et portant à mon cœur des atteintes plus rudes,
> Me fait un long récit de mes ingratitudes.
> (*Britannicus* 484–8)

In his article on 'The Theatricality of Discourse in Racinian Tragedy' H. Phillips has demonstrated in some detail the attentiveness of Racine's characters to what they and their opponents have to say. Their rhetorical self-consciousness invites the critic to undertake a rhetorical analysis of their verbal actions.

2

Formal Oratory: Trials, Embassies, and Councils

> Judge, prosecutor, advocate, plaintiff, defendant—what play
> could not be written with these five characters and a witness
> or two? Court-room language is a dramatic language in that
> it finds itself under the dual compulsion of the theatre: to
> keep things moving and to be at each moment esthetically
> impressive.
>
> (E. Bentley, The Life of the Drama, 87)

The obvious places to look for the application of the precepts of
rhetoric are formal speeches in courts of law, in political assem-
blies, and in churches. It is in these contexts that the formal orator
traditionally operates. Yet these contexts are public ones and as
such are not usually associated with seventeenth-century tragedy,
in which it is the representation of private struggles that pre-
dominates. Indeed the importance attached by theorists to the
closeness of the relationship between characters in tragedy would
almost seem to preclude any representation of formal oratory.[1]
It is not likely that mothers and sons, husbands and wives, or
brothers and sisters would have occasion to practise formal oratory on each other.

Formal oratory is not, however, absent from Racinian tragedy.
Some of Racine's characters are, in fact, formal orators. In this
chapter I isolate examples of formal oratory, examine the characters' use of *inventio* and *dispositio*, and comment on the theatrical
qualities of such oratory. Whereas P. France writes of the 'un-

---

[1] Corneille e.g. quotes Aristotle on this particular feature of tragedy: 'Pour nous
faciliter les moyens d'exciter cette pitié qui fait de si beaux effets sur nos théâtres,
Aristote nous donne une lumière. Toute action, dit-il, se passe ou entre des amis,
ou entre des ennemis, ou entre des gens indifférents l'un pour l'autre . . . quand les
choses arrivent entre des gens que la naissance ou l'affection attache aux intérêts
l'un de l'autre, comme alors qu'un mari tue ou est prêt de tuer sa femme, une mère
ses enfants, un frère sa sœur; c'est ce qui convient merveilleusement à la tragédie'
(*Writings*, 37–8).

dramatic, non-tragic pleasure' to be had out of the debating,[2] it is
the theatrical potential of formal debates that is foregrounded
here.

1. FORENSIC ORATORS IN *LES PLAIDEURS*

A discussion of Racine's use of formal oratory in the dramatic
context should begin not with the tragedies, but with *Les Plaideurs*.
Both the title and the subject of this comedy evoke forensic oratory.
Yet it is only in the third and final act of the play that any forensic
oratory is represented. Although the scene in question (III. 3) is
the main source of dramatic interest in the final act for the audience, its occurrence is something of a surprise. For the occasion
which gives rise to it has only the most tenuous relationship with
the activities of the two lovers, Léandre and Isabelle, and with the
schemes of the determined litigants, Chicanneau and the Comtesse
de Pimbêche, which had promised to be the predominant focus of
the audience's attention throughout the whole play. A scene of
forensic oratory might not be unexpected given the subject of the
play, but when there looms on the horizon the trial of a dog
accused of killing a capon, the audience has every right to be
surprised. The apparently gratuitous nature of this scene is the
first of many differences between Racine's representation of oratory in *Les Plaideurs* and his use of the same technique in his
tragedies. It is possible to account for these differences with reference to his comic purposes in *Les Plaideurs*, where the desire to
provoke laughter makes Racine employ irrelevance and incongruity
in his representation of formal oratory.

The seeds of the trial are sown at the end of Act II when Petit-
Jean, Dandin's porter, announces the apparently inconsequential
news that his master's dog, Citron, has eaten a capon (621–2).
Léandre is quick to interpret this news as an opportunity to
occupy his father Dandin, the judge who refuses to stop judging
(624–5). Dandin falls in instantly with his son's plan and the
judge intends the trial to be conducted as he sees fit (629–30):

> Mais je veux faire au moins la chose avec éclat.
> Il faut de part et d'autre avoir un avocat.

[2] *Racine's Rhetoric* (Oxford, 1965), 238.

Léandre, who has been described as a 'colourless' character,[3] fulfils an interesting and vital role in the preparation for and in the conduct of the trial. Of all the characters involved he is the only one to show a degree of ironical detachment. He is in a sense the producer of the trial scene, the *meneur du jeu*, manipulating the other characters and inviting the audience to find fun in an absurd trial executed with full seriousness by most of those participating in it. To supply the judge with a prosecution and a defence counsel Léandre indulges in a little casting (632–4):

> Voilà votre portier et votre secrétaire:
> Vous en ferez, je crois, d'excellents avocats;
> Ils sont fort ignorants.

The suggestion that ignorance goes hand in hand with forensic excellence sets the satirical tone for the scene which will follow in the next act. Dandin concludes the second act by refining Léandre's casting (641–2):

> Vous, maître Petit-Jean, serez le demandeur;
> Vous, maître l'Intimé, soyez le défendeur.

Thus everyone has a role for the trial scene. Dandin will be the judge. His porter will be the prosecution, his secretary the defence. To help the incompetent barristers there will be a prompter in case their command of *memoria*, the fourth part of rhetoric, should fail them. Léandre casts himself as the public (668).

Given this distribution of roles, it is easy to appreciate why P. Butler described the trial scene as 'une version ... de la comédie dans la comédie'.[4] Yet to describe this scene as a play-within-a-play is perhaps misleading. For it is not the case that all the characters involved consciously enter a theatrical world and suddenly adopt roles different from those that they have played so far. Racine's comic oratory is remarkable in that it mingles the real with the imaginary.[5] The court (in front of Dandin's house) is not a real court and the trial (of a dog) is clearly absurd and fantastic. But the judge is a real judge, who takes the trial seriously

---

[3] P. J. Yarrow, *Racine* (Oxford, 1978), 44.

[4] *Classicisme et baroque dans l'œuvre de Racine* (Paris, 1959), 123.

[5] It is because of this that I think that it is also slightly misleading of G. Forestier to make the opposite point from Butler that the trial scene is rooted in the same level of reality as all the preceding scenes (*Le Théâtre dans le théâtre sur la scène française du XVIIᵉ siècle*, 348).

and shows no sign of distinguishing it from genuine trials. The barristers on the other hand are not real; they are servants pretending to be barristers. Yet they too take the trial seriously, pleading determinedly, if incompetently. The prompter appears to be playing a role given to him by Léandre (III. 2); but his status must remain ambiguous, as he has no reality for the audience other than that of prompter in the trial. Léandre, as producer or instigator of the scene, serves as the link between the imaginary world towards which the trial veers and the real world which for some of the characters seems to have been temporarily suspended. Racine's comic art lies in making the scene balance uncertainly between the supposedly real world of Acts I and II and the imaginary world into which the scene occasionally bursts.

The trial gets under way when the audience has seen the barristers arrive in robes and when the judge has asked for proceedings to begin (669). The direction 'en robe' at the beginning of Scene 3 is significant. In his tragedies too Racine sometimes takes care to offer a visual sign to denote cases of formal oratory. The sign is usually slight, but a producer may emphasize the formality of the oratory by further visual means. In *Les Plaideurs* III. 3, for example, the characters, as well as being appropriately dressed, might also be so positioned on stage as to give prominence to the judge, with the two opposing counsels facing each other. The formality of the words can thus be visually reinforced.

In the course of the trial scene many aspects of judicial proceedings are parodied, most notably the formal orations of the counsels. It may also be that Racine is to some extent parodying the formal oratory to be found in tragedy. For the two counsels delivering their speeches for and against the accused draw on the same range of rhetorical precepts as the orators in the tragedies. The use that they make of these precepts, of course, distinguishes them from their counterparts in the tragedies.

Neither Petit-Jean, who speaks first and against the accused, nor l'Intimé is allowed to speak without interruption. The interruptions are invariably used by Racine for comic effect. There is Dandin's fussing over formalities, which forces Petit-Jean to begin his speech three times over; there is Petit-Jean's failure to understand the prompter, which results in an altercation; and there is Dandin's unhappiness with l'Intimé's oratorical style, his criticisms of it, and his attempts to make him change it.

Despite these interruptions the speeches of both barristers are readily assimilable to the form suggested for the judicial speech by rhetoricians. Petit-Jean has an extensive *exordium* which, how-ever, is remarkable for his failure to address his audience and involve them directly, a major task in the opening part of a speech according to the rhetoricians. He begins inappropriately by reveal-ing that he is pleased with his introduction:

> Ce que je sais le mieux, c'est mon commencement,
> Messieurs, quand je regarde avec exactitude
> L'inconstance du monde et sa vicissitude;
> Lorsque je vois, parmi tant d'hommes différents,
> Pas une étoile fixe, et tant d'astres errants;
> Quand je vois les Césars, quand je vois leur fortune
> Quand je vois le soleil, et quand je vois la lune;
> > (*Babyloniens*)
> Quand je vois les États des Babiboniens
> > (*Persans*)   (*Macédoniens*)
> Transférés des Serpans aux Nacédoniens;
> > (*Romains*)   (*despotique*)
> Quand je vois les Lorrains de l'état dépotique,
> > (*démocratique*)
> Passer au démocrite, et puis au monarchique;
> Quand je vois le Japon . . .
> > (*Les Plaideurs* 674–85)

The theatre audience is surely meant to be struck by the irrelevance of this *exordium* to the case against the dog. For instance, the *exordium* is not the place to indulge in an extensive exploitation of the *loci*. Yet Petit-Jean (or rather his speech-writer) seems to have paid a visit to the *loci speciei* and *partium enumerationis*, and indiscriminately to have brought back with him everything that he found there, producing an unfinished list of some kinds of inconstancy to be found in the world, none of which has any obvious connection with the crime of Citron. According to rhetor-icians the *exordium* should aim to capture the goodwill and atten-tion of the audience by flattering them (especially if one of them is a judge) and by insisting on the brevity and clarity of the presenta-tion that is to follow. Petit-Jean is incompetent in his *exordium* in that he acts on neither of these suggestions. Yet ironically the judge is indeed favourably impressed and his attention is captured. For when l'Intimé interrupts Petit-Jean with the suggestion that

the speech is irrelevant (685), Dandin is eager to defend the prosecutor and hear the rest of the *exordium* (687–92). The comic
climax of this part of the scene comes when Petit-Jean declares
that he cannot remember the rest of his introduction, and no
amount of prompting is able to help him.

Racine is also able to extract comedy from the *actio* of rhetoric.
Léandre ventures to give Petit-Jean advice on the use of gesture
(694–6):

> Mais que font là tes bras pendants à ton côté?
> Te voilà sur tes pieds droit comme une statue.
> Dégourdis-toi. Courage! allons, qu'on s'évertue.

Petit-Jean attempts to resume his *exordium*, but his words falter
(697):

> Quand . . . je vois . . . Quand . . . je vois . . .

And the direction '*remuant les bras*' invites the actor to make
Petit-Jean's gestural rhetoric as awkward as his verbal rhetoric.
The poor porter cannot combine the two aspects simultaneously
(698):

> Oh dame! on ne court pas deux lièvres à la fois.

After his argument with the prompter and encouragement by
the judge to deal with the facts of the case, Petit-Jean comments
unfavourably on the rhetoric that has been foisted upon him and
proceeds with the accusation in a manner which is more recog-
nizably that of the porter in him (709–14):

> Pour moi, je ne sais pas tant faire de façon
> Pour dire qu'un mâtin vient de prendre un chapon.
> Tant y a qu'il n'est rien que votre chien ne prenne,
> Qu'il a mangé là-bas un bon chapon du Maine,
> Que la première fois que je l'y trouverai,
> Son procès est tout fait, et je l'assommerai.

In the space of a few lines Petit-Jean accomplishes the task of
narratio, *confirmatio*, and *peroratio*. Hence Léandre's ironical
comment (715):

> Belle conclusion, et digne de l'exorde!

This comment, drawing on rhetorical terminology, makes it clear
that the features of rhetoric play an important part in the text and

are not simply in the eyes of the literary critic. In 710 the crime is narrated as baldly as possible. The *confirmatio* follows in 711–12 with an argument based on the *locus comparationis minorum*: the dog will eat absolutely anything, so there can be no doubt that it ate a tasty chicken from Maine. Rather than offering a *peroratio* in which he might try to convince his audience of Citron's guilt, Petit-Jean presumptuously assumes the role of judge and condemns the creature. His spontaneous oratory, carefully contrived by Racine, is as ridiculous as his prepared version. The one is as inadequately thin and insubstantial as the other is expansive and irrelevant.

Before l'Intimé's defence there is an inconsequential attempt by the judge to solicit real proof (*probationes inartificiales*) in the form of witnesses. All that Petit-Jean can produce are the head and feet of the chicken, which l'Intimé refuses to accept as evidence on the grounds of the bird's geographical origins. L'Intimé takes advantage of the dead-end into which the pursuit of witnesses has led them in order to start his defence.

His *exordium* is in content, though not in delivery, more promising than that of Petit-Jean (727–33):

> Messieurs, tout ce qui peut étonner un coupable,
> Tout ce que les mortels ont de plus redoutable,
> Semble s'être assemblé contre nous par hasard:
> Je veux dire la brigue et l'éloquence. Car
> D'un côté, le crédit du défunt m'épouvante;
> Et de l'autre côté l'éloquence éclatante
> De maître Petit-Jean m'éblouit.

This first half of the *exordium* demonstrates a willingness to act on the recommendations of the rhetoricians. L'Intimé is concerned with the image of himself and his client, Citron, trying to appear modest and humble (*mores*). The crime was committed against such an esteemed victim and the prosecutor's case was pleaded so eloquently as to make the task of the defence very difficult. In the proper context this would not be a bad *exordium*. In the present context it is ridiculous, because incongruous. The highly esteemed victim was a chicken and the prosecutor's case was appallingly pleaded. Moreover, l'Intimé's *actio* is also meant to be inappropriate. He says these lines '*d'un ton finissant en fausset*'. It is the overdone delivery rather than the incongruity of the content to which Dandin objects in an interruption. As a result, the remainder of the *exordium* is delivered '*du beau ton*':

> Mais quelque défiance
> Que vous doive donner la susdite éloquence,
> Et le susdit crédit, ce néanmoins, Messieurs,
> L'ancre de vos bontés nous rassure d'ailleurs.
> Devant le grand Dandin l'innocence est hardie:
> Oui, devant ce Caton de Basse-Normandie,
> Ce soleil d'équité qui n'est jamais terni,
> *Victrix causa diis placuit, sed victa Catoni.*
>
> (*Les Plaideurs* 735–42)

In this second half l'Intimé accomplishes another task of the *exordium*, that of flattering the audience and, in particular, the judge. Once again the incongruity between Cato, whose qualities are attributed to Dandin, and the crazy old judge himself creates laughter, laughter which is reinforced by Dandin's approving interruption (743):

> Vraiment, il plaide bien.

L'Intimé now signals that he is moving on to the next part of his speech, which, in theory, should be the *narratio*. But what he says, or rather tries to say (for he is not allowed to finish a sentence), seems to be either a digression leading up to the *narratio* or a preview of the *confirmatio*. He attempts to impress the judge with *probationes inartificiales*, citing ancient and medieval authorities. Uncharacteristically sceptical about the relevance of Aristotle, Pausanias, Rebuffe, 'le grand Jacques', and Armeno Pul to the crime of the hungry Citron,[6] Dandin repeatedly insists that l'Intimé deal with the facts of the case. Only the threat of an instant judgement (754) prompts l'Intimé to start his *narratio* and finish it as quickly as he can. Hence a third oratorical style, characterized by Racine as '*vite*':

> Un chien vient dans une cuisine;
> Il y trouve un chapon, lequel a bonne mine.
> Or celui pour lequel je parle est affamé,

---

[6] Pausanias (2nd cent. AD) wrote a *Description of Greece*; Rebuffe (1487–1557) was a French jurisconsult; 'le grand Jacques' is usually identified as the famous jurisconsult Jacques Cujas (1520–90); and Armeno Pul was a 14th-century Greek jurisconsult.

Celui contre lequel je parle *autem* plumé;
Et celui pour lequel je suis prend en cachette
Celui contre lequel je parle. L'on décrète:
On le prend. Avocat pour et contre appelé;
Jour pris. Je dois parler, je parle, j'ai parlé.

(*Les Plaideurs* 755–62)

Though heavy with legal jargon, l'Intimé's *narratio* is almost as bare as that of Petit-Jean and it is less appropriate in two ways. First, it is an objective statement of what happened, whereas it ought to have been constructed in such a way as to include a defence of l'Intimé's client. Secondly, it exceeds the normal limits of a judicial *narratio* by relating events between the crime and l'Intimé's own speech. 'Jour pris. Je dois parler, je parle, j'ai parlé' is comic in its irrelevance. Dandin's tastes have evidently changed since his approval of Petit-Jean's expansive *exordium*, as he now expresses approval of l'Intimé's clipped oratory (763–6).

L'Intimé himself, however, states a preference for the earlier more ponderous style (766) and it is this to which he returns when he resumes his speech and launches into the *confirmatio*, delivered '*d'un ton véhément*' (769–88):

Qu'arrive-t-il, Messieurs? On vient. Comment vient-on?
On poursuit ma partie. On force une maison.
Quelle maison? maison de notre propre juge!
On brise le cellier qui nous sert de refuge!
De vol, de brigandage on nous déclare auteurs!
On nous traîne, on nous livre à nos accusateurs,
A maître Petit-Jean, Messieurs. Je vous atteste:
Qui ne sait que la loi *Si quis canis*, Digeste,
De vi, paragrapho, Messieurs, *Caponibus*,
Est manifestement contraire à cet abus?
Et quand il serait vrai que Citron, ma partie,
Aurait mangé, Messieurs, le tout, ou bien partie
Du dit chapon: qu'on mette en compensation
Ce que nous avons fait avant cette action.
Quand ma partie a-t-elle été réprimandée?
Par qui votre maison a-t-elle été gardée?
Quand avons-nous manqué d'aboyer au larron?
Témoin trois procureurs, dont icelui Citron
A déchiré la robe. On en verra les pièces.
Pour nous justifier, voulez-vous d'autres pièces?

L'Intimé's *confirmatio* contains three points. The first is an elaboration of the words 'On le prend' found in the *narratio* (761). The elaboration is based on the *locus adiunctorum*, that is to say that l'Intimé gives details of the circumstances of Citron's arrest and he does so in such a way as to arouse pity for the persecuted pet, identifying himself with Citron ('notre... nous... nous... nous... nous... nos') and using emotive language ('refuge... brigandage... traîne'). L'Intimé's second point is rather curious in that it remains deliberately unclear. He cites a (fictitious) legal authority impressively (*probatio inartificialis*) and asserts that this law is 'manifestement contraire à cet abus'. But what does he mean? What he wants his audience to believe is that there is a law against pursuing dogs who have eaten capons. This is perhaps Racine satirizing the fuzzy and tendentious citation of legal authorities. L'Intimé's third point is based on *mores*, the good character of the dog and the service he has rendered his owner. As evidence of Citron's qualities as a guard-dog, l'Intimé proposes the real evidence of legal robes ripped, he suggests, by the teeth of his client. Citron's crime, if indeed he committed one, has to be weighed against his domestic services. L'Intimé's *confirmatio* offers Citron only a slender defence: a tattered robe, an obscure citation, and pity for the captured criminal.

At this point there comes an interruption from Petit-Jean, who feels moved to comment on l'Intimé's voice, which is once again straining for effect. Then Dandin invites l'Intimé to start his *peroratio* (791). This the barrister does '*d'un ton pesant*'. The *peroratio* promises to take a long time as l'Intimé explains at unnecessary length that his recapitulation of the main points will be brief (791–6):

> Puis donc qu'on nous permet de prendre
> Haleine, et que l'on nous défend de nous étendre,
> Je vais sans rien omettre, et sans prévariquer,
> Compendieusement énoncer, expliquer,
> Exposer à vos yeux l'idée universelle
> De ma cause et des faits renfermés en icelle.

A further injunction to conclude induces l'Intimé to indulge in a verbose and irrelevant exploitation of the *locus causarum*, a description of nature before the creation of the world (800–10). The *peroratio* is the place to sum up and make a final appeal on behalf of the client. It is the worst place to lose the attention of the judge as he will be left with a poor final impression. Yet lose the judge is precisely what l'Intimé does: Dandin falls asleep.

There is a comic distortion of legal procedure when Dandin wakes up and pronounces judgement, condemning Citron to the galleys (815). Not only is the sentence inappropriate for a dog, but it is not the result of any formal consideration by the judge of any of the issues raised; nor has the judge let the defence barrister even finish his speech. Aware of this inadequate sentence, Dandin for a third time asks l'Intimé to bring his speech to a conclusion.

The *peroratio* is generally deemed to be the most suitable part of a speech in which to appeal to the passions of the hearers (*affectus*). Accordingly l'Intimé now adopts a new approach which depends upon *affectus*. He seeks so to arouse Dandin's pity as to make an adverse judgement impossible. This he does with the help of a visual stimulus (*probatio inartificialis*), Citron's offspring (818–24):

> Venez, famille désolée,
> Venez, pauvres enfants qu'on veut rendre orphelins,
> Venez faire parler vos esprits enfantins.
> Oui, Messieurs, vous voyez ici notre misère:
> Nous sommes orphelins; rendez-nous notre père;
> Notre père, par qui nous fûmes engendrés,
> Notre père, qui nous...

The judge is presented with a living image of desolate orphanage. Prosopopœia allows the puppies to make an eloquent plea for the return of their father. L'Intimé's idea is rhetorically sound, but rendered ridiculous in its application to puppies. Moreover the comedy is heightened when the little dogs destroy the favourable impression created for them by the barrister: they begin to yelp and urinate (825–6):

> Quels vacarmes!
> Ils ont pissé partout.

L'Intimé's final word shows his wit and inventive powers when their urine is portrayed as a symbol of their tears (826):

> Monsieur, voyez nos larmes.

At this point the *peroratio* ends and Dandin, whose reactions have been fitful and inconsistent throughout the trial, now declares himself moved to pity. Parody of rhetoric in the tragedies seems especially acute here. 'Larmes', 'compassion', and 'toucher' are all terms associated with tragedy.

In three lines (830–2) Dandin sums up the case for and against condemning Citron:

> Le crime est avéré; lui-même il le confesse.
> Mais s'il est condamné, l'embarras est égal.
> Voilà bien des enfants réduits à l'hôpital.

But there, inconclusively, the trial ends. For the supposedly real and pressing concerns of Acts I and II take over with the arrival of Chicanneau and Isabelle. All the pleading has been in vain. No conclusion has been reached. The participants in the trial shed their roles with an ease which reveals the utter inconsequentiality of the proceedings, the real justification for which lies in their enormous comic potential.

From this analysis of *Les Plaideurs* III. 3 there emerges a number of conclusions about Racine's representation of formal oratory in a comic context.

First, this scene of forensic oratory has an unusual relationship with the other scenes in the play. It does not form part of the linear progression of the main dramatic action. Racine prepares for the scene at the end of the preceding act, but this preparation strikes the audience as strangely tangential to the main action. Though tangential, it is not so removed from the main action as to become a play-within-a-play. The unstable relationship which the scene enjoys with the surrounding dramatic action contributes to the fun that it engenders both for Léandre and for the theatre audience. Secondly, the two orators deliver speeches which lend themselves to an analysis based upon the recommendations of rhetorical theory. Indeed such an analysis proves to be especially helpful because, although Petit-Jean and l'Intimé do not always put the recommendations properly into effect, the critic can refer specifically to the gap between precept and practice and so point precisely to some sources of comedy. In those cases where l'Intimé does seem to act upon the recommendations of the rhetoricians, the critic can then look elsewhere for the source of the comedy, and find it in the incongruity between sound rhetorical strategy and ridiculous application.

Thirdly, Racine makes special use of Dandin as the immediate audience of the two orators. He is the judge whom they are trying to persuade. He is a fickle interlocutor, now responding, now falling asleep, at one moment showing a degree of acuity, at the next appearing slow-witted, often inconsistent and uncertain in his judgement. His lack of coherence as an interlocutor is manipulated for comic effect. Fourthly, Racine uses the visual aid of legal robes to reinforce for the audience the transition into formal oratory.

And finally, some general comment needs to be made on how persuasion works in this scene as a source of dramatic interest. The attention of the audience is not directed towards characters' vigorous attempts at deploying rhetorical strategies in order to achieve a persuasive aim, which, if successfully attained, will have important repercussions on the lives of all the characters involved. Rather the art of persuasion in *Les Plaideurs* III. 3 is employed in such a way as to extract laughter from the audience, whose attention is focused on individual rhetorical strategies, each incompetently or incongruously executed. The scene is given shape by the two speeches of the barristers which, in fits and starts, follow the recommendations for *dispositio*. But the many and often irrelevant interruptions make the scene deliberately disjointed and this feature contributes to the audience's interest in a series of individual moments, each funny in its own way. Interest in any total persuasive effect is much less important.

In retrospect, *Les Plaideurs* III. 3 turns out not to be an obvious example of the representation of formal oratory in Racine's dramatic works. For '*Les Plaideurs* sont une délicieuse caricature, mais non pas un portrait'.[7] It is the parody of oratory rather than the representation of oratory which is Racine's dramatic means in this scene. It is in his tragedies that he represents oratory without any subversive intent, and seeks to hold the attention of his audience with such a representation. His dramatic use of persuasion in the tragedies will be all the clearer for the contrast with *Les Plaideurs*.

---

[7] C. Du Pasquier, '*Les Plaideurs*' *de Racine et l'éloquence judiciaire sous Louis XIV* (Paris, 1919), 16.

II. THREE AMBASSADORS: MATHAN, ÉPHESTION, AND ORESTE

Formal oratory is often in the background in certain of Racine's tragedies in the form of references to ambassadorial activity or references to persuasion in the senate house.[8] But the representation of formal oratory on stage as part of the dramatic action occurs unambiguously in only three plays, *Alexandre*, *Andromaque*, and *Athalie*, where Éphestion, Oreste, and Mathan all play the role of ambassador. In *Alexandre* II. 2 Éphestion puts Alexandre's offer of peace to the two Indian kings, Porus and Taxile. In *Andromaque* I. 2 Oreste, as Greek ambassador, attempts to persuade Pyrrhus to hand over to the Greeks Astyanax, the son of their deceased enemy, Hector. And in *Athalie* III. 4 Mathan comes on a mission superficially parallel to that of Oreste: he has been sent by Athalie to ask that Éliacin be entrusted to the queen's care.[9]

All three scenes have two major features in common which distinguish them markedly from the comic oratory of *Les Plaideurs*. First, they are all very much part of the linear progression of the dramatic action. The formal oratory is pivotal in that it ensures communication between two parties who, unless ambassadors were employed, could not have been brought together without offending *vraisemblance*. Alexandre's formal offer of peace to Taxile and Porus could not reasonably be made in person; geographical considerations in *Andromaque* require that an envoy should approach Pyrrhus on behalf of the Greeks; and, as Athalie has already made one unaccustomed appearance in her enemies' temple, a second shortly after the first would appear too obviously as the triumph of convenience over *vraisemblance*. It should not be thought, however, that ambassadors are used by Racine *faute de mieux*. For specific dramatic effects are to be had from the introduction of formal orators. The scenes in question are also

---

[8] See e.g. *Andromaque* 134, 175, 765, 1288, 1503, 1557, 1572; *Britannicus* 94, 101, 793, 905, 1136, 1241, 1367, 1530; *Bérénice* 170, 299, 570, 1241, 1248, 1376; *Mithridate* 808.

[9] In *Athalie* V. 2 Abner comes to speak to Joad as Athalie's ambassador. But this is not a scene of formal ambassadorial oratory, because Abner does not discharge his duties as an ambassador should. He proceeds to speak on his own account rather than on that of someone wishing to promote Athalie's interests.

pivotal in that the subject of debate is in all cases central to the concerns of the major characters.

A second feature which these scenes have in common is the dramatic function of persuasion within them. Whereas in *Les Plaideurs* it is the comic effect of individual rhetorical strategies that holds the attention of the audience, in formal oratory in the tragedies it is the overall effect of the persuasive speeches which matters: how, if at all, will the world of the characters be changed as a result of the persuasive efforts of the orators? Individual rhetorical strategies are interesting, but above all for their cumulative effect. Consideration of these scenes most readily reveals how Racine creates theatrical interest in scenes in which the action is predominantly verbal.

Mathan uses his embassy to further his own ends. In this respect he resembles Oreste, but not Éphestion. He arrives in the temple with his confidant Nabal and asks to see Josabet in order to deliver a message from the queen (III. 1–2). Alone with Nabal in III. 3 Mathan explains how he has actually instigated this embassy himself. Athalie had started to waver in her plans for vengeance against the Jews. So Mathan, wishing to crush his archrival Joad and see the ruin of the temple of Jerusalem, made her afraid of Éliacin by suggesting that the Jews secretly saw in him 'un autre Moïse' (891). Whereupon Athalie granted Mathan the mission that he had desired: he is to demand Éliacin as a hostage from Josabet; and, if the child is withheld, he is to threaten to attack the temple. Mathan is pleased with this mission because he is sure that it will fail and that failure will allow him finally to take vengeance on Joad:

> Ils le refuseront. Je prends sur moi le reste,
> Et j'espère qu'enfin de ce temple odieux
> Et la flamme et le fer vont délivrer mes yeux.
> (*Athalie* 912–14)

Mathan will deploy his oratory deliberately to induce in Josabet a refusal of his apparent claim.[10]

---

[10] The audience is assured of Mathan's rhetorical skills by Mathan himself as he sketches his career as a courtier (939–44): 'Autant que de Joad l'inflexible rudesse | De leur superbe oreille offensait la mollesse, | Autant je les charmais par ma dextérité, | Dérobant à leurs yeux la triste vérité, | Prêtant à leurs fureurs des couleurs favorables, | Et prodigue surtout du sang des misérables.'

Mathan cleverly, and with a subtlety not usually attributed to him, makes sure that he appears to carry out his embassy, while at the same time using *inventio* so as to bring about its failure. It is noticeable that Josabet does not even offer counter-arguments. She simply unmasks his superficial ambassadorial politeness, as he had clearly wanted her to do. Her refusal of his request is implicit in this scene, though it is made visually explicit in the next scene (III. 5), when Joad drives Mathan off stage.

Mathan's embassy is a cunning and perverse use of oratory. Though he is well-known as an enemy of Josabet's husband, he delivers an *exordium* which exploits *mores* by laying such great stress on his own personal support of the Jews that it must inevitably be received with suspicion:

> De Joad contre moi je sais les injustices,
> Mais il faut à l'offense opposer les bienfaits.
> Enfin je viens chargé de paroles de paix.
> Vivez, solennisez vos fêtes sans ombrage.
> De votre obéissance elle ne veut qu'un gage:
> C'est (pour l'en détourner j'ai fait ce que j'ai pu)
> Cet enfant sans parents qu'elle dit qu'elle a vu.
> (*Athalie* 972–8)

After he has teased her a little more in this suspicious persona of a well-wisher, Josabet implicitly strips off the mask which his manipulation of *mores* had painted with deliberate lavishness (987–90):

> J'admirais si Mathan, dépouillant l'artifice,
> Avait pu de son cœur surmonter l'injustice,
> Et si de tant de maux le funeste inventeur
> De quelque ombre de bien pouvait être l'auteur.

Josabet is not taken in by his purely apparent ambassadorial politeness and Mathan proceeds to deploy threatening arguments which attempt to probe the ancestry of Éliacin. This approach makes Josabet very angry. So when she has expressed her fury and when he has been rudely dismissed by Joad, Mathan can feel that, from a personal point of view, his oratory has been eminently successful, even though in his duty as an ambassador he has apparently failed.

The theatrical qualities of this particular embassy lie in the perverse manipulation of formal oratory by Mathan, which gives rise to an unreasoned display of passion first in Josabet, then in Joad. It is in the earlier embassies of Éphestion and Oreste that audiences find two or more orators clashing on equal, or relatively equal, terms, with argument followed by counter-argument.

In *Alexandre* II. 2 Éphestion begins his attempt to persuade Taxile and Porus to accept peace on Alexandre's terms. The introduction of formal oratory is marked visually for the audience by the use of two chairs for the kings and a stool for the ambassador.[11] It is important for the reader of the play to bear this picture in mind. For later in the scene Racine produces a specific effect from the combination of the visual and verbal aspects of the formal oratory.

It is significant that the views of all three participants in the debate have been made known to the audience beforehand: Taxile's inclination to accept Alexandre's offer of peace (I. 2), Porus's refusal to entertain it at all seriously (I. 2–3), and Éphestion's determination to do all he can to persuade both parties to accept the offer (II. 1). With the attitude of each participant already sketched in, the audience is better placed to appreciate the rhetorical strategies of each when they meet formally.

Éphestion speaks first, putting the offer and trying to sell it. His speech is composed according to the traditional pattern of *dispositio*. There is an *exordium* (445–8), followed by a *narratio* (449–52), a *confirmatio* (453–68), and a *peroratio* (469–72):

> Avant que le combat qui menace vos têtes (445)
> Mette tous vos États au rang de nos conquêtes,
> Alexandre veut bien différer ses exploits,
> Et vous offrir la paix pour la dernière fois.
> Vos peuples, prévenus de l'espoir qui vous flatte, (449)
> Prétendaient arrêter le vainqueur de l'Euphrate;
> Mais l'Hydaspe, malgré tant d'escadrons épars,
> Voit enfin sur ses bords flotter nos étendards.
> Vous les verriez plantés jusque sur vos tranchées, (453)
> Et de sang et de morts vos campagnes jonchées,
> Si ce héros, couvert de tant d'autres lauriers,
> N'eût lui-même arrêté l'ardeur de nos guerriers.
> Il ne vient point ici souillé du sang des princes,
> D'un triomphe barbare effrayer vos provinces,

---

[11] 'Theatre est des tentes de guerre et pavillons. Il faut deux fauteuille [*sic*] et un tabouret' (*Le Mémoire de Mahelot*, ed. H. C. Lancaster (Paris, 1920), 112).

Et cherchant à briller d'une triste splendeur,
Sur le tombeau des rois élever sa grandeur.
Mais vous-mêmes, trompés d'un vain espoir de gloire,
N'allez point dans ses bras irriter la Victoire;
Et lorsque son courroux demeure suspendu,
Princes, contentez-vous de l'avoir attendu,
Ne différez point tant à lui rendre l'hommage
Que vos cœurs, malgré vous, rendent à son courage;
Et recevant l'appui que vous offre son bras,
D'un si grand défenseur honorez vos États.
Voilà ce qu'un grand roi veut bien vous faire entendre,   (469)
Prêt à quitter le fer, et prêt à le reprendre.
Vous savez son dessein: choisissez aujourd'hui,
Si vous voulez tout perdre ou tenir tout de lui.

Racine has composed Éphestion's speech in such a way as to give the impression of a skilful orator seeking to win over his interlocutors by avoiding contentious issues. Accordingly, there is little reasoning in the speech, and the main part of *inventio* drawn on is *mores*, with an element of *affectus*. Éphestion secures the attention of the kings in the *exordium* by suggesting, with words both tactful and menacing, that it is their safety which is at stake; he secures their goodwill by implying that his own party, Alexandre, is sympathetic to them; and he renders them receptive by spelling out the significance of the occasion of the speech: the last offer of peace. In the second part of his speech he narrates the present state of affairs which the kings and their peoples have to face up to, and again he injects an element of fear for their safety. The *confirmatio*, rather than pursuing the logical consequences of a rejection of Alexandre's offer (as Oreste will do with Pyrrhus in *Andromaque* 162–8), concentrates on the *mores* of Alexandre, while none the less managing once again to provoke a degree of fear: it is thanks to Alexandre, he suggests, that the kings have not already been conquered. Further painting of Alexandre in terms which invite veneration leads Éphestion, by way of an enthymeme, to the conclusion that the offer must be accepted. The *peroratio* recapitulates his points, reminding Taxile and Porus of the alternatives, recalling the worthy character of Alexandre, and asking them to reach a decision. Éphestion's oratory, though not aggressive, is distinctly condescending: he is kindly offering the kings what he implies is their only option. He has not, for instance, bothered to argue his case strongly and has omitted any hint of a *refutatio*.

How will Taxile, as spokesman, reply? Given the audience's knowledge of the way in which Taxile's views have evolved in Act I, it is clear that he would be expected to want to accept the offer. This means that, for Taxile by himself, Éphestion's speech would easily suffice to secure persuasion. There would be no need for debate, because there would be no disagreement. Porus's presence, however, alters the situation significantly and makes Taxile's reply particularly interesting. For Taxile wants his own view to prevail, he wants to accept the offer of peace, but he does not, at this stage, want to alienate Porus. Taxile, then, has to walk a tightrope. He does not succeed, and it is this speech which prepares for the change of mood of the confrontation from superficial politeness to direct expression of hostility.

The opening of his reply is for the ears of Éphestion. He secures his goodwill by accepting his picture of Alexandre and by contributing to it himself (473–80). What he goes on to say is meant for the ears of both Éphestion and Porus. It is ostensibly addressed to Éphestion as a corrective measure to the peace offer, suggesting the need for Alexandre to stress his friendship towards them. But in practice this element of correction amounts to nothing tangible, and the speech can be viewed as an attempt by Taxile to persuade Porus that he (Taxile) is, after all, right-minded, even though he may appear to be yielding to Alexandre. It is to convince Porus of this that he draws on the *locus dissimilitudinis* to differentiate between the adoring states that Alexandre believes himself to have under his control and the servile states that they actually become. This statement Taxile supports with the real proof (*probatio inartificialis*) of *exempla*, which, however, remain unspecified (481–6). At this point he suggests a compromise solution: they should become Alexandre's friends, and not his worshippers or slaves (487–8). To back up his view of the situation further he develops a *definitio per descriptionem* whereby Alexandre's empire is described in terms of the master–slave relationship (483–94), and a *probatio inartificialis* (the discontented Scythians) is adduced as evidence (495–6). Taxile reiterates his plea for friendship, this time tentatively adding the practical consequence of mutual trust: no formal agreement should be necessary (497–8). A *peroratio* (501–4) shows him again trying to perform a balancing act,

reminding Éphestion of his admiration for Alexandre and reminding Porus that his acceptance of Alexandre's offer is conditional
upon the establishment of a friendly partnership. The evident care
and caution with which Taxile speaks, and, in particular, his
production of *probationes inartificiales* to support his claims, go
some way towards establishing the soundness of his view and
prevent the audience from seeing him as a coward. The conflict of
the two apparently sound views of Taxile and Porus makes the
debate more gripping.

Éphestion might well have spoken here to reassure Taxile that
he and Porus would indeed be Alexandre's friends. But the ambassador knows that Taxile's reply is in fact as favourable to
Alexandre as he might have hoped for. In any case, Porus's response at this juncture allows the situation to be developed more
interestingly. For Porus rejects the reply of Taxile and, tipping the
scales against ambassadorial decorum, raises issues which the previous speakers have either ignored or swept aside. The debate
becomes heated.

At the beginning of his speech Porus dismisses Taxile by drawing on the *locus generis* to evoke the type of ruler Taxile should
be: one who, like his allies, desires to defend his peoples against
Alexandre's tyranny. Taxile no longer fits the mould, so Porus
claims the right to speak in his stead. He starts his response
proper to Éphestion by implicitly questioning the generosity of
character to which Éphestion had tried to attribute the activities of Alexandre (*mores*, 513–16). To support this attack on
Alexandre's motivation he draws on the *locus antecedentium*,
painting a picture of a formerly peaceful region (517–20), the
locus causarum, suggesting the unlikeliness of finding sound
reasons for Alexandre's conquering exploits (521–8), and the
locus effectorum, claiming that the master–slave relationship
between Alexandre and the rest of the world is the result of
his exploits (529–36). All the material Porus uses is couched in
enthymemes which invite the conclusion that Alexandre's aims
cannot be justified. To terminate his treatment of the renowned
warrior he offers an unflattering explanation of his exploits: his
overweening pride (537).

Whereas Éphestion's and Taxile's speeches had aimed at persuasion, Porus's is simply a statement of defiance. For him there is
no question of dissuading Alexandre from pursuing his policies

and, though Porus's arguments might be expected to have some effect on Taxile, there is no indication in the text that Porus is seeking to make Taxile change his mind. His expansive rhetoric concludes with an apparently impressive justification of his attitude. He claims to be behaving as an independent monarch must against a conquering tyrant. He is in search of *gloire*. Such at least is the motivation he wishes to claim in his capacity as a formal orator. The audience, however, is in a position to think of an alternative motivation for his hostile attitude towards Alexandre. For he might think that defeating Alexandre would be a good way of winning Axiane, the object of his, as well as Taxile's, affections.

Porus's lengthy rejection of the offer of peace turns Éphestion's formerly condescending tone into one of haughty contempt and sarcasm. The ambassador's reply is highly provocative and includes a personal attack on Porus (551–2):

> Si le monde penchant n'a plus que cet appui [Porus],
> Je le plains, et vous plains vous-même autant que lui.

Éphestion seems to assume that his persuasion has been unsuccessful, but rather than end his embassy forthwith he continues rudely to demonstrate why Porus is foolish to reject Alexandre's offer. He starts to adopt an inductive argument: none of Alexandre's previous exploits has failed, so neither will this one.

Before he can list Alexandre's previous successes, however, Porus interrupts him in mid-sentence. At this point Racine makes Porus perform a rhetorical manœuvre as provocative as that just performed by Éphestion. The king adopts the same inductive framework which Éphestion was about to employ, but fills it with material interpreted in a very different way from the way in which Éphestion would have interpreted it. Porus manipulates the material so as to reach the opposite conclusion to Éphestion. The recollection of Alexandre's previous successes now comes across as a demonstrative piece attacking Alexandre. Then, instead of drawing a parallel between his previous and present exploits, he uses the *locus dissimilitudinis* to differentiate the peoples Alexandre has already conquered from those he now wishes to conquer, who, Porus suggests, are made of sterner stuff (571). A *definitio* of Alexandre puts him firmly in his place as a human tyrant (572–4) and a joint exploitation of *effecta* and *dissimilitudo* warns Éphestion that the results of Alexandre's presence will not be the

easy successes with which he has met before (575–82). This
brings Porus to the point which he reached at the end of his
earlier speech, a statement of the driving force behind him: the
need for *gloire*.

Porus has taken advantage of the fact that he is formally superior
to Éphestion in order to give a hostile and negative response to the
offer and to air his disapproval of Alexandre's deeds. The rhetorical
situation which Éphestion established at the start of his embassy
was such as required from Porus and Taxile a sign of agreement or
disagreement, or an attempt to persuade Alexandre, via Éphestion,
to adopt a different position himself. Taxile takes the first of these
three options, while trying to make it seem, for Porus's sake, that
he has adopted the third. The audience's interest in the oratory is
renewed when Porus refuses to adopt any of the obvious options.
Although he certainly expresses disagreement with the proposal,
he goes well beyond this to deliver barely veiled insults. After
Taxile's attempt at conciliation, the discussion becomes increasingly hostile.

Porus's attitude supplies ample motivation for Éphestion's ex-
asperation, which leads him to interrupt the king, to stand up,
and, moving away from persuasion based ostensibly on *mores*
(Alexandre's good character), to exploit *affectus* instead, attempting to prompt considerable fear in his interlocutors. His last words
are both a threat of violence (593–5) and an assertion that
Alexandre, like Porus, is in search of *gloire*. The debate has cul-
minated in verbally violent disagreement and this is reinforced
visually by the ambassador's rising from his stool and leaving
without having been formally dismissed by the kings.

How does Racine seek to ensure the interest of the audience
from the start of the scene and all the way through to the end?
Consciously or not, the audience can keenly follow the rhetorical
strategies of the characters and especially the way in which
these strategies work to make the debate progress. But Racine also
tries to make the issue at stake seem of great importance for the
characters involved. This is not difficult in this particular scene,
for the scene is the culmination of all that has gone before.
Announced in I. 2 (136), discussed in I. 3 (341–4), imminent in
II. 1 (345–6), this embassy has long been awaited by the audience. It is to be the moment of decision. Moreover, in the scene

itself Éphestion can secure the attention of the audience as well as
that of the kings by stressing the urgency of the decision:

> Alexandre veut bien différer ses exploits,
> Et vous offrir la paix pour la dernière fois.   (447–8)
>
> Vous savez son dessein: choisissez aujourd'hui,
> Si vous voulez tout perdre ou tenir tout de lui.   (471–2)
>
> Mais, Seigneur, c'est bien tard s'opposer à l'orage.   (550)

And, with Porus's decision made, Éphestion points out that time
has finally run out (593–4):

> Vos yeux, dès aujourd'hui, témoins de sa victoire,
> Verront de quelle ardeur il combat pour la gloire.

His departure marks the apparent end of any hopes of peace.

In his next play, *Andromaque*, Racine offers his audience another scene of ambassadorial oratory (I. 2). The placing of this
scene close to the beginning of the play means that the audience is
not able to experience the same sense of expectation of formal
oratory as in *Alexandre*. In *Andromaque* Racine uses different
techniques for securing the interest of the audience in the formal
debate.

In the first scene of the play he establishes the conflict of interests between Oreste the ambassador and Oreste the admirer of
Hermione. Already this makes Oreste, like Mathan, a more dramatically interesting ambassador than Éphestion, who has no
personal motives in his oratory. For although, when he meets
Pyrrhus, Oreste must appear to persuade him to hand over Astyanax to the Greeks and marry Hermione, his fiancée, he actually
wants Pyrrhus to refuse the request. The audience also has foreknowledge of Pyrrhus's desires. Pylade has informed them and
Oreste of Pyrrhus's vacillations. Though he wants to save Astyanax, marry Andromaque, and reject Hermione, he is prepared to
threaten Andromaque with the loss of Astyanax unless she is
prepared to marry him:

> Il peut, Seigneur, il peut, dans ce désordre extrême,
> Épouser ce qu'il hait, et punir ce qu'il aime.
> *(Andromaque* 121–2)

The three orators in *Alexandre* II. 2 have a known fixed stance on the subject of the debate. In *Andromaque* the stance of the orators is known to be complex and unstable. This must increase the curiosity of the audience as to what will happen.

Another means used by Racine to interest the audience in the debate is to allow Pylade to offer Oreste specific rhetorical advice for his confrontation with Pyrrhus. The scene in question, and in particular Oreste's speeches, must then be received in the light of this advice which is dispensed just as Pyrrhus comes on stage to meet the ambassador (135–40):

> Vous attendez le roi: parlez, et lui montrez
> Contre le fils d'Hector tous les Grecs conjurés.
> Loin de leur accorder ce fils de sa maîtresse,
> Leur haine ne fera qu'irriter sa tendresse.
> Plus on les veut brouiller, plus on va les unir.
> Pressez, demandez tout, pour ne rien obtenir.

Oreste must exaggerate his arguments and play excessively on Pyrrhus's supposed fears, thereby arousing his contempt and provoking a rejection of the proposal. Oreste successfully puts this advice into effect, while remaining on the surface an official orator:

> Avant que tous les Grecs vous parlent par ma voix,   (143)
> Souffrez que j'ose ici me flatter de leur choix,
> Et qu'à vos yeux, Seigneur, je montre quelque joie
> De voir le fils d'Achille et le vainqueur de Troie.
> Oui, comme ses exploits nous admirons vos coups:
> Hector tomba sous lui, Troie expira sous vous;
> Et vous avez montré, par une heureuse audace,
> Que le fils seul d'Achille a pu remplir sa place.
> Mais, ce qu'il n'eût point fait, la Grèce avec douleur   (151)
> Vous voit du sang troyen relever le malheur,
> Et vous laissant toucher d'une pitié funeste,
> D'une guerre si longue entretenir le reste.
> Ne vous souvient-il plus, Seigneur, quel fut Hector?   (155)
> Nos peuples affaiblis s'en souviennent encor.
> Son nom seul fait frémir nos veuves et nos filles,
> Et dans toute la Grèce il n'est point de familles
> Qui ne demandent compte à ce malheureux fils
> D'un père ou d'un époux qu'Hector leur a ravis.
> Et qui sait ce qu'un jour ce fils peut entreprendre?   (161)
> Peut-être dans nos ports nous le verrons descendre,

Tel qu'on a vu son père embraser nos vaisseaux,
Et, la flamme à la main, les suivre sur les eaux.
Oserai-je, Seigneur, dire ce que je pense?   (165)
Vous-même de vos soins craignez la récompense,
Et que dans votre sein ce serpent élevé
Ne vous punisse un jour de l'avoir conservé.
Enfin de tous les Grecs satisfaites l'envie,   (169)
Assurez leur vengeance, assurez votre vie;
Perdez un ennemi d'autant plus dangereux
Qu'il s'essaiera sur vous à combattre contre eux.

Oreste's speech follows closely the recommendations of rhetoricians regarding *inventio* and *dispositio*. As far as the arrangement is concerned, there is an *exordium* (143–50) followed by a *narratio* (151–4), which in turn is followed by a *confirmatio* (155–68), and the speech concludes with a *peroratio* (169–72).

In the *exordium* Oreste performs his duty as if he were sincere. He draws on *mores* to create a favourable impression of himself as the submissive ambassador, thereby winning the benevolence of Pyrrhus. He then pursues a flattering *definitio* of his interlocutor, comparing him with his father, Achilles. This ensures Pyrrhus's attention.

With the *narratio*, however, Oreste starts to put into practice the advice of Pylade. The event narrated is the point at issue, namely that Pyrrhus is allowing Astyanax to live. But Oreste mentions this in a way which suggests a retraction of the previous flattering comparison with Achilles. This along with the words 'vous laissant toucher d'une pitié funeste' (153) imputes a certain weakness to Pyrrhus. Oreste is deliberately trying to ruffle him.

This process continues in the *confirmatio*, which is composed of three movements. In the first (155–60) Oreste exploits the *locus adiunctorum* to suggest that the child, however innocent, is inevitably associated, in the eyes of the Greeks, with the deeds of his father, Hector. The second movement (161–4) develops the idea of this association through the *locus consequentium* to imply the danger which a vengeful Astyanax might represent for the Greeks when he has grown up. The possibility of such a threat is supported by inductive reasoning: like father, like son. So far, there has been a disproportion between the reasoning and the object of the reasoning, a small child. A similarly exaggerated argument forms the third movement of the *confirmatio* (165–8). Oreste exploits the *locus consequentium* from the point of view of Pyrrhus, while at the same time pretending to appeal to the king's sense of fear. The suggestion that Pyrrhus should be afraid of a prisoner-child is clearly designed to provoke dissent.

In the *peroratio* Oreste recapitulates his claim (169) before summing up the arguments advanced in the *confirmatio* and dwelling particularly on the danger to Pyrrhus (*affectus*). This produces from Pyrrhus precisely the reaction that Oreste desires: a rejection of his claim. It is with formal politeness coloured with contemptuous irony that Pyrrhus first responds to Oreste's exaggerated, fear-inspiring arguments (173−4):

> La Grèce en ma faveur est trop inquiétée.
> De soins plus importants je l'ai crue agitée.

Just as the spectators are able to distinguish between the apparent meaning of Oreste's words and the personal persuasive aim that the words are designed to attain, so they appreciate the difference between the noble motives that Pyrrhus advances for rejecting the claim and the personal motive which they know to lie behind the rejection.

Pyrrhus's speech has no formal *narratio* as the subject under discussion is now well known to both orators. But like Oreste's oration, it has an *exordium* (173−80), a *confirmatio* (181−216), and a *peroratio* (217−20). After flattering Oreste in double-edged terms, Pyrrhus argues first that the Greeks have no rights over his captive; secondly that fear of Astyanax is absurdly exaggerated; and thirdly that it would be cruel to dispose of the child at this late stage. His *peroratio* dismisses the Greeks, states his refusal to hand over the child, and stresses his own essentially good character as his main reason for this decision (219):

> De mes inimitiés le cours est achevé.

Oreste made it easy for Pyrrhus to refute the Greek claim and Pyrrhus has taken advantage of the opportunity. However, both to allow Oreste to appear to Pyrrhus as a determined Greek ambassador, and to produce a crescendo of heated debate, Racine extends the interview by drawing further on the resources of *inventio* and making his characters develop more arguments.

Now that Pyrrhus has declared his hand and has done so with such apparent relish, Oreste can produce more arguments for the Greek cause which will make Pyrrhus adopt an even more entrenched position. Oreste's response to the king's first argument is that the Greeks do indeed have some rights over Astyanax because they had ordered his death in Troy, and it was only by some subterfuge that he escaped it. This reasonable argument is suffixed by a threatening conclusion, for which, as far as is known from I. I, Oreste has no authority. The Greeks, he claims, will make war on Pyrrhus in order to take the child.

Oreste has so successfully angered Pyrrhus that the king does not trouble himself to reason with the ambassador. The debate has reached a moment of defiance and insult, and the pace of the confrontation is articulated through the use of a brief stichomythic exchange (237–8). Oreste's last taunt as ambassador is that Hermione will put an end to Pyrrhus's defiance (239–40). This is the closest either character comes in this scene to mentioning the issues which really motivate him. Yet Oreste, far from wanting Hermione to take any further interest in Pyrrhus, really wants her for himself. He uses her name in order to irritate Pyrrhus even more. For he has been told in I. I that Pyrrhus is neglecting his duty towards Hermione and lavishing his attention on Andromaque.

When Pyrrhus, in a rather unsatisfactory way, has dismissed this reproach of neglect, he steps aside briefly from the rhetorical situation to sow the seeds of a future scene between Hermione and Oreste (245–6):

> Vous pouvez cependant voir la fille d'Hélène:
> Du sang qui vous unit je sais l'étroite chaîne.

Stepping back into the rhetorical situation, he curtly dismisses the ambassador with his negative response to the claim (247–8):

> Après cela, Seigneur, je ne vous retiens plus,
> Et vous pourrez aux Grecs annoncer mon refus.

Oreste leaves the stage and his departure marks visually the end of the formal oratory, along with the apparent success of Pyrrhus in rejecting the claims of the ambassador.

E. Vinaver concludes that Pyrrhus 'sort triomphant de ce débat, ayant acquis à nos yeux, et, il l'espère du moins, aux yeux d'Andromaque, le prestige d'un homme qui au risque d'une guerre s'oppose à l'inhumaine cruauté des Grecs'.[12] Though true as an account of what appears to happen in this scene, the conclusion is inadequate for two reasons. First, Pyrrhus may be pleased with the way in which his exploitation of *mores* in the debate has projected his self-image, but Pyrrhus himself, along with Oreste and the audience, knows that it is a fragile self-image. All are aware that Pyrrhus is less an adversary of cruelty to children than a would-be lover of Andromaque. This is made clear in his meeting with Andromaque in I. 4, where he is prepared to use a threat to Astyanax's life as a means of persuading her to marry him. Pyrrhus's exploitation of *mores* is a rhetorical ploy with little substance in fact.

Moreover, Pyrrhus is less the victor in the debate than Vinaver suggests. Pyrrhus certainly appears to triumph, and Oreste appears to lose. But that is what Oreste wanted. It is Oreste who is in control throughout the debate. His exaggerated arguments provoke Pyrrhus to contemptuous rejections of the Greek offer. When the ambassador exits dismissed, he exits with the scent of victory in the air.

But Oreste does not savour victory for very long. For the unforeseen arises, and it brings about a reversal of rhetorical roles. In their first meeting Pyrrhus appears to win through, while Oreste is the real victor. When they meet again (II. 4), Pyrrhus appears to give in to Oreste, and Oreste then emerges as the real loser: what appears to be Oreste's victory is actually his defeat.

When Oreste meets Hermione (II. 2), she tells him that she will leave Epirus with him on two conditions. The first is that he should see Pyrrhus again, and remind him of his duty to Hermione. The second is that Pyrrhus should reject her in favour of Andromaque. The audience is prepared for another confrontation in which Oreste will deploy the same strategies as before in order to obtain from Pyrrhus a rejection of the claim being put to him.

But the expectations of the audience are defeated. For when Oreste sees Pyrrhus, the king forestalls Oreste's renewal of the debate, and announces simply that, after reflecting upon Oreste's earlier arguments, he has changed his mind. He will hand over Astyanax and marry Hermione. So intent is he on securing a rejection from Pyrrhus and so surprised at this sudden change of

---

[12] *Entretiens sur Racine* (Paris, 1984), 79.

mind, that Oreste interrupts the king rather clumsily with an overt discouragement, using the moral argument that Pyrrhus had used earlier himself:

Seigneur, par ce conseil prudent et rigoureux,
C'est acheter la paix du sang d'un malheureux.
(*Andromaque* 615–16)

But this, or any other attempt at counter-persuasion, must be unlikely to succeed, because this time Oreste is unaware of the real reasons which lie behind Pyrrhus's stance. Oreste is now the victim of irony. He does not know that Pyrrhus has changed his mind not as a result of the weightiness of Oreste's earlier arguments, but because of Andromaque's rejection of the king. Oreste must now think that his rhetoric, which had previously seemed so successful in its subtlety, was faulty. Aimed at obtaining a rejection from Pyrrhus, it has finally produced an acceptance. As a consequence of his own arguments, so Oreste thinks, Pyrrhus will now marry Hermione. Oreste is horrified at the prospect: 'Ah dieux!' (625).

Analysis of the scenes of formal oratory in *Athalie*, *Alexandre*, and *Andromaque* provides a basic demonstration of the way in which Racine creates verbal action. It is clear that in the tragedies, but not in *Les Plaideurs*, the scene of formal oratory forms an essential component in the linear progression of the main dramatic action, and that, within the scene itself, the central focus of the audience's interest is on the overall persuasive effect of the strategies employed by the orators. Rhetorical analysis is useful as it allows the critic to see how Racine uses the building bricks of *inventio* and *dispositio* to construct dramatically interesting scenes.

The initial meeting of Oreste and Pyrrhus is generally recognized as the most obvious example of the use of rhetoric in his tragedies. It has provoked many analyses and much admiration.[13] By contrast the embassies in *Alexandre* and *Athalie* are virtually

[13] 'La rhétorique théâtrale de l'époque amenée ici à son plus haut point de perfection' (Vinaver, *Entretiens*, 78; the scene is analysed on pp. 77–9). For other analyses see: Butler, *Classicisme et baroque*, 128–9; G. Declercq, 'L'Énonciation et la personne de l'orateur dans le texte dramatique', in G. Maurand (ed.), *Pouvoir et dire* (Toulouse, n.d.), 268–94; France, *Racine's Rhetoric*, 208–9; J. P. Houston, *The Rhetoric of Poetry in the Renaissance and the Seventeenth Century* (Baton Rouge, La., 1983), 259–60; and B. Weinberg, *The Art of Jean Racine* (Chicago, 1963), 86–9.

ignored. Yet theatrically they have much in common with the embassy in *Andromaque*.

The scene in *Athalie* effectively exploits in a new context the technique of Oreste's double-edged oratory. And, in some ways, Racine seems in *Andromaque* to be exploiting a scene which worked well in his previous play, *Alexandre*. He rewrites it for a new context, but uses a broadly similar framework and capitalizes on features which are nascent in the scene in *Alexandre* but which flourish in *Andromaque*. For both scenes the audience has been given foreknowledge of the views of the characters. In both these scenes the ambassador speaks first in a speech built along the lines of the rhetoricians' recommendations for *dispositio*. In both scenes there is a reply (or replies) of similar rhetorical stature, before this lengthy form of expression eventually gives way to shorter thrusts indicative of an even hotter rhetorical atmosphere and increasing impatience on the part of the orators. In *Andromaque* I. 2 Racine has more or less repeated the exciting dramatic structure of *Alexandre* II. 2.

What he has added and what makes the formal oratory of *Andromaque* and that of *Athalie* more interesting than that in *Alexandre* is the distinction between the characters' role as orators and their role as passionate individuals. This distinction underlies all the oratory in *Andromaque* I. 2 and *Athalie* III. 4. Although the ambassador in *Alexandre* has no personal desires to intertwine with his public message, there is some potential for play upon this sort of distinction. For Taxile's oratory is performing two functions (persuading both Éphestion and Porus) while appearing to perform one (persuading Éphestion alone), and Porus's arguments may be motivated by his amorous, as well as by his military, desires. These are features, however, on which Racine does not deliberately play for effect. In *Andromaque*, on the other hand, Racine has built into his preparation of the scene (I. 1), into his execution of it (I. 2), and into its follow-up (II. 4) a requirement that the audience appreciate the ambiguous position of Oreste and Pyrrhus as formal orators, with both characters having to use words convincingly and plausibly, but with neither character giving away his real feelings. Presenting formal oratory in such a context is a way of creating suspense and is a technique which Racine may well have learnt from the famous deliberation scene in Corneille's *Cinna* (II. 1), where the emperor seeks advice from his counsellors, who are conspiring against him and who therefore have suddenly to assume the orator's mask of carefully weighed words with which both to protect themselves and to advance their aims. Formal orators have great theatrical potential, which Racine fully realizes in *Andromaque* as Corneille had done in *Cinna*.

A contemporary writer offers an excellent analysis of how scenes like these appealed to the seventeenth-century audiences. All these scenes are examples of deliberative oratory. Deliberative oratory is particularly suited to the theatre because implicit in it is uncertainty about an important decision. The audience wants to know how the uncertainty will be resolved and so listens keenly. D'Aubignac acknowledges that 'le Theatre n'est presque remply que de Deliberations, et que qui les en retrancheroit, en osteroit tout ce qu'il y a de plus agréable et de plus ordinaire' (*Pratique*, p. 305). But despite this acknowledgement, he expresses the view that deliberations are out of place in drama, unless they are treated very carefully. In particular, care should be taken to allow the audience to engage with the motivation and passions of the speakers. He explains in these terms how well the deliberation scene in *Cinna* works, while lamenting the dramatic coldness and incompetence of the deliberation scene at the beginning of *Pompée*. In summing up the qualities of a good deliberation scene, he makes a comment which suggests the potential dramatic impact of scenes of persuasion. A deliberation, he says (pp. 310–11), must above all be

tellement attachée au sujet du Poëme, et ceux qui donnent conseil si fort interessez en ce qu'ils se proposent, que les Spectateurs soient pressez du desir d'en connoistre les sentimens; parce qu'alors ce n'est plus un simple conseil, mais une Action Theatrale; et ceux qui donnent avis ne sont pas de simples Discoureurs, mais des gens qui agissent dans leur propre Faict où méme ils tiennent le Spectateur engagé.

D'Aubignac is describing the theatricality of verbal action. In his ambassadorial oratory in *Alexandre* Racine seems to try to engage with d'Aubignac's advice. In the scenes of ambassadorial oratory in *Andromaque* and *Athalie* he produced nothing to disappoint the demanding abbé.

III. A FAMILY EMBASSY: RACINE'S
AND DU RYER'S *ESTHER*

Éphestion, Oreste, and Mathan supply the only scenes of unambiguously formal oratory in Racine's tragedies. These characters have a purely formal relationship with the characters to whom they address their planned speeches. Yet Esther is also, in a sense, an ambassador. When she speaks at length to her husband, Assuérus, in III. 4, she speaks not only as a wife, but also as the ambassador of the Jewish people. It was with the aim of securing for the Jews a secret foothold in the corridors of power that her uncle Mardochée sent her incognito, as it were, to compete with other hopeful candidates for the attentions of the king, Assuérus, whose previous wife had left in disgrace. The king's choice fell on Esther, who became his queen (49—76). In I. 3 the known Jew Mardochée boldly penetrates the women's quarters of the king's palace to speak urgently to his niece and prompt her to carry out the rhetorical mission which will be the culmination of his scheme. For the plight of the Jews is now desperate. The king, under the influence of the evil counsellor Aman, has signed an edict leading to the extermination of the Jews in ten days' time (166—80). Esther's ambassadorial status must now be made manifest to Assuérus. She must declare herself and risk the consequences:

> Toute pleine du feu de tant de saints prophètes,
> Allez, osez au roi déclarer qui vous êtes.
> (*Esther* 189—90)

After some initial hesitation, Esther is persuaded to act.

Mardochée's scheme in using Esther as a political pawn relies largely upon the persuasive strategy of *mores*. If Esther has won the confidence and admiration of the king, any cause for which she pleads should in theory be viewed favourably by him. That this theory works in practice can be appreciated by the audience during Esther's initial approach to Assuérus in II. 7 and at the beginning of her confrontation with him and Aman in III. 4. For, to bring out Assuérus's trust in Esther, Racine adopts an unusual way of presenting an instance of persuasion. He has Assuérus agree in advance to any claim that Esther may make. In II. 7 he tells her (683—4):

> Parlez: de vos désirs le succès est certain
> Si ce succès dépend d'une mortelle main.

And in III. 4 Assuérus's admiration for her and his granting of her, as yet unknown, request are made explicit in almost fulsome terms before she has even opened her mouth to speak (1022−5):

> Mais dites promptement ce que vous demandez:
> Tous vos désirs, Esther, vous seront accordés,
> Dussiez-vous, je l'ai dit et veux bien le redire,
> Demander la moitié de ce puissant empire.

It might seem on the surface that Esther's persuasion of Assuérus should probably work theatrically in a completely different way from the persuasive acts of Racine's other ambassadors, that it might even be undramatic. For, if Assuérus has agreed to grant Esther's wishes before he has even heard them, where will be the dramatic interest for the spectators as they listen to Esther's plea? Perhaps these two moments in *Esther* (II. 7 and III. 4) might be evidence for those who believe that Racine 'had largely abandoned suspense and surprise as dramatic weapons'?[14]

In fact *Esther* shows Racine trying out a new way of building suspense into scenes of persuasive action. This happens in two ways. First, there is the way in which the audience's expectations are built up and then defeated in II. 7. In I. 3 Esther is persuaded by Mardochée to approach Assuérus on behalf of the Jews and to declare herself, and she agrees to act the following morning (244−6). Aman's words at the start of Act II make it clear that a new day is dawning (373−4):

> Hé quoi? lorsque le jour ne commence qu'à luire,
> Dans ce lieu redoutable oses-tu m'introduire?

When, therefore, later in the act, Esther makes her dramatic entrance into the throne-room of Assuérus, the audience expects her to make her revelation and begin her plea. But her fear at having approached Assuérus unbidden results in fainting and hesitation, and the persuasion that ensues is undertaken not by

---

[14] P. France, 'Racine', in J. Cruickshank (ed.), *French Literature and its Background*, ii. *The Seventeenth Century* (Oxford, 1969), 169. In ch. 4 of *The Tragic Drama of Corneille and Racine* (Oxford, 1982), H. T. Barnwell shows how skilfully Racine deploys these very weapons of surprise and suspense.

Esther, but by Assuérus attempting to prevail upon his wife to speak. When she does so, the curiosity of the audience and of Assuérus is aroused but not satisfied. For she simply requests a subsequent meeting with Assuérus in the presence of Aman. The king agrees, thus prolonging his own and the audience's expectation of Esther's revelation.

The other way of creating suspense in both II. 7 and III. 4 depends specifically on Mardochée's exploitation of *mores* through the personality of Esther. The audience is shown how such a strategy can be an easy route to rhetorical success when Assuérus twice gives his assent before even hearing Esther's plea. But Assuérus's prior agreement does not deprive the audience of suspense. The audience cannot be sure that Assuérus's consent will remain firm throughout, and at the end of, Esther's plea. Indeed Racine contrives to show the audience that Esther's particular mission is such as will stretch the device of *mores* to the very limits of its persuasive powers and perhaps beyond. In other words, the audience is made to be all the more fearful by Assuérus's all too early assent to a request the enormity of which he cannot possibly imagine. This element of fear is built into Racine's presentation of Esther's rhetorical mission early in the play. In I. 3 she tells Mardochée how much she fears appearing unsummoned before Assuérus's eyes (191–204). Mardochée himself recognizes that her mission could well result in the loss of her life (205–8). There is danger because Esther's good character is based on deceit. She has acquired a favourable reputation in the eyes of Assuérus by hiding her racial origins. Her plea requires the revelation of this deceit.

The audience first enjoys the mixture of hope in Esther's *mores* and fear that the strategy might not work, when she appears before the king in II. 7. In the event the strategy suffices to secure her a ready pardon for her unexpected intrusion and a willing assent to a further interview.

It is in the second interview that the mixture of hope and fear will be most intensely felt. For it is then that the strategy will be severely tested and that her pleading will have to be at its most eloquent. The interview may well open with Assuérus's agreeing to whatever Esther desires. But how can Esther plead to an enemy of the Jews so that the decree condemning them all to death might be revoked? How will she make best use of her resources of *mores?* What supplementary strategies can she employ? These questions subconsciously tax the minds of the spectators and ensure that they are gripped by Esther's long plea. An analysis of her plea will be followed by an analysis of a comparable scene in Du Ryer's *Esther*. The details of the analyses will highlight the differences in the verbal action of the two dramatists.

Perhaps her most difficult task is to break the news to her husband that she is Jewish, thus running the immediate risk of accusations of deceit and of loss of all her credit in his eyes. This task she undertakes with startling suddenness in an *exordium* which aims at a most economical *captatio benevolentiae*, followed immediately by a blunt statement of news which is so shocking as to arouse the acute interest of Assuérus (1026–31):

> Je ne m'égare point dans ces vastes désirs.
> Mais, puisqu'il faut enfin expliquer mes soupirs,
> Puisque mon roi lui-même à parler me convie,
>   (*Elle se jette aux pieds du roi*)
> J'ose vous implorer, et pour ma propre vie,
> Et pour les tristes jours d'un peuple infortuné
> Qu'à périr avec moi vous avez condamné.

Her first line replies directly to Assuérus's offer of half his empire should she want it. Her comment is calculated to disarm Assuérus, suggesting that her demand will be much more modest and more easily granted. Then come two lines which suggest hesitation and hence reinforce the idea of modesty, which is also promoted by her use of *actio* as she falls at his feet to make her request. The whole substance of her rhetorical mission is made plain in her next three lines, which, though strictly periphrasis rather than direct statement, reveal unmistakably that she is a Jewess and that she wishes to plead for her own life and for that of all others of her race.

The *exordium* is interrupted by four agitated questions from Assuérus which demonstrate his degree of interest (1032):

> A périr? Vous? Quel peuple? Et quel est ce mystère?

At the same time he helps her to her feet, a gesture which urgently invites a response to his questions. His apparent incomprehension of her plea is the result of his confident belief that Esther is not Jewish, which does not tally with what she has just said. Assuérus's shock is shared by Aman, whose 'Je tremble' (1032) indicates fear that Esther's persuasive armoury may include accusing arrows directed against himself.

When she continues her *exordium* by reiterating the substance of her earlier periphrasis in terms of direct statement (1032–3), the two men register their shock openly. Aman is even more afraid, while Assuérus expresses painful disappointment at the deceit which the apparently innocent Esther is now admitting (1035–40). This is the moment when her dependence on *mores* might collapse. But Esther quickly takes charge of the situation and concludes her *exordium* with a request that she be heard out and in particular that Aman should not be allowed to interrupt her (1040–3). Assuérus's response, 'Parlez' (1044), indicates that Esther's revelation has probably not lost her the king's good-will, an indication which will be reinforced in the middle of her speech when Aman ventures to interrupt and is rudely put down by Assuérus (1089–91).

Esther's main aims are to save the Jews from extermination and to rescue Mardochée whose assassination is imminent. The strategy which she adopts is similar to that of Agrippine in *Britannicus* IV. 2. Esther's speech is composed largely of *narratio* (1044–88, 1092–9, 1114–20, 1120–35) with a short *confirmatio* inserted in the middle (1100–13). She will narrate a series of events in such a way as to alter the perspective on them of the man whom she is trying to persuade. Unlike Agrippine, however, Esther operates subtly, never spelling out in imperatives the actions required of her interlocutor as a result of the new perspective. Esther draws no conclusions; Agrippine draws them insistently. Rather Esther weaves *mores* and *affectus* into the texture of her *narratio* so that the cumulative effect might lead Assuérus to draw his own conclusions. Her strategy is both a result and a reinforcement of her modesty.

In presenting her sketch of the history of the Jewish people Esther is of course careful to take every opportunity to paint a favourable picture of them. Their origins lay in the worship of their god (1048); this god punished them when they transgressed (1060–1); they had admiration for the new king Assuérus and pinned their hopes on him (1078–82); they prayed for God to watch over Assuérus, even as he was planning their destruction (1109–11). She paints the Jews as an innocent, humble race, whose destruction could not possibly be of any benefit to the king.

She is also careful to make the most of Aman's treachery (1083−103), showing Assuérus how this counsellor deceived him into hostile action against the Jews. It is this part of the story which is supported by a *confirmatio*. She exploits both the *locus consequentium* and the *locus contrariorum* together (1100−4):

> On verra, sous le nom du plus juste des princes,
> Un perfide étranger désoler vos provinces,
> Et dans ce palais même, en proie à son courroux,
> Le sang de vos sujets regorger jusqu'à vous!

The consequence of allowing Aman's advice to be put into effect will be the king's horrible assassination of his subjects, graphically described. The *locus causarum* offers a defence of them against Aman's accusations (1105−8):

> Et que reproche aux Juifs sa haine envenimée?
> Quelle guerre intestine avons-nous allumée?
> Les a-t-on vus marcher parmi nos ennemis?
> Fut-il jamais au joug esclaves plus soumis?

There can, she implies, be no grounds for royal hostility towards the Jews.

Her account of Aman's deceits, along with her description of the role of Mardochée and a moving evocation of his present plight (1118−35), is a second revelation to Assuérus in this scene. His trusted minister is revealed as a traitor, while the Jew who is about to die on his orders is a loyal supporter, who saved his life and is the adoptive father of Esther.

Esther's story, moving from the early history of the Jews to their imminent destruction, skilfully interweaves elements of deliberative and judicial oratory. Assuérus is being persuaded to revoke his condemnation of the Jews; he is also being persuaded to reconsider the case of Mardochée, and pass judgement on Aman. Esther argues the case for the Jews, defends Mardochée, and accuses Aman, mostly by means of *narratio*.

Her consummate skill as an orator, however, is best seen in her presentation of God and in the manner in which this is intertwined with her subtle flattery of Assuérus himself. She perceives that any defence of the Jews must embrace a defence of their God. She wastes no time in inserting such a defence shortly after the beginning of her *narratio* (1050−7):

> Ce Dieu, maître absolu de la terre et des cieux,
> N'est point tel que l'erreur le figure à vos yeux.
> L'Éternel est son nom, le monde est son ouvrage;
> Il entend les soupirs de l'humble qu'on outrage,
> Il juge tous les mortels avec d'égales lois,
> Et du haut de son trône interroge les rois.
> Des plus fermes États la chute épouvantable,
> Quand il veut n'est qu'un jeu de sa main redoutable.

Esther's thumbnail sketch of God makes it plain that she is correcting Assuérus's image of Him and includes both His kindly as well as His more fearsome characteristics. It is important that His personality is understood by Assuérus, for Esther makes Him the principal agent in her story. God punished the Jews when they turned away from Him (1060–1). He reassembled them and restored His worship under Cyrus (1062–73). God dispensed with Cyrus's son and chose to put Assuérus on the throne (1074–7).

> 'Dieu regarde en pitié son peuple malheureux,
> Disions-nous: un roi règne, ami de l'innocence.'
> Partout du nouveau prince on vantait la clémence;
> Les Juifs partout de joie en poussèrent des cris.
>
> (*Esther* 1078–81)

Here Assuérus is invited to perceive a relationship between God, the Jews, and himself, a relationship which places him firmly in the camp of the good and innocent Jews. Epithets applied to Assuérus contrast with those soon to be applied to Aman, for Aman belongs to a different camp from which Assuérus must keep clear. Indeed the Jews prayed that God would save Assuérus from 'des méchants les trames criminelles' (1112). Finally Esther spells out the agency of God in Assuérus's imperial successes and in his recent escape from two conspirators through the divinely inspired intervention of Mardochée (1114–19):

> N'en doutez point, Seigneur, il [Dieu] fut votre soutien.
> Lui seul mit à vos pieds le Parthe et l'Indien,
> Dissipa devant vous les innombrables Scythes,
> Et renferma les mers dans vos vastes limites;
> Lui seul aux yeux d'un Juif découvrit le dessein
> De deux traîtres tout prêts à vous percer le sein.

The implication behind Esther's presentation of God's agency in these events is that Assuérus, recognizing that God has chosen to favour him, should not act in a way likely to offend His apparent design.

Esther has assembled a strong case. She has, in addition, had the verbal, and no doubt facial, reactions of Aman as supporting evidence for her accusation against him. Whatever fears the audience had towards the beginning of the scene must have been gradually dissipated by this careful display of persuasive power. But there must be some uncertainty until the king finally responds to her revelations and persuasion. Will he still grant her wishes, as he has promised? Will he perhaps call on Aman to defend himself?

Esther's speech does not end with a recapitulatory *peroratio*. This may be because Assuérus is prompted to interrupt by the description of the suffering which Mardochée faces within the next hour. Alternatively Esther may formally close her speech now that she has brought the story up to the present moment, depriving herself at the end, as throughout, of any overt statements of her claims. In the absence of textual evidence, both options are open to producers of the play. In any case, what Assuérus says reveals him to have been favourably impressed, indeed disturbed, by Esther's plea (1137–8):

> Tout mon sang de colère et de honte s'enflamme.
> J'étais donc le jouet... Ciel, daigne m'éclairer.

But although Esther's demands will be met and will supply the denouement to the plot, the audience's confidence in her persuasion is not entirely justified. For Racine has further surprise and suspense in store for the moments which follow.

Rather than showing complete conviction in Esther's story and acting upon that conviction, Assuérus takes a moment to pause and reflect, and to do this he leaves the stage. This is after he has decided to call another witness, who will supply further evidence before a final decision is reached (1140):

> Appelez Mardochée: il faut aussi l'entendre.

Assuérus has clearly assumed the role of judge and he is not yet ready to pronounce judgement. His performance as judge, however, is forestalled by the sight which greets him when he returns in III. 6.

He sees Aman on his knees at Esther's feet with his hands touching the queen. Although Aman is actually pleading with

Esther to save him from Assuérus's imminent fury, Assuérus misinterprets the gesture. To him this sight must recall his nightmare recounted earlier by Hydaspe (387–90):

> J'ai couru. Le désordre était dans ses discours.
> Il s'est plaint d'un péril qui menaçait ses jours:
> Il parlait d'ennemi, de ravisseur farouche;
> Même le nom d'Esther est sorti de sa bouche.

Aman has become the 'ravisseur farouche' before the eyes of the judge, who pronounces an immediate death sentence, while at the same time revoking that of Mardochée (1172–5):

> Qu'à ce monstre à l'instant l'âme soit arrachée,
> Et que devant sa porte, au lieu de Mardochée,
> Apaisant par sa mort et la terre et les cieux,
> De mes peuples vengés il repaisse les yeux.

So Esther's pleading is resolved in a way which neither she nor the spectators can have anticipated. Her skilful oratory goes some way to persuading Assuérus, but it is his accidental confrontation with Aman apparently *in flagrante delicto* that finally convinces him. It is ironical that the evidence by which he has been persuaded to save the Jews is false.

Esther's oration is the culmination of a drama which has throughout built up and played on the audience's expectations of this crucial act of persuasion. When she finally comes to her plea, the audience trembles as she makes her initial revelation, before growing in confidence as she deploys her powers of *inventio* and appears to secure the conviction of Assuérus. Assuérus's unexpected departure and his return to find Aman at Esther's feet and to deliver a swift condemnation form a final surprise and resolve the long suspense of Esther's rhetorical mission.

Despite the claims of its recent editors, there is no comparably rich concentration of dramatic features to be found in the treatment of the same episode in Du Ryer's *Esther*.[15] It is true that the two plays are not exactly comparable. For Du Ryer fits in far more of the biblical story than Racine. Most notably, his first

---

[15] 'La pièce n'est certes pas parfaite, mais elle doit ennuyer beaucoup moins à la représentation que n'importe quelle autre version française, y compris celle du grand Racine' in P. Du Ryer, *Esther*, ed. P. Gethner and E. J. Campion (Exeter, 1982), p. xix.

three acts are taken up by the question as to whether or not Esther
will finally supplant Vasthi in the king's affections. Du Ryer's
Esther, then, has not yet become queen. But, like Racine's, Du
Ryer's Esther has to defend the Jews against the decree of their
extermination and to do this she must reveal her own Jewish
origins to the king.

Du Ryer handles the verbal action with less varied means of
maintaining the interest of his audience. In Du Ryer's play Esther's
plea is less carefully prepared for the audience; her powers of
inventio are comparatively slight; and the plea is presented with
little regard for those elements of suspense and surprise which
contribute so effectively to the dramatic impact of Racine's presentation of this act of persuasion.

In I. 2 of Du Ryer's play there is a discussion between Mardochée
and Esther about the advantages and disadvantages of revealing
her Jewish origins. Mardochée wants her to continue to dissimu-
late, while Esther would like to speak the truth to the king. This
discussion gives rise to a theme which is central to Racine's presentation of Esther's mission, namely the persuasive impact of
mores if Esther should eventually plead with the king. Thamar, a
confidant, suggests that Esther should conceal her identity in order
to build up a stock of good impressions which will ultimately help
her cause:

> Si par nostre mal-heur jusqu'icy manifeste
> Il brusla pour les Juifs d'une haine funeste,
> Par un effet d'amour qui peut tout surmonter
> Il aimera les Juifs parce qu'il aime Esther.
> (Du Ryer, *Esther* 165–8)

Esther expresses the opposite view that such a scheme is based on
deceit and, by implication, that it would be perilous to put one's
trust in it (169–72):

> Peut-on dire qu'il m'aime, & que son cœur me suive,
> Puisqu'il ne pense pas brusler pour une Juifve,
> Et que je luy serois un objet odieux
> Sans le voile trompeur qui me cache à ses yeux?

This contrast lies at the heart of the suspense which Racine builds
into his presentation of Esther's persuasion: hope in a strong
strategy and fear because of the deceit involved. Yet, though Du
Ryer makes his characters articulate this contrast more overtly

than Racine's do, the earlier dramatist does not make theatrical capital out of it. For Esther simply agrees to keep quiet about her identity for the moment and the issue is not revived until Act IV, when the idea that she may have a reserve of *mores* on which to draw has been forgotten.

Her revelation to the king and her plea on behalf of the Jews occupies the last scene of the play, v. 5. But Du Ryer's Esther is a rather slow and laborious orator, not adept at weaving together different threads of persuasion as Racine's is. She does not begin by making a dramatic revelation of her identity. Rather it emerges at the end of her plea, when its theatrical potential is least great. For once the king has registered the necessary surprise: 'Quoy vous sortez des Juifs?' (1808), his next words are an unconditional granting of her request (1817–24).

Moreover, Esther's speech, which so readily secures the persuasion of the king, has but one major thread: the accusation against Haman, who had conspired to assassinate the king. This serves as a defence of the Jews in that her *narratio* includes favourable comments on them, instrumental as they were in stopping the conspiracy.

This judicial element is only one part of the persuasive strategy of Racine's Esther, who argues on a much wider front, promoting the God of the Jews and associating Him in a subtle way with the position of Assuérus. God and the religious activities of the Jews are almost entirely absent from the speeches of Du Ryer's Esther.

In the earlier play, Esther argues less interestingly and less persuasively, yet secures persuasion immediately, bringing the play to an end. In the later play Esther argues more skilfully, yet is left uncertain as to the outcome of her persuasion, Assuérus's mind being made up only later.

iv. FAMILY ORATORY IN *BRITANNICUS* AND *MITHRIDATE*

There are so few examples of formal oratory in Racine's plays because most of the characters are closely related either by family ties or by personal friendship. They deal with each other on a private level and cannot therefore be formal orators. Esther's formal embassy to her husband is a notable exception to this general principle.

The principle breaks down, however, in two other cases. *Mithridate* III. 1 and *Britannicus* IV. 2 beg to be received as instances of formal oratory even though the participants are, respectively, father and sons, and mother and son. Both scenes have similar features to those occurring in the scenes of ambassadorial oratory. They depict a controversial discussion of an issue which is central to the play, be it Agrippine's desire to control the power vested in Néron, or the political and amorous conflicts of Mithridate and his sons. In both scenes the first speaker is allowed an extensive oration following the traditional recommendations for *dispositio*. The first speech is followed by similarly expansive responses before the discussion becomes more heated and breaks up into shorter ripostes. In both scenes the formality of the oratory is marked visually. Agrippine, Néron, and Mithridate are all seated for their formal interviews. In both scenes, as in the embassies of Oreste and Mathan, though in different ways, there is some play on the gap between the desires to which the characters admit as orators and those to which they admit elsewhere. Above all, these family debates are scenes of formal oratory because the characters treat them as such. Agrippine is less a mother talking to her son than a disgraced political counsellor trying to defend and re-establish her reputation before the emperor. Mithridate is at first more the elderly king cautiously and warily addressing two generals than a father confronting his sons; eventually, of course, the audience realizes that Mithridate's aim is a family one: he wants to marry off Pharnace.

The scene in *Mithridate* in which, in the longest speech in any play of Racine's, the king expounds his plans to attack Rome has often been compared to Auguste's discussion of his future with Cinna and Maxime in *Cinna* II. 1. Without referring specifically to Corneille, Racine's preface conveys the dramatist's evident pleasure at the success of the scene on stage.[16] The preface to the 1741 edition of his plays advertises the quality of this scene and claims that it is equal to any scene in the plays of Corneille.[17] More recently comparisons have not always been so favourable towards

[16] 'Ce dessein [de Mithridate] m'a fourni une des scènes qui ont le plus réussi dans ma tragédie' (p. 447).
[17] 'La premiere Scene du troisiéme Acte est d'une grande beauté. Je ne pense pas qu'elle doive céder à la plus belle scéne des Piéces du grand Corneille.' See F. and C. Parfaict, *Histoire du théâtre françois* (Amsterdam and Paris, 1747), xi. 270.

Racine. Yarrow[18] is more prepared to admire the scene than Pocock, who thinks it much 'inferior' to *Cinna* II. 1,[19] or Adam[20] and Abraham,[21] who criticize it on grounds of implausibility.

A sketch of the rhetorical moves made by father and sons already exists in the notes to G. Rudler's edition of the play (pp. 82–6). What I should like to point out is the difference in dramatic effects achieved by the two playwrights in these scenes. It is a difference which comparisons between the scenes have tended to overlook.

The dramatic essence of Corneille's scene lies in the fact that throughout the discussion no character lets his orator's mask slip. The audience is all the time left with the puzzle as to why Auguste should, with apparent sincerity, be consulting those conspiring against him and why the conspirators should respond with such conflicting advice. Why, in particular, should Cinna argue so persuasively against Auguste's abdication? These orators skate on thin ice and it is the sense of danger which propels the audience's interest. In the scene itself the ice is not broken. Oreste and Pyrrhus are similarly daring and careful skaters. But Mithridate and his sons are not. Mithridate is wily, to be sure, but both he and Pharnace are impulsive. Hence the novel dramatic effect in this scene when the ice cracks. For, after Mithridate has failed to persuade Pharnace, with specious reasons, to leave for a wedding in Parthia, the king is ready to take off his orator's mask (a notional action reinforced visually by the stage direction '*se levant*' (947)) and he commands Pharnace to leave (952–8), even explaining the real reasons for the command, which are his suspicions of Pharnace's designs on Monime (973–4). This cracking of the ice, or lifting of the orator's mask, results in the calling of guards and the arrest of Pharnace (III. 2), who, in turn, spitefully lifts Xipharès's mask, which has so far remained in place (994–8). It is usual for representations of formal oratory to begin sedately and to end with a degree of verbal bustle or even verbal violence. Corneille's scene is unusual in remaining reasonably sedate throughout and in ending with agreement, while main-

[18] *Racine*, 63

[19] *Corneille and Racine: Problems of Tragic Form* (Cambridge, 1973), 223.

[20] *Histoire de la littérature française au XVIIe siècle*, 5 vols. (Paris, 1948–56), iv. 352.

[21] *Racine* (Boston, Mass., 1977), 110.

taining dramatic interest. The scene in *Mithridate* is equally unusual in passing from verbal violence to physical violence, which is surely at least as effective a way of gripping the audience. Any comparison of these two scenes must take account of this essential difference. It is with very different dramatic effects in mind that the two dramatists manipulate the rhetorical strategies of their characters.

All the scenes of formal oratory examined so far have been examples of mainly deliberative oratory, though there were important judicial elements in Esther's oration. The meeting of Néron and Agrippine in *Britannicus* IV. 2 is of special interest for the predominance in it of formal judicial oratory. Agrippine is the defendant. She has been arrested by her son's guards and now has to face the emperor to answer for her actions. Its dramatic interest, however, lies in the way in which Agrippine deploys her judicial strategies in such a way as to toss the accusation back to Néron himself and eventually turn judicial oratory into demonstrative and then deliberative oratory, persuading her son to do as she wants. This is a meeting for which Agrippine has been waiting throughout the play. It is her chance to speak alone and at length with her son. She is a clever and manipulative orator, but turns out to be not quite clever enough.

Before the defendant meets her judge and prosecutor, Burrhus announces the interview to her and gives her some advice (VI. 1). She should recognize that Néron rules and that she should not expect power for herself. Rather than making demands of her son, she should be mindful that she is under arrest and concentrate on defending herself and perhaps showing Néron some affection (1104–6):

> Ne vous souvenez plus qu'il vous ait offensée:
> Préparez-vous plutôt à lui tendre les bras;
> Défendez-vous, Madame, et ne l'accusez pas.

Néron arrives, and Burrhus departs, leaving them together. The audience has had its expectations shaped by Burrhus's advice and it is now keen to discover whether or not Agrippine will act on it. The dramatic device is similar to that used immediately before the ambassadorial scene in *Andromaque*. Oreste uses to good effect the advice given to him. Agrippine is a rather different case. She speaks first, beginning with an *exordium* (1115–18) in which, having rudely invited the emperor to take a seat,[22] she announces her subject (1115–18):

> Approchez-vous, Néron, et prenez votre place.
> On veut sur vos soupçons que je vous satisfasse.
> J'ignore de quel crime on a pu me noircir:
> De tous ceux que j'ai faits je vais vous éclaircir.

Her simple words are ambiguous, and it is only in the course of the speech that the correct interpretation of them becomes evident: 1116 might suggest that she sees Néron as a judge, whom she is keen to satisfy; 1117 might be a proclamation of innocence, followed by 1118, which might suggest a sincere confession of everything she can remember having done that might give Néron cause for concern. But this turns out to be the wrong interpretation of these lines. The crimes which she enumerates in this bitterly ironic manipulation of the judicial framework, occupying the first part of her speech (1119–94), are crimes which she has committed to help Néron, and for which she expects recognition.

She certainly does not treat Néron with the tact that Burrhus proposed. But at least the judicial framework that she has adopted focuses on herself, and does not look too much like a direct attack on the emperor. Indeed it could be seen as a demonstrative oration in which Agrippine flaunts all her worth. Like a demonstrative speech, it is composed principally of *narratio* rather than *confirmatio*. It is a *narratio* which illustrates the statement that she makes immediately after the *exordium* (1119–20):

> Vous régnez: vous savez combien votre naissance
> Entre l'empire et vous avait mis de distance.

She traces chronologically the steps which led to Néron's occupancy of the throne: her seduction of Claudius (1123–35); their marriage (1136–8); Néron's adoption into the imperial family (1139–42); Néron's becoming Claudius's heir in preference to Britannicus (1143–8); Agrippine's machinations to remove suspicious courtiers (1149–58); her choice of Néron's advisers

---

[22] 'The formula "prenez votre place"... suggests that, Emperor or no, he should know his place, and is reminiscent of the defendant's being required to sit on the "sellette" in a seventeenth-century lawcourt... Agrippine behaves like the presiding judge, seating herself first, and not waiting for Néron even to greet her verbally' (Barnwell, *Tragic Drama*, 202).

(1159–66); her attempts to win support for him (1167–72); and the conclusive step, the most dangerous one, and the one to which Agrippine devotes most space, her manipulation of the news of Claudius's death and the proclaiming of Néron as emperor (1173–94).

This is crowned, as any confession of guilt might be, by a protestation of sincerity (*mores*) (1195):

> C'est le sincère aveu que je voulais vous faire.

This is a highly ironical and sarcastic use of this strategy, however. For Agrippine has not tried to think of crimes which she may have committed against Néron. Rather she has revelled in a demonstrative speech proclaiming all the crimes which she has committed for him. With her next line, her rhetorical strategy becomes clear (1196):

> Voilà tous mes forfaits. En voici le salaire.

What at first seemed like a judicial speech of self-accusation, and then a demonstrative speech extolling Agrippine's deeds, can now be seen for what it is, a coolly executed attack on Néron's ingratitude. The previous *narratio* of Agrippine's good deeds carried out for Néron is balanced by a shorter *narratio* of Néron's recent, but increasing, crimes against his mother (1197–1219). Agrippine's argumentative strategy is arrogantly simple. Her whole speech is based on a single enthymeme: 'I have been kind to you; you should be kind to me.' It is significant that she does not yet draw on any of the *loci* to develop her argument. She conducts her case solely by means of *narratio*, in which real events are adduced as evidence. The predominance of real over artificial proof is characteristic of *Britannicus*. Perhaps because Racine is inspired by Tacitus' substantial historical account, and perhaps because his conception of his subject requires more judicial oratory than his other plays, characters more frequently draw upon the past to support their arguments.

The audience may think that Agrippine can frighten Néron into submission. Certainly that is what Néron himself had been afraid of earlier in the play (496–510). In any case, her *peroratio*, far from being a careful appeal to win Néron over, is a brief statement of withering contempt, a rejection of the view that the

emperor's mother should ever have been asked to give an account
of herself at all (1220–2):

> Et lorsque, convaincu de tant de perfidies,
> Vous deviez ne me voir que pour les expier,
> C'est vous qui m'ordonnez de me justifier.

Thus she acts as judge and proclaims the emperor guilty.

In a speech which shows Néron to be more a master of the
spoken word than some have allowed,[23] the emperor responds to
his mother in terms which are just as sarcastic and accusatory as
those that she has used with him. Moreover, the fact that he
adopts a very similar rhetorical strategy to the one which she had
used makes his reply all the more cutting. Like his mother, he
pretends not to accuse, while doing just that. It is noteworthy that
one of the proofs which he employs is the quotation of popular
rumour (1231–5). This is the very device with which he will
finally be persuaded by Narcisse, two scenes later, to murder
Britannicus (1468–78).

To hear herself accused of plotting against Néron is too much
for Agrippine to take, and she interrupts in order to refute the
accusation. To help her to do this she draws on two *loci*, first
effecta (1259–60):

> Quel serait mon dessein? qu'aurais-je pu prétendre?
> Quels honneurs dans sa cour, quel rang pourrais-je attendre?

and then *comparatio minorum* (1261–4):

> Ah! si sous votre empire on ne m'épargne pas,
> Si mes accusateurs observent tous mes pas,
> Si de leur empereur ils poursuivent la mère,
> Que ferais-je au milieu d'une cour étrangère?

At this point the audience realizes just how manipulative Agrippine
is, playing Néron off against Britannicus while she pursues her
own self-interest. Having answered her son's accusation, she does
not attempt to win him over to her point of view, but continues in

---

[23] C. Venesoen makes the case for Néron's verbal impotence, though he rather
overstates it: 'Crainte de lui parler [à Agrippine] ou incapacité de parole; incapacité
de convaincre par le discours ou de se servir de mots efficaces pour régner ou pour
séduire' ('Le Néron de Racine: Un cas curieux d'impuissance verbale', *IL* 33
(1981), 132).

belligerent mood with the same unrestrained personal attacks that Néron has just delivered to her (1269–70):

> Vous ne me trompez point, je vois tous vos détours:
> Vous êtes un ingrat, vous le fûtes toujours.

She finishes this speech with an appeal to *affectus*. Like so many of Racine's heroes and heroines, she offers to surrender her life. It is the last card that she can play in order to get her own way. Normally the threat of suicide is couched in terms which arouse pity. Agrippine, however, is still on the war-path against Néron, and her threat is accompanied by an intimation that Néron's own life is far from secure (1283–6). The audience might well think that Agrippine's belligerence would infuriate Néron even more. But he pretends to be persuaded by her arguments and asks her what she would like him to do (1287). She has now done all that Burrhus told her not to do. She finishes by crowning her overassured oratory with another overconfident move. She makes demands, and she makes them authoritatively (1288–94). When Néron has agreed to these demands and restored his mother's position of authority, she leaves as a triumphant orator. It therefore comes as a horrific surprise to the audience when, shortly afterwards, Néron reveals to Burrhus his deceit and his real intentions (1313–14): he will murder Britannicus.

Agrippine has put too much trust in her own rhetoric, and Néron, perceiving this weakness, agrees to be persuaded so that he can escape the situation of formal oratory. This occurrence and the end of *Mithridate* III. 1 are two of several chilling moments in Racine's depiction of persuasion, when the audience is bleakly reminded that power is always stronger than words. The example in *Britannicus* is bleaker, because it is more bathed in deceit.

Any attempt to engage in rhetorical criticism of a work of drama must focus initially on those scenes in which formal oratory is represented. It emerges from my analyses of such scenes that scrutiny of characters' *inventio* and *dispositio* allows the critic to give an account of the shape of scenes and to lay bare characters' persuasive techniques, with which Racine is attempting to hold the attention of the audience. Comparison of formal oratory in the tragedies with the trial in *Les Plaideurs* highlights the distinctive quality of persuasion as action in the former. The rhetorical manœuvres of the characters in the tragedies interest the audience because the outcome of the formal oratory is in all cases made to seem of vital importance to the lives of those involved.

There are only six such scenes in Racine's tragedies: *Alexandre* II. 2, *Andromaque* I. 2, *Britannicus* IV. 2, *Mithridate* III. 1, *Esther* III. 4, and *Athalie* III. 4. This may not seem to be many scenes out of the total corpus, but both their pivotal importance in the plays and their number do seem great when set against Corneille's reminder that dramatic characters are not, or even should not be, orators (*Writings*, 19).

Corneille's remark might seem all the more puzzling when his own plays are scrutinized. Three of his four best known tragedies contain representations of formal oratory. In addition to the political deliberations in *Cinna* (II. 1), there are judicial scenes in *Le Cid* (II. 8, IV. 5), *Horace* (V. 2–3), and *Cinna* (V. 1–3).[24] The trial of Horace must rank as one of the most prominent representations of formal oratory in any seventeenth-century tragedy, occupying almost the whole of the last act and serving as the denouement of the play.

Moreover it is not only in the well-known plays of the period that formal oratory can be found. From Hardy's *Coriolan* early in the century, where there are examples of formal oratory of both a judicial and a deliberative nature (III. 3, IV. 4, V. 2), from the trial of the eponymous hero in Du Ryer's *Thémistocle* (III. 1), and from the judicial oratory of Thomas Corneille in *Stilicon* (IV. 3), to the political oratory in his brother's *Sertorius* (III. 1), there are plenty of orators to be found on the seventeenth-century tragic stage, be they ambassadors, counsellors, judges, defendants, or prosecutors.

What Corneille opposes is, of course, not the judicious and sparing representation of oratory which is well integrated into the overall dramatic action and used as a dramatic highlight, but the clumsy character whose oratory is not clearly aimed at an interlocutor but is directed only too clearly at the audience. For when that happens the theatrical illusion is broken.

It is tempting to point to an example of this type of oratory in

[24] For comments on the characters' rhetoric in these scenes see S. Harwood, *Rhetoric in the Tragedies of Corneille* (New Orleans, 1977), 52–8 (*Le Cid* II. 8), 66–74 (*Horace*); H. Barnwell, *Tragic Drama*, 183–90 (*Horace*), 191–3 (*Cinna* V. 1–3); and W. J. Dickson, 'Corneille's Use of Judicial Rhetoric: The Last Act of *Horace*', SCFS 10 (1988), 23–39.

one of Racine's tragedies: the speech delivered by La Piété in *Esther*. The speech of this allegorical character occurring at the beginning of the play is a demonstrative oration, addressed directly to the audience and praising Louis XIV for his support of Saint-Cyr and his leadership of the nation. What twentieth-century tastes would dismiss as a clumsy piece of propaganda and literary flattery can be excused on two grounds. First, La Piété does not actually disrupt the dramatic action, for she is not part of it. The play makes sense without her speech, though what she has to say is essential for an appreciation of the historical circumstances of the play's first performances. Secondly, La Piété appears not to be a character planned by Racine as part of his conception of the play. The role was conceived as an afterthought so that Madame de Caylus could be introduced into the performance.[25] It is better not to view the speech of La Piété alongside the instances of formal oratory discussed already, not least because its status is in fact very different from the ambassadorial addresses of Oreste and Éphestion. Their speeches are *representations* of formal oratory within the world of the play. The speech of La Piété is an *actual* instance of formal oratory, prefixing the play to which it belongs. It is therefore unfair to see this speech as an example of the sort of oratory to which Corneille might object. The speech is almost exceptional in Racine's tragedies as an example of undramatic rhetoric.[26] It is precisely the sort of speech which might provoke the 'undramatic pleasure' mentioned by P. France.[27]

In using the representation of formal oratory for dramatic purposes Racine followed the example of his predecessors and contemporaries. The modern audience should not be surprised at the recurrence (however infrequent) of this feature in plays of the period. For it is an obvious source of dramatic pleasure for playwrights whose dramatic action depends largely upon the spoken word. And it is a source of dramatic pleasure which writers and others continue to exploit today; witness the popular film *Kramer*

---

[25] See H. Lyonnet, *Les 'Premières' de Racine* (Paris, 1924), 185.

[26] *Almost* exceptional, because Taxile's speech announcing the arrival of Alexandre in *Alexandre* III. 3 and singing the emperor's praises also smacks of undramatic demonstrative oratory. It is the demonstrative oratory in praise of Louis XIV in Act V of Molière's *Tartuffe* that makes some critics feel the ending of that play to be rather awkward.

[27] *Racine's Rhetoric*, 238.

versus Kramer, which focuses on a fight in court between divorced parents for the custody of their child; witness also the broadcasting of trials in the USA and of parliamentary debates in Great Britain, whose audiences are as much entertained as informed.

Formal oratory is a dramatic language; so too, the seventeenth-century playwrights observed, is informal oratory, which is the subject of the next two chapters.

3

Informal Oratory: The Protagonists

[La Rhétorique] se fait paroître dans les chaires de nos Eglises, dans le Barreau, dans toutes les negociations, dans les conversations; en un mot le but que nous avons dans le commerce de la vie est de persuader ceux avec qui nous traittons, & de les faire tomber dans nos sentimens.

(Bernard Lamy, *L'Art de parler*, 279–80)

If Racine perceived clearly the dramatic potential of the representation of formal oratory on stage, he saw too that oratory as a dramatic resource need not be restricted to formal juridical and political proceedings. While traditional rhetoric books catered principally for such formal situations, a rhetorician like Bernard Lamy, writing in French, could state explicitly that persuasion was an art of value to all people in their daily lives.[1] Since Oreste the ambassador can interest an audience with the persuasive strategies which he uses against a foreign king, why should he not be an equally interesting orator when using similar strategies to attempt to win the affection of his loved one? Here is the essence of Racine's dramatic technique. A theatre essentially of words is made gripping by the extension of persuasive action beyond the normal situations of formal oratory.

For much of the time the spectators of a seventeenth-century tragedy witness scenes of conflict between protagonists. In most of these scenes the characters do not adopt the role of formal orator; they are not ambassadors or barristers. Yet they nearly always behave like orators.

In this chapter I examine examples of such behaviour with a number of questions in mind. Can scenes of informal oratory be analysed in the same way as scenes of formal oratory? What variety of treatment is accorded to these scenes? And does Racine treat them differently from his contemporaries?

---

[1] See the epigraph to this chapter.

1. MASKED AND UNMASKED ORATORS: *IPHIGÉNIE* AND *ASTRATE*

Scenes of informal oratory between protagonists combine with scenes of formal oratory to make up a large proportion of the text of Racine's plays. Throughout a series of debates Racine can interest his audience in a vital question. In *Iphigénie* that question is: will the heroine be sent to her death or not? The audience, however, is not simply presented with a series of repetitious confrontations. There are many ways in which variety can be introduced. The position of a particular debate in the play ought to confer on it a certain uniqueness, if the plot is advancing and if participants take account in their arguments of any developments. Clytemnestre, for instance, has new arguments to wield against Agamemnon in *Iphigénie* IV. 4 since their earlier confrontation in III. 1. Different combinations of characters will permit different perspectives on issues debated more than once: Iphigénie's arguments relating to the sacrifice vary according to whether she is addressing Agamemnon or Achille. Moreover the structure of the debate can vary enormously. Characters may be given long speeches containing all the main parts of a traditional oration and these may be followed by quick-fire debate. Alternatively, speeches may be shorter and the debate may have interruptions and perhaps changes of direction. Such structural variations are numerous.

There is, however, a further and important source of variety in the presentation of rhetorical confrontations, which, though it is, strictly speaking, a product of the dramatist's handling of plot, has significant consequences for the characters' choice of rhetorical strategies and for the audience's appreciation of them. It concerns the degree to which characters involved in a debate are aware of their interlocutor's motives, and the degree to which they are willing to declare their own motives. The speeches of all characters invite rhetorical analysis; but the speeches of those characters who deliberately hide their feelings invite it all the more pressingly. For if they are not speaking from their heart, they have clearly to make a special effort at *inventio*, finding plausible reasons in order to keep the real ones hidden, and drawing on *mores* to present an image of themselves which is not genuine.[2] Rhetorical analysis is

---

[2] See G. Declercq, 'La Ruse oratoire dans les tragédies de Racine', *DSS* 150

well suited to revealing characters' deviousness. Such deviousness is, of course, what Oreste practises in *Andromaque* I. 2, Mathan in *Athalie* III. 4, and Mithridate, at least initially, in *Mithridate* III. 1. But they are far from being the only ones.

Often, two characters will meet in a debate which requires deliberate deceit on the part of one of them, and this deceit can vary in intensity. One of the most deceitful of all Racine's characters, Atalide in *Bajazet*, attempts to persuade Roxane of Bajazet's love for the sultana, knowing full well that such love does not exist; she wears the mask of the helpful go-between, eager to promote Roxane's interests (I. 3; III. 6).[3] Atalide's exploitation of false arguments and *mores* is given an edge by the fact that she behaves thus in front of a woman who has all power over Bajazet and herself. Atalide's rhetorical role-playing, then, arouses a degree of fear from which Racine extracts the maximum dramatic effect by showing what happens when the role becomes too great for Atalide and her mask slips (IV. 3).

Phèdre too wears a mask when she approaches Hippolyte in II. 5. It is the mask of the queen wishing to plead with Hippolyte for the defence of her little son and full of regret for any offence which she may have caused her stepson in the past. But gradually, ever so gradually, in the course of the scene, Phèdre's mask slips to reveal the married woman passionately in love with her stepson, who stands before her. Her feelings declared, she delivers a judicial speech accusing herself and inviting Hippolyte to punish her.

A very different use of the mask occurs in *Andromaque* III. 5, the confrontation between the desperate Andromaque and the haughty Hermione. Revealing her deepest feelings as a frightened mother, Andromaque pleads with Hermione to prevail upon Pyrrhus to save her son. Hermione, now Pyrrhus's betrothed, does not intend to enter into a debate with Andromaque. So, hiding her real feelings of joy at her forthcoming marriage and irritation with

(1986), 43–60, an article which examines the vocabulary of imposture in the tragedies and makes the distinction between real and plausible arguments. It is to this feature that H. T. Barnwell alludes when he says that in some scenes 'the armoury of rhetoric is used on two levels, one apparently political and rational, the other personal and passionate' (*The Tragic Drama of Corneille and Racine* (Oxford, 1982), 211).

[3] It is true that Atalide jealously suspects Bajazet of loving Roxane in III. 3–4; but the suspicion is soon cleared up.

Andromaque, she briefly dons the mask of a political bride without any personal influence over Pyrrhus. It is a mask through which Andromaque and the audience see very clearly.

It rarely happens in Racine's tragedies that all parties in a debate hide their real feelings, no doubt because of the potential confusion for the audience.[4] It could be said that neither Oreste nor Pyrrhus really speaks the truth in *Andromaque* I. 2 and II. 4. This pattern is not found elsewhere. It is true that in *Phèdre* II. 5 Hippolyte is in a sense hiding his love for Aricie, but that is not central to the discussion or to any opinions which Hippolyte expresses in the scene. Usually only one character in a debate will wear a deliberately misleading mask.

Sometimes, by contrast, all characters involved will unleash all their feelings. Such heated displays of emotion would lose their effect if repeated too frequently, a risk which Racine runs in his first play, *La Thébaïde*. Aware perhaps of the potential of such scenes to stir the audience, Racine uses them repeatedly in this play. Jocaste battles with Étéocle in I. 3, with Polynice in II. 3, and again with Étéocle in III. 4, battles which culminate in the three-way confrontation between Étéocle, Polynice, and Jocaste in IV. 3. In later plays Racine tends to save these outbursts of candid oratory for the fourth and final acts. It is in *Alexandre* IV. 2 and 3 that Axiane comes to verbal blows with Alexandre and Taxile. It is in *Andromaque* V. 3 that Oreste, honest as always with Hermione, finds Hermione distressingly honest with him for the first time in the play. It is in *Britannicus* IV. 2 that Agrippine and Néron speak the truth to each other, before Néron retreats into the relative safety of deceit, pretending to be convinced by his mother's arguments. It is in *Bérénice* IV. 5 that Titus and Bérénice first attempt to persuade each other of the rightness of the diametrically opposed courses of action which each wishes the other to pursue. Handled sparingly, outbursts of honesty by both protagonists in a debate can provide a stunning display of rhetorical fireworks, effective because of their rarity and because in them the audience sees some of the major conflicts and tensions come into sharp focus.

---

[4] It is the use of monologues and confidants that allows the audience to be sure of the real feelings and wishes of the characters. The absence of confidants from *Alexandre* results in some uncertainty on this score. It is sometimes hard to know just when Cléofile is revealing herself truthfully and when she is drawing on *mores* deliberately to alter the way in which she is perceived.

In whichever way protagonists argue with each other, with or without an orator's mask, Racine is nearly always careful to let the audience know beforehand what a character's persuasive aim will be and what mask, if any, will be worn. Armed with this knowledge, the audience can take a closer and better-informed interest in the implementation of rhetorical strategies during the scene of persuasion itself. This point is illustrated by the example of Oreste, whose strategy against Pyrrhus in *Andromaque* I. 2 was spelt out for him by Pylade at the end of I. I.

To this general principle there are a few exceptions. When the spectators first see Narcisse advising Britannicus to put his trust in Agrippine, they do not appreciate the dramatic irony of Narcisse's double-dealing (I. 4). Narcisse appears simply to be the *gouverneur* of Britannicus, proffering probably sensible advice. But if Racine deprives his spectators of this dramatic irony at the end of Act I, it is to shock them at the beginning of Act II when Narcisse is shown to be betraying Britannicus to the emperor. The mask that he wore in I. 4 is made visible only in retrospect.[5]

Similarly, when Atalide first pleads to Roxane on behalf of Bajazet, the audience cannot know that her arguments are not genuine. The mask slips momentarily when Roxane says that she wishes to be married to Bajazet forthwith. Atalide's exclamation might serve as a clue to the audience that there is more to her feelings than there has so far appeared to be:

> Vous épouser! O ciel! que prétendez-vous faire?
> (*Bajazet* 289)

It is only upon Roxane's departure, however, that Atalide rips off her mask to reveal her own love for Bajazet in explicit terms.

In the case of both Narcisse and Atalide, Racine seems to withhold the sight of the mask from the spectators to create a specific dramatic effect, plunging them suddenly into unexpected complexities of the situation. His handling of Créon's mask in *La Thébaïde* is less assured. Whatever Créon may appear to argue for in the presence of other protagonists, his aim is always to stir up

---

[5] Racine might be thought to contradict himself about the proper description of the role of Narcisse. In the list of characters he is 'gouverneur de Britannicus' (p. 260). In the first and second prefaces he is 'confident de Néron' (p. 254, and see p. 258). The two descriptions, of course, bear witness to Narcisse's double-dealing.

the mutual hatred of Polynice and Étéocle so that they might destroy each other and hence leave the throne open to himself; with the throne he might also win Antigone. None of this emerges clearly until III. 6 when he reveals his desires to his confidant, Attale. This is after he has participated in four scenes with other protagonists (I. 4–5; III. 4–5), which show him mysteriously, it would seem, shifting his ground, arguing first that Étéocle should do battle with Polynice, next that he should grant his brother an interview to make peace. There is a hint of Créon's love for Antigone at the end of I. 5, but it is only in III. 6 that the motives behind Créon's apparently inconsistent arguments become clear. Racine may well have been aiming to engage his audience in the mystery of Créon's motivation, but it is perhaps significant that he does not use such a technique again except in the more circumscribed and sharply focused instances of *Britannicus* and *Bajazet*. He perhaps realized that, by and large, spectators better appreciate a scene of oratory when the motivation of the orators is known to them in advance.

An analysis of two scenes from *Iphigénie* (III. 1 and IV. 4) will illustrate some of the points that I have been making in more general terms: how Racine's characters behave like orators even when they are most definitely not formal orators; how Racine can renew interest in debates on what is essentially the same subject; and in particular how the declaration and non-declaration of motives contribute to this renewal of interest.

H. T. Barnwell makes the point that *Iphigénie* IV. 4–9 form a series of scenes which exploit the procedures of judicial oratory to dramatic effect: 'This sequence of scenes represents a further adaptation . . . by Racine of the rhetoric of judicial procedures, not in a formal juridical context, but in a dramatic form of judgement and self-judgement arising out of accusation and defence with the production and interpretation of evidence.'[6] I should like to approach two of these scenes in the same spirit, but from a different angle. First, if the confrontation between Clytemnestre, Iphigénie, and Agamemnon in IV. 4 and that between Agamemnon and Achille in IV. 6 are based on rhetorical procedures, so too are the earlier ones between Clytemnestre and Agamemnon in III. 1 and between Achille and Agamemnon in I. 2. The later scenes are

---

[6] *Tragic Drama*, 205.

replays of the earlier ones after Agamemnon's mask of deceit has
been stripped away. Secondly, if the scenes in Act IV are based
largely on judicial oratory, this is intertwined with an important
deliberative function. The aim of all three of Agamemnon's opponents is, from Iphigénie's first gentle plea to Achille's furious
and defiant departure, to persuade the father not to go ahead with
his daughter's sacrifice. Their judgement of him is in a sense a
foretaste of the judgement which they would pass if he carried out
his criminal act. For the accused has not yet committed the crime.
The torrent of judicial oratory is in effect an exploitation of
affectus: fear of adverse judgement might prompt Agamemnon to
change his mind about the sacrifice of Iphigénie.

In both III. 1 and IV. 4 Agamemnon's rhetorical aim is to secure
the opportunity to go ahead with the sacrifice of his daughter. In
III. 1 he sets about achieving this aim by devious means, for the
aim itself is not made known to Clytemnestre. Agamemnon pretends to have a different aim, which, if achieved, should go some
way to achieving his real, undeclared aim.

There are two acts of persuasion in this scene, the first quickly
dispatched. Clytemnestre apparently persuades Agamemnon to
pursue plans for the wedding of Iphigénie and Achille. The doubts
which he had expressed in his letter about Achille's commitment
to the marriage are, she says, groundless. To support her case
she uses a *narratio* which points to the *probatio inartificialis* of
Achille's own testimony:

> Mais lui-même, étonné d'une fuite si prompte,
> Par combien de serments, dont je n'ai pu douter,
> Vient-il de me convaincre, et de nous arrêter!
> Il presse cet hymen qu'on prétend qu'il diffère,
> Et vous cherche, brûlant d'amour et de colère:
> Prêt d'imposer silence à ce bruit imposteur,
> Achille en veut connaître et confondre l'auteur.
> (*Iphigénie* 770–6)

The success of Agamemnon's strategy involving the letter de-
pended upon Clytemnestre's receiving it before she reached the
camp and before she spoke to Achille. Faced with the overwhelming evidence of Achille's reported enthusiasm for the marriage,
Agamemnon cannot take this strategy any further. This evidence,
along with the hints of his possibly being discovered as the author

of the ploy (774–6), is enough to persuade Agamemnon to abandon the strategy and to pretend to authorize the marriage.

Agamemnon's new technique is to try to keep Clytemnestre away from the altar so that a mother's fury will not impede the conduct of the sacrifice. To do this he draws carefully on *mores* and adduces specious reasons. His apparently easy agreement to the marriage and recognition of his mistake, glossed over vaguely with the first person plural pronoun rather than the singular, serve him well as a *captatio benevolentiae* as he begins his new strategy (778–83):

> Madame, c'est assez. Je consens qu'on le croie.
> Je reconnais l'erreur qui nous avait séduits,
> Et ressens votre joie autant que je le puis.
> Vous voulez que Calchas l'unisse à ma famille;
> Vous pouvez à l'autel envoyer votre fille,
> Je l'attends.

He is already starting to wear his new mask of the father happy at the prospect of his daughter's wedding. Only the phrase 'autant que je le puis' casts a slight and ambiguous shadow over the sincerity of his projected image. Then, arguing from the *locus adiunctorum* and describing the physical and atmospheric features associated with a military camp, he extends his mask further to project an image of the husband concerned for his wife's comfort and dignity. This whole development is rendered more plausible by an introduction suggestive of husbandly intimacy (783–92):

> Mais avant de passer plus loin,
> J'ai voulu vous parler un moment sans témoin.
> Vous voyez en quels lieux vous l'avez amenée:
> Tout y ressent la guerre, et non point l'hyménée,
> Le tumulte d'un camp, soldats et matelots,
> Un autel hérissé de dards, de javelots,
> Tout ce spectacle enfin, pompe digne d'Achille,
> Pour altérer vos yeux n'est point assez tranquille,
> Et les Grecs y verraient l'épouse de leur roi
> Dans un état indigne et de vous et de moi.

All this is invention in the ordinary as well as in the rhetorical sense of the word. Agamemnon is presenting arguments based on a fictional situation as if it were the real situation.

The consequence for Clytemnestre is that, although she would

argue fervently against Agamemnon's real rhetorical aim, if she
knew it, she is going unwittingly to argue with her hand tied
behind her back; she is going to expend rhetorical effort on a
battle which is virtually irrelevant in comparison with the real and
hidden point at issue. Although she puts up convincing arguments,
Agamemnon soon grows tired of the debate and brings it to an
end by issuing an order.

Clytemnestre's first argument, delivered in the form of incre-
dulous exclamations and rhetorical questions (795–801), is based
implicitly on the *probatio inartificialis* of custom: mothers always
accompany their daughters at the wedding ceremony. To this
Agamemnon can only start feebly to repeat the argument which he
has already developed, based essentially on the *locus adiunctorum*,
though now accompanied by the *locus dissimilitudinis* (802–3):

> Vous n'êtes point ici dans le palais d'Atrée.
> Vous êtes dans un camp . . .

Clytemnestre interrupts with a sharp response, turning upside
down Agamemnon's *locus dissimilitudinis* to present the same
material via the *locus similitudinis* (803–8):

> Où tout vous est soumis,
> Où le sort de l'Asie en vos mains est remis,
> Où je vois sous vos lois marcher la Grèce entière,
> Où le fils de Thétis va m'appeler sa mère.
> Dans quel palais superbe et plein de ma grandeur
> Puis-je jamais paraître avec plus de splendeur?

Clytemnestre clearly has the better arguments, but Agamemnon
cannot give in and allow her to attend the marriage, because there
is to be no marriage, only a sacrifice. So this is the point at which
he loses patience and makes a final mysterious and tyrannical plea,
totally lacking in persuasive force (810–11):

> Daignez à mon amour accorder cette grâce.
> J'ai mes raisons.

This induces Clytemnestre not to give in, but to try a third approach, humbling herself and appealing for her husband's pity
(*affectus*) (812–13):

> D'un spectacle si doux ne privez point mes yeux.
> Daignez ne point rougir de ma présence.

Unmistakably defeated, but unable to concede, Agamemnon asserts his authority (816–19):

> Puisque enfin ma prière a si peu de pouvoir,
> Vous avez entendu ce que je vous demande,
> Madame: je le veux, et je vous le commande.
> Obéissez.

His departure ensures that he has the last word.

Throughout this scene the audience must wonder if Clytemnestre will say anything to penetrate Agamemnon's rhetorical mask. She does not do so. But she does, when alone in the next scene, significantly exploit the *locus causarum* in an attempt to perceive the reason for what she evidently thinks is a peculiar aim of Agamemnon's. She does not, of course, come up with the right answer, because the truth is too horrible to be simply guessed. Although something has impressed her as odd about her husband's behaviour, she does not yet see the devious mask which he was wearing. For the moment she decides to obey (827).

The other response of the audience to III. 1 is surely a sense of frustration that the superior arguments are being deployed in vain, because Clytemnestre is kept in the dark about the real issue to which she should be applying her rhetoric.

The same sense of frustration is absent from her next confrontation with her husband in IV. 4. For then Clytemnestre is fully apprised of the central issue. Her husband's mask having been stripped off, she can tackle him on an equal footing. His aim is still essentially the same as in III. 1, namely to be able to proceed with the sacrifice without too much disruption. But the present scene is very different, because the changed circumstances require a new approach from Agamemnon and permit a properly focused and informed approach from Clytemnestre. Moreover, the presence of Iphigénie adds an extra and different voice to the case against Agamemnon and the sacrifice.

The father's intention to sacrifice his daughter has been made known to Clytemnestre and Iphigénie by Arcas. When Clytemnestre probes her husband in a game of cat-and-mouse in IV. 3, Agamemnon cannot properly understand her point, for he does not yet know of Arcas's betrayal. This dawns on him when Iphigénie arrives in tears (1167–70):

Que vois-je? quel discours? Ma fille, vous pleurez,
Et baissez devant moi vos yeux mal assurés.
Quel trouble! Mais tout pleure, et la fille et la mère.
Ah! malheureux Arcas, tu m'as trahi!

From this moment on all three characters can speak with a full
and equal awareness of the end to which they must bend their
rhetoric. Each character speaks in turn: Iphigénie, Agamemnon,
and Clytemnestre.

There is no suggestion of judicial oratory in Iphigénie's speech,
no hint of accusation. It is a deliberative speech, based on a subtle
strategy. Iphigénie explicitly states her willingness to be sacrificed,
but implicitly argues for her release from this duty. Throughout
she is careful to present an image of herself as a loving and dutiful
daughter.

She begins with an *exordium* based on *insinuatio*, saying things
which will not alienate Agamemnon or make him feel that his
design is being opposed (1170–80) and there is certainly a hint
of irony as she recollects Agamemnon's promise to marry his
daughter and stresses the innocence of the person that will be
offered to Calchas's whetted blade. Nevertheless, Iphigénie's
words are those of a submissive, if fearful, daughter, not of a
hostile one. Such words are calculated to secure the attentive
interest of Agamemnon.

After the *insinuatio* Iphigénie tentatively begins a *confirmatio*,
arguing with great caution for the safety of her life (1181–8).
Her first argument is based on *affectus* and is an appeal to
Agamemnon's paternal affection. She reminds him of this blood-
relationship in three separate ways (1189–94):

Fille d'Agamemnon, c'est moi qui la première,
Seigneur, vous appelai de ce doux nom de père;
C'est moi qui, si longtemps le plaisir de vos yeux,
Vous ai fait de ce nom remercier les dieux,
Et pour qui tant de fois prodiguant vos caresses,
Vous n'avez point du sang dédaigné les faiblesses.

Her appeal continues with a *narratio* evoking past occasions of her
eager interest in her father's military successes. When Agamemnon's
affections have been stirred, Iphigénie closes the *narratio* by contrasting former happiness with her present distress (1197–200):

> Et déjà d'Ilion présageant la conquête,
> D'un triomphe si beau je préparais la fête.
> Je ne m'attendais pas que pour le commencer,
> Mon sang fût le premier que vous dussiez verser.

Here is the first sign in Iphigénie's speech of determined opposition to Agamemnon's plan and, lest this should anger him or put
him ill at ease, she follows it with reassuring comments suggestive
of the submissive daughter of the *exordium* (1201–4):

> Non que la peur du coup dont je suis menacée
> Me fasse rappeler votre bonté passée.
> Ne craignez rien. Mon cœur, de votre honneur jaloux,
> Ne fera point rougir un père tel que vous.

This further statement of a willingness to obey, however, leads
subtly into another argument against the sacrifice. This argument
is drawn from the *locus generis*: Iphigénie is one of a group of
those who would suffer if she were killed, the other two in the
group being Achille and Clytemnestre (1205–12). Use is again
made of *affectus* (1213–14):

> Il [Achille] sait votre dessein; jugez de ses alarmes.
> Ma mère est devant vous, et vous voyez ses larmes.

Iphigénie gently invites Agamemnon to fear the consequences of
his deception of the now shocked Achille and also to take pity on
his wife, who is visibly distressed. But, most of all, with such a
display of self-denial, Iphigénie is silently asking her father to be
impressed by, and to take pity on, *her*. Her self-denial is reinforced in her concluding remark. An elaborate *peroratio* is shunned
in favour of a statement which, like her *exordium*, plays down the
rhetorical aim of her speech (1215–16):

> Pardonnez aux efforts que je viens de tenter
> Pour prévenir les pleurs que je leur vais coûter.

The expression of reluctance to use rhetoric on her own behalf
establishes Iphigénie as one of Racine's more self-effacing orators.
Whether the self-effacement is genuine or simply a ploy will depend upon individual actresses. But the audience is surely meant
to be moved by the daughter's unselfishly phrased plea for her

life.[7] Moreover, an audience so moved will expect Agamemnon to be equally moved.

But Agamemnon's reaction is not quite what an optimistic audience might have expected. For he takes advantage of the modesty of Iphigénie's speech to reassert the need for the sacrifice, without starting up a dialogue with either of her main arguments. His aim seems to be to accomplish the sacrifice without stirring up too much obstructive hostility on the way. He is careful, therefore, not to appear openly to contradict Iphigénie. He exploits *mores*, not, in this scene, to cover up deceit, but to reinforce his image as a sympathetic and distressed father. His immediate response capitalizes on Iphigénie's claim to be willing to be sacrificed (1217–20):

> Ma fille, il est trop vrai: j'ignore pour quel crime
> La colère des dieux demande une victime,
> Mais ils vous ont nommée; un oracle cruel
> Veut qu'ici votre sang coule sur un autel.

To bolster his image and ward off any potential accusations, he moves into a *narratio* which makes much of his former efforts to prevent the sacrifice (1221–32). In support of his case comes just one brief argument drawn from the *locus comparationis maiorum*: Agamemnon's power is as nothing, compared to the combined force of the people and the gods (1233–6). A *peroratio* repeats the conclusion that he had already drawn in his *exordium*, reinforcing his own grief at his daughter's imminent death.

Iphigénie's conciliatory approach has allowed Agamemnon not to change his mind at all and has even dispensed him from arguing strenuously for his position. The main purpose of his speech has been to defend his image as a caring father. He has sought to avoid bitter conflict in the way that Iphigénie was avoiding it. But he has miscalculated his strategy. For, by saying little and arguing little, he has made his position weak, a weakness which Clytemnestre thoroughly exposes.

---

[7] It might be supposed that the tears of Iphigénie and Clytemnestre in this scene are intended to move the audience to weep as well. Praising himself and aligning himself with the Greeks in his preface, Racine was pleased to report the tears of the spectators (without, however, specifying the moments at which they occurred): 'Mes spectateurs ont été émus des mêmes choses qui ont mis autrefois en larmes le plus savant peuple de la Grèce' (p. 511). See the comparable confrontation between the three main protagonists in Euripides' *Iphigeneia at Aulis* 1141–275.

Her speech is judicial to the extent that she takes up her husband's attempt at self-defence and undermines it, condemning him as a cruel murderer. But her intention is basically deliberative, the attack on Agamemnon being part of her strategy to prevent her daughter's death even at this late stage. There is no careful manipulation of *mores* by Clytemnestre. She comes across simply as the mother trying to shame Agamemnon into doing as she desires. Appropriately, then, she begins with a virulent personal attack, based on the *locus generis* (1245−8):

> Vous ne démentez point une race funeste:
> Oui, vous êtes le sang d'Atrée et de Thyeste.
> Bourreau de votre fille, il ne vous reste enfin
> Que d'en faire à sa mère un horrible festin.

Iphigénie's understated approach, on which Agamemnon capitalized, meant that the full horror of the sacrifice had remained unspoken. Clytemnestre makes it her business to fill the lacunae left by the earlier speeches: Agamemnon will be the murderer of his child and, as such, will be following in the footsteps of his ancestors. Whereas Iphigénie understated, Clytemnestre overstates. Hence the reference to the gruesome meal of Thyestes's three sons, killed by Atreus and served to his brother, their father.

The next part of her speech (1249−60) justifies her description of Agamemnon as a murderer by undermining his presentation of himself as an anxious and distressed father (1253):

> Pourquoi feindre à nos yeux une fausse tristesse?

It is impossible to know how artificial Agamemnon's use of *mores* has been in this scene. On the evidence of his tortured mental state in I. 1 and elsewhere, it is reasonable to suppose that the distress is genuine, but that it may have been specially manipulated in this scene in an attempt to avoid criticism. By firmly believing his grief to be pure artifice and exposing it as such, Clytemnestre is no doubt hoping to bully her husband into a genuine display of paternal affection which would manifest itself in the cancellation of the sacrifice. Certainly she is not prepared to accept as evidence of such affection a few tears and his reported efforts to save Iphigénie; she wants more convincing *probationes inartificiales* (1254−60):

> Pensez-vous par des pleurs prouver votre tendresse?
> Où sont-ils ces combats que vous avez rendus?
> Quels flots de sang pour elle avez-vous répandus?
> Quel débris parle ici de votre résistance?
> Quel champ couvert de morts me condamne au silence?
> Voilà par quels témoins il fallait me prouver,
> Cruel, que votre amour a voulu la sauver.

Having undermined most of Agamemnon's speech, she goes on to present positive arguments against the sacrifice. The first is drawn from the *locus generis* (1261–72): if Helen provoked the war against Troy, her own daughter and her own husband should suffer, not Iphigénie, Agamemnon, or Clytemnestre. A second argument comes from the *locus causarum* (1273–5): Helen's adulterous behaviour is the basic cause of their troubles and she is not worth their grief. This is developed in a *narratio* (1276–82) detailing Helen's crimes and reminding Agamemnon that he has known about them all along.

Then comes a twist in Clytemnestre's strategy as she swerves away from the positive argument of deliberative oratory to a further personal attack on her husband, suggestive of judicial oratory. She continues to exploit the *locus causarum*, but in such a way as to designate not Helen but Agamemnon himself as the cause of their troubles (1283–96). Blame lies with Agamemnon's character, his lust for power, and his pride (1285–8):

> Cette soif de régner, que rien ne peut éteindre,
> L'orgueil de voir vingt rois vous servir et vous craindre,
> Tous les droits de l'empire en vos mains confiés,
> Cruel, c'est à ces dieux que vous sacrifiez.

Whereas her first two arguments made a case against the sacrifice explicitly, the third does so implicitly. Agamemnon should demonstrate the falseness of her accusation by refusing to go ahead with his plan.

With a fourth and final argument based on the *locus consequentium* and on *affectus* she appeals for the first time for Agamemnon's pity (1297–304):

> Un prêtre, environné d'une foule cruelle,
> Portera sur ma fille une main criminelle,
> Déchirera son sein, et d'un œil curieux,

> Dans son cœur palpitant consultera les dieux?
> Et moi, qui l'amenai, triomphante, adorée,
> Je m'en retournerai seule et désespérée?
> Je verrai les chemins encor tout parfumés
> Des fleurs dont sous ses pas on les avait semés?

This is the same technique as Esther uses at the end of her long plea to Assuérus (III. 4). Both women conjure up a picture of the imminent murder in order to move their hearer. Clytemnestre goes further, by contrasting her solitary journey away from the camp with the happy journey that had brought mother and daughter to it. The rhetorical questions in which this argument is framed are meant to invite Agamemnon to reach a decision against the sacrifice.

But in a *peroratio*, in which she takes her leave of rhetoric, Clytemnestre defiantly answers the questions herself. The conciliatory mood with which Iphigénie began the persuasion of her father has now been completely overturned. Clytemnestre simply asserts that the sacrifice will not take place, unless Agamemnon murders his wife as well as his daughter. She may still hope that her persuasion will have some effect on Agamemnon, but she does not give him the opportunity to reply. She accompanies her daughter off stage, a gesture which signifies that, having exhausted all her resources of verbal protection, she will henceforth protect her daughter physically.

Agamemnon does not have time in his short monologue in IV. 5 to say to what extent he has been moved by the oratory of Iphigénie and Clytemnestre. For Achille arrives and, forgetful of a *captatio benevolentiae*, harangues Agamemnon with such aggressive oratory that any good that wife or daughter might have achieved, is spoilt and Agamemnon's mind is decided upon the sacrifice. In a monologue following this scene (IV. 7), he interestingly contrasts the effects of the two different rhetorical approaches of Iphigénie and Achille (1421–4, 1427):

> Et voilà ce qui rend sa perte inévitable.
> Ma fille toute seule était plus redoutable.
> Ton insolent amour, qui croit m'épouvanter,
> Vient de hâter le coup que tu veux arrêter.
>
> Achille menaçant détermine mon cœur.

Heavy-handed oratory has not worked.

This sequence of scenes in *Iphigénie* IV reveals the dramatic excitement which can be aroused by scenes of almost entirely verbal action based on persuasive activity.[8] Three very different approaches to dissuade Agamemnon from the sacrifice contrast with each other in both technique and effect, and also with Agamemnon's feeble responses, rhetorically weak but actually powerful, because behind the weak oratory lies the authority to order the sacrifice. The audience watches all these forces at play, hoping that each new argument, each new strategy will be the one that will save Iphigénie.

Judicial oratory certainly plays a part in these scenes, but the deliberative element is perhaps prevalent and is vital to an understanding of the audience's appreciation of the scenes. The audience is interested in Clytemnestre's judgement of Agamemnon only in so far as it might persuade him against the sacrifice of his daughter.

Antoine Adam notices a marked difference in Racine's dialogue in *Iphigénie*:

Comme chez Sophocle ou Euripide, il arrive chez Racine que l'acteur ne s'adresse plus à un partenaire, mais se tourne vers le public et déclame pour lui son rôle. Nous devrions dire plutôt qu'il le chante. Car le mot de déclamation supposerait que les vers d'*Iphigénie* sont de la rhétorique alors qu'ils sont tout chargés d'une beauté lyrique. Ce sont des plaintes qui s'épanchent, ou des colères.[9]

He sees some speeches as essentially lyrical addresses to the audience and dismisses their rhetorical aspect, but he does not give specific examples. He does, however, suggest the sort of things he has in mind (p. 362): 'La plainte d'une jeune fille condamnée à mourir, d'un père réduit à immoler son enfant. Les colères et la douleur de Clytemnestre.' This seems to identify as lyrics directed at the audience precisely those speeches which I have analysed

---

[8] It should be added that the visual rhetoric of Clytemnestre has a significant theatrical impact as is suggested by the 18th-cent. engraving by Moreau, reproduced in D. Achach's Classiques Larousse edn. of the play (p. 103). Clytemnestre is depicted in a defiant stance, one arm protectively clutching her daughter, the other held out appealingly to Agamemnon, whose hand covers his face in despair.

[9] *Histoire de la littérature française au XVIIe siècle* (Paris, 1948–56), iv. 361–2.

from *Iphigénie* IV. 4. This is a very different reading of this scene from the one presented here, in which the speeches are seen as urgent attempts to communicate between characters facing imminent catastrophe, with the characters speaking very much to each other, not to the audience. In my reading it is on the rhetorical, or persuasive, element that the audience's enjoyment depends.

Whatever variations Racine may introduce into his presentation of scenes of informal oratory, the pleasure of the audience can lie largely in watching characters deploy rhetorical strategies and in experiencing the effect of these strategies. Nearly always the spectators are able to appreciate the implementation of particular strategies, because Racine makes it clear in advance what the real aims and desires of the debating characters are. This fact is important in understanding what is characteristically Racinian about the verbal action of Racine's tragedies. For his contemporaries are often less keen to let their audiences share in the exciting rhetorical manœuvres of their characters—sometimes, perhaps, because their rhetorical manœuvres are not very exciting.

A popular play in its time, Quinault's *Astrate*, first performed in the season 1664–5 and hence contemporary with *La Thébaïde*, provides a useful illustration of this point. The dramatic structure of *Astrate* hangs upon mistaken identity. Only Sichée, Astrate's supposed father, and presumably the other shadowy conspirators know that Astrate is the legitimate ruler. Neither Astrate, nor Élise, the queen by usurpation, nor the other characters, nor the audience know his identity, which begins to be published only in Act IV. Inevitably Quinault wishes to play on such general ignorance, but such play comes at the expense of clearly focused and gripping verbal action. Racine too has tragedies involving mistaken identity: *Iphigénie*, *Esther*, and *Athalie*. But Racine manages his verbal action very differently from Quinault.

Whereas Racine nearly always contrives to let the audience know the real stance of a character, even if that character is to wear a mask, Quinault seems to feel no need to transmit such information. The result is that his characters' words and behaviour are often puzzling to the audience. It may be that *Astrate* is best appreciated as a kind of game, in which the audience plays the role of detective, fishing through the murky waters of unexplained actions and obscure motivation. The verbal action of *Astrate*, though superficially similar to Racine's, is really quite different.

Quinault certainly builds his scenes out of acts of persuasion. Act I has three major confrontations: Scenes 1, 3, and 5. The first scene is composed of a discussion between two opposing protagonists, Agénor and Astrate, in the course of which Astrate accuses himself of loving the queen, whom Agénor is contracted to marry. Astrate begs that Agénor punish him. In 1. 3 Sichée speaks to Agénor in his capacity as royal messenger, bearing the news that Élise wishes to postpone the wedding, and appearing to persuade Agénor to rise up against Élise and take the throne for himself; Agénor will have none of this. Lastly, in 1. 5, Sichée attempts to rouse Élise against Agénor and then, on being told that she wishes to marry Sichée's son, he offers arguments against this, and she attempts to refute them. He has finally to agree to send Astrate to her.

These acts of persuasion cannot be appreciated by the audience in the same way as they might appreciate those in Racine's tragedies. For instance, not only do the spectators not know in 1. 1 that Astrate is the legitimate ruler (an insignificant gap in knowledge at this stage, in any case); more importantly, they must be puzzled by Agénor's poverty of argument and apparent lack of concern in the face of Astrate's revelation of his love for Élise and his consequent self-accusation. What might on the surface promise to be an exciting opening scene of argument and conflict peters out because of the apparent indifference of one of the participants. With the debatable exception of *Alexandre*, Racine never uses two opposing protagonists in an opening scene and, in the light of *Astrate* 1. 1, the reason seems clear: the audience at this point cannot be adequately apprised of the motivation of two protagonists to be able to savour a rhetorical confrontation. It might be said that Agénor's inexplicable response to Astrate serves to arouse the curiosity of the audience. This is satisfied in the following scene, when Agénor explains to his confidant why he did not become angry with Astrate: he did not want to drive him into the camp of the conspirators led by the legitimate ruler. The irony of this explanation is necessarily missed by the audience. Moreover, Agénor's explanation of his earlier inexplicable behaviour is less exciting, because less disturbing of the audience's perception of the situation, than the parallel revelations of Créon, Narcisse, and Atalide.

It is through a similar mist that the audience witnesses the persuasion in I. 3. For there is no way of knowing why Sichée, having delivered the queen's message about the postponement of the wedding, should appear to prompt rebellion in Agénor's heart. Light is thrown on this only in I. 5, when he tells Élise:

> Le Prince a sceu vostre ordre; & malgré sa surprise,
> Il m'a fait voir une ame au dernier point soûmise.
> J'ay voulu vainement, en m'offrant contre Vous,
> Penetrer ses desseins, & sonder son couroux;
> Et soit qu'il me neglige, ou soit qu'il me soupçonne,
> Je n'ay rien veu de Luy qu'un respect qui m'étonne.
>
> (*Astrate* 191–6)

Even this explanation is inadequate. For it remains unclear whether Sichée's attempted corruption of Agénor was his own or Élise's idea, and why, in any case, it was undertaken.

After speaking to Agénor in I. 3, but before speaking to Élise in I. 5, Sichée exchanges a few words with two men whom the audience will henceforth assume to be in cahoots with him. One of them, Bazore, says to him (185–7):

> Vostre entreprise est belle, & vos projets sont grands;
> Mais il faut desunir la Maison des Tyrans;
> Sans quelque trouble entr'eux, l'issuë est incertaine.

The audience is alerted to Sichée's having some great plan which is hidden from Agénor and from the queen and which depends on breaking up the planned union between the pair. This information is of retrospective help in interpreting Sichée's dealings with Agénor and will also help the audience to appreciate some of Sichée's words to Élise. But his plans will remain a mystery for some time yet and, in his discussion with Élise, the spectators soon find themselves lacking sufficient knowledge to perceive what he is about.

When he tells the queen to be wary of Agénor's apparent respect (191–213), it is clear that he is exploiting *mores*, painting a black picture of Agénor, even though he has evidence from his recent meeting only for a favourable portrait. The audience realizes that he is trying to set Élise against her intended. But when Élise, in a surprise move, announces that she would like to marry Sichée's son Astrate, the audience is puzzled to find Sichée arguing against this, for it would seem on the surface that Élise's wish would admirably suit Sichée's purpose in separating the interests of Agénor from those of the queen.

Throughout Act I, then, Quinault persistently blocks the audience's appreciation of the rhetorical strategies of the characters. But the strategies would not, anyhow, necessarily be interesting in their own right. When Agénor expresses surprise at being told of the delay to his marriage and asks what Élise's arguments might be, Sichée shows no willingness to engage in persuasion (138–42):

> Qu'Elle le veut ainsi, Seigneur, & rien de plus.
> En cherchant des raisons, la fierté de la Reyne
> Croirait trop abaisser la Grandeur Souveraine,
> Et pretend qu'en tous lieux, & qu'en toutes saisons,
> Les volontez des Rois tiennent lieu de raisons.

It may be realized in retrospect that Sichée may have been deliberately using this relatively poor argument in order to anger Agénor (in this he does not succeed); but, at the time, the audience cannot see the point of this argument which must seem merely capricious.

Similarly, when he debates with Élise, Sichée's arguments can seem insubstantial and even comic. For the audience cannot see, and will not for a long time be allowed to see, the reasons behind them. Élise argues persuasively for her marriage to Astrate, who has proved to be such a great help in securing her position on the throne. Sichée's refutation is a curious one for a courtier and a father (273–7):

> Astrate fût heureux, & peut cesser de l'estre;
> C'est un Fils qui m'est cher, mais je le dois connestre:
> Loin comme il est de Vous, pouriez-vous aujourd'huy,
> Sans vous trop abaisser, descendre jusqu'à Luy?
> Il a sans doute un Cœur qui ne cede à nul autre,
> Mais il n'a point de Sceptre à joindre avec le vostre,
> Point de Rang qui merite un si glorieux soin.

This might make sense in the mouth of a humble and overwhelmed subordinate, but Sichée intends this exploitation of the *locus generis* to be an effective objection to the marriage. Élise is not persuaded.

The game-playing required of the audience may point to a further difference between Racine and Quinault. By refusing to allow his spectators thoroughly to understand the arguments of his characters, Quinault is keeping them at a distance from that rather unfathomable situation being represented on stage. The spectators are onlookers trying to make sense of what is happening. Their curiosity is certainly aroused, but not their emotions. Racine, on the other hand, by giving his spectators a privileged insight into the aims and feeling of his characters before he shows them in debate, is able to awaken an acute interest in their desires and in the rhetorical techniques which they employ to achieve them. This ensures that spectators follow all arguments and strategies, being moved by each in turn. So in Act I of *Iphigénie* the audience can be moved to pity for the father whom an opponent is persuading to sacrifice his daughter. Racine's approach provides a surer means of making an emotional impact on the audience.

11. INQUISITORIAL ORATORY: ANAXIMENES AND *MITHRIDATE*

The three kinds of oratory (judicial, deliberative, and demonstrative) provide a useful way of describing and understanding the verbal actions executed by Racine's characters. It is no doubt significant that speeches based entirely on demonstrative oratory are, with the exception of La Piété's speech as the prologue to *Esther* and Taxile's praise of Alexandre, absent from the tragedies. For such speeches are undramatic. They do not lead to an important decision. It is the promise of some such decision that keeps the audience interested in scenes of deliberative and judicial oratory. It is again no doubt significant that, of this pair, deliberative oratory is more frequent. For any decision taken after judicial oratory is a judgement on the past, whereas a decision taken after deliberative oratory affects the as yet uncertain future of the characters, which the audience is keen to discover.

Some confrontations between protagonists, however, cannot easily be described as one of these three kinds of oratory. When Athalie confronts the child Joas in *Athalie* II. 7, when Roxane shows Atalide the letter from the sultan effectively requiring Bajazet's death in *Bajazet* IV. 3, and when Mithridate induces Monime to tell him of her love for Xipharès in *Mithridate* III. 5, what sort of verbal actions are they carrying out? Could this be the point at which rhetoric ceases to help the critic to understand the way in which Racine's predominantly verbal theatre is made dramatic?

In a backwater of the rhetorical tradition there is to be found reference to another type of oratory, which I shall call inquisitorial. In the *Rhetorica ad Alexandrum*, a treatise of the fourth century BC, wrongly attributed to Aristotle and still to be found in editions and translations of his complete works, oratory is divided into three classes (judicial, deliberative, and demonstrative) and into seven species (persuasion, dissuasion, eulogy, vituperation, accusation, defence, and inquiry).[10] Quintilian in the *Institutio Oratoria* 3. 4. 9 says that Anaximenes makes such a division, and on the basis of this remark the *Rhetorica ad Alexandrum* is now attributed to him.

Six of Anaximenes' seven species clearly belong to the three kinds of oratory. Persuasion and dissuasion combine to make deliberative oratory; accusation and defence make judicial oratory; eulogy and vituperation make demonstrative oratory. But what he calls inquiry seems to be a kind of its own. Quintilian is perhaps right, in the final analysis, to insist that all species of oratory suggested by rhetoricians should ultimately fall under the headings of the three basic kinds (3. 4. 15) and, in this light, inquiry is considered as the part of judicial oratory which deals with the examination of witnesses. None the less, much of what Anaximenes says about inquiry and Quintilian about the examination of witnesses is of help in understanding the rhetorical behaviour of Roxane in *Bajazet* IV. 3, of Mithridate in *Mithridate* III. 5, and of Athalie in *Athalie* II. 7.

Three relevant points emerge from the discussion of the rhetoricians. First, before beginning his inquiry, the orator must give plausible reasons for it (*Rhetorica ad Alexandrum* 37). Secondly, the orator should begin with questions of an apparently innocent nature and should then compare replies to these questions with subsequent replies. In this way inconsistencies often occur and the orator can 'frequently lead witnesses into such a position that it becomes possible to extort useful admissions from them against their will' (Quintilian, *Institutio Oratoria* 5. 7. 27: 'saepe eo

---

[10] I quote from the trans. by E. Forster in *The Works of Aristotle*, xi, ed. W. D. Ross (Oxford, 1924). For an account of the treatise and discussion of its attribution see G. Kennedy, *The Art of Persuasion in Greece* (London, 1963), 114−24.

perducit homines, ut invitis quod prosit extorqueat'). Thirdly, the orator will conduct his inquiry 'not in a bitter but in a gentle spirit; for words if thus spoken will appear more persuasive to our hearers, and those who utter them will be less likely to bring prejudice upon themselves' (*Rhetorica ad Alexandrum* 37).

There are clearly important differences between the situation of the inquiring orator evoked by the rhetoricians and the situation of Racine's characters. The latter do not question someone in order to impress on a judge or jury the guilt or innocence of a third character. The inquiring characters in Racine are themselves the judge and jury. But the technique of questioning described by the rhetoricians is very close to the technique used by Racine's characters in their dramatic context. For in inquisitorial oratory the orator seeks to make his interlocutor reveal a fact which will often serve to absolve or, more usually, to condemn a third party.

In describing what often happens Quintilian implies the theatricality of inquisition:

Turbantur enim [testes] et a patronis diversae partis inducuntur in laqueos et plus deprehensi nocent quam firmi et interriti profuissent (5. 7. 11).

(For the opposing counsel have a way of making a witness lose his head or of leading him into some trap; and once a witness trips, he does more harm to his own side than he would have done good, had he retained his composure and presence of mind.)

This remark, copied by Racine into his book of extracts from Quintilian (p. 331), conjures up the picture of a witness being led unwittingly by a devious orator into a trap from which he and others may not emerge unscathed. The theatrical potential of this situation is obvious. An audience is excited by fear for the character as he is progressively wrong-footed.

It is this situation that is found in the three scenes in *Bajazet*, *Mithridate*, and *Athalie*. Mithridate is the most efficient of the inquiring orators as his efforts result in the prompt revelation of the information which he needs. In III. 2 Pharnace has angrily asserted before Mithridate that Xipharès loves, and is loved by, Monime. In the following scene the king assures Xipharès that he will not believe his brother's tempestuous accusation. But in his monologue in III. 4 Mithridate makes it clear that he intends to find out the truth about any relationship between his fiancée and his sons. Has he been wrong to blame Pharnace? Is it not rather

Xipharès who is his rival and who should be accused, sentenced, and punished? Like an examining magistrate, Mithridate prepares to question his witness:

> Non, ne l'en croyons point, sans trop nous presser,
> Voyons, examinons. Mais par où commencer?
> Qui m'en éclaircira? quels témoins? quel indice? . . .
> Le ciel en ce moment m'inspire un artifice.
> Qu'on appelle la reine. Oui, sans aller plus loin,
> Je veux l'ouïr. Mon choix s'arrête à ce témoin.
> L'amour avidement croit tout ce qui le flatte.
> Qui peut de son vainqueur mieux parler que l'ingrate?
> Voyons qui son amour accusera des deux.
> S'il n'est digne de moi, le piège est digne d'eux.
>   (*Mithridate* 1021–30)

The vocabulary is that of rhetorical theory, and of the theory of inquiry in particular: 'examinons', 'témoin(s)', 'indice', 'artifice', 'accusera', 'piège'. As the theorists recommend, Mithridate is going to trap Monime into revealing what he wants to know. The audience is now prepared for a scene of inquisitorial oratory.

As the inquiring orator is supposed to do, Mithridate begins by giving plausible reasons for his inquiry. In effect, the orator exploits *mores* to don a sympathetic mask. Mithridate claims to be too old and too committed to military and naval matters away from home to be a suitable husband (1035–50). He then pretends to know of an attachment between Pharnace and Monime, which he insists must come to an end (1051–6). This is a good way of securing the trust of his witness, because Monime, if she does not love Pharnace, will be made to feel secure that Mithridate knows and suspects nothing of her real love for Xipharès. The final part of his preparatory speech is to state that he intends to make Monime queen and Xipharès her husband (1057–62). This is ample justification for the questions which he will go on to ask her about her feelings for Xipharès.

With her immediate response to Mithridate's apparent wish, Monime takes the first step into the trap of revelation: 'Xipharès! Lui, Seigneur?' (1061), surely a combination of surprise, delight, but also anxiety about what may be afoot. Mithridate has much further to go before Monime will unambiguously speak the truth.

His first questions seize on her exclamation, asking for an interpretation of it and, by describing Xipharès in fulsome terms, prompting her to feel safe in expressing joy at the prospect of such a marriage (1061–72). Monime's reply, however, suggests that she is aware of Mithridate's propensity for crafty dealing and believes that he may not now be behaving in an altogether straightforward manner. She starts off by almost giving herself away, but soon speaks with caution (1073–6):

> Que dites-vous? O ciel! Pourriez-vous approuver...
> Pourquoi, Seigneur, pourquoi voulez-vous m'éprouver?
> Cessez de tourmenter une âme infortunée.
> Je sais que c'est à vous que je fus destinée.

At this point she tries to stop the inquisition by inviting him to accompany her to the marriage altar for her own wedding (1079).

Unabashed by the lack of co-operation on the part of his witness, Mithridate remains in order to pursue his inquiry by attributing to Monime feelings which she does not have and which he hopes she will therefore deny. He pretends to interpret her words and behaviour as a sign of her love for Pharnace and scorn for Xipharès (1079–82). Her slender reaction to this ('Je le méprise?' (1083)) is virtually ignored by Mithridate who presses on relentlessly with his devious interpretation of her words, hoping to pressurize her to state explicitly the opposite and so fall into his trap. The conclusion which he draws from his wilful misinterpretation is that he should allow her to marry Pharnace, the traitor, as a punishment for her supposed obstinacy. In reply to her earlier movement, he now pretends to usher Monime off stage (1089, 1093) hastily to accomplish the marriage to Pharnace.

This is the last straw. Monime now gives in to the pressure of the inquisitor, pointing out that his inquisition has been so persistent that his declared wish for her and Xipharès must be genuine (1097–8). Drawing this illogical consequence is Monime's downfall and she goes on, still cautiously, but quite explicitly, after a final prompt from Mithridate ('Vous l'aimez?' (1109)), to deliver into his hands the very information which he has been trying to elicit throughout the whole confrontation (1109–12):

> Si le sort ne m'eût donné à vous,
> Mon bonheur dépendait de l'avoir pour époux.
> Avant que votre amour m'eût envoyé ce gage,
> Nous nous aimions.

Though Mithridate's words do not give away the use to which he is going to put this information, his facial reaction (1112) tells Monime that Mithridate's questioning was, after all, probably not innocent. She leaves in a state of panic.

This scene amply illustrates the theatrical potential of inquisitorial oratory, as the audience watches the victim gradually accept the noose with which to hang herself. The two other instances are different and less complete examples of this process. In *Bajazet* IV. 3 Roxane has clearly prepared her method of questioning as thoroughly and as deviously as Mithridate (1118–22, 1162). To test out her suspicions about a possible relationship between Atalide and Bajazet she has as her pretext the letter sent by Amurat, who assumes that Bajazet is dead. Roxane deftly avoids Atalide's attempt to start up a deliberative debate in which the sultana would be encouraged to mount an instant coup (1177–81). Three well-timed questions lead to Atalide's revelatory faint. After Atalide has read the dreadful letter, Roxane prompts her with 'Eh bien?' (1193) and 'Que vous semble?' (1194), and, having cruelly said that Bajazet must now of course be killed, she nonchalantly asks:

> Et que faire en ce péril extrême?
> Il le faut.
>
> (*Bajazet* 1202–3)

Atalide becomes increasingly agitated and, when Roxane announces that she has already given the order for Bajazet's death, Atalide cannot help but implicitly reveal her feelings for Bajazet in her faint. Explicit evidence comes only later, when Roxane's servant has found the incriminating letter from Bajazet hidden in Atalide's dress (IV. 5). Roxane's task is easier than that of Mithridate because her pretext, Amurat's letter, is so overwhelmingly genuine that Atalide, who recognizes the handwriting (1184), cannot doubt it and inevitably responds to its urgency. Atalide's faint is no less a triumph for the inquisitor than Monime's explicit self-exposure.

It takes the innocence of youth to resist a Racinian inquisitor. *Athalie* shows the triumph of the witness in the person of Joas. Mathan has encouraged Athalie to believe that Joas is the threatening child of her vision. To find out if this is so she wishes to examine Joas, both scrutinizing his appearance and questioning him about himself:

> Laissez-moi, cher Mathan, le voir, l'interroger.
> *(Athalie* 614)

More brusque than either Mithridate or even Roxane, Athalie makes the mistake of not offering a likely pretext for her inquiry. Indeed it would appear from her words that her immediate re-action upon Joas's entrance is to go up to him and spend some time staring carefully at all his features (620–1):

> O ciel! plus j'examine, et plus je le regarde...
> C'est lui!

This imperious and unfriendly action, followed by her rude re-joinder to Josabet, who attempts to speak on Joas's behalf (626–7), is not calculated to inspire trust in her witness. The result is that Joas's answers to her questions are, though truthful, not at all incriminating; indeed they suggest an innocence and charm which almost captivates the would-be captor (651–4):

> Quel prodige nouveau me trouble, et m'embarrasse?
> La douceur de sa voix, son enfance, sa grâce,
> Font insensiblement à mon inimitié
> Succéder... Je serais sensible à la pitié?

At this point Abner draws the conclusion that Joas cannot be the child of her vision and Josabet makes as if to leave with Joas. As in the scene in *Mithridate* the suggestion of departure is used to heighten the tension of the interrogation. Athalie calls them back: she has not finished with her witness. When questioned about his daily activities, Joas reveals himself to be a devoted servant of God. Without explaining why, though the audience realizes that it is because she is suspicious of the child, Athalie now adopts the deliberative kind of oratory, attempting to persuade Joas to go and live with her in her palace. Her technique depends on *affectus* and *mores*. She tries to appeal to what she assumes must be Joas's desire for a more pleasurable lifestyle, one more suitable for a child (687):

> Hé quoi? vous n'avez point de passe-temps plus doux?

Far too late she tries to impress him as a well-wishing maternal figure (689):

Je plains le triste sort d'un enfant tel que vous.

This attempted persuasion shows that, while Athalie may well have correctly deduced that Joas is not what he appears to be, she has singularly failed to learn from her inquiry what it demonstrates to everyone else and to the audience: namely that Joas's devotion to his God is so firm as to preclude any temptation to yield to Athalie's offer of vain pleasures. To delight his audience Racine lets Joas make his distaste for Athalie clear in a cruel, child-like way (699–700):

> JOAS   Quel père
>   Je quitterais! et pour . . .
> ATHALIE   Eh bien?
> JOAS   Pour quelle mère!

With this the witness dismisses his interrogator and is spared any further questioning.

The rhetorical theorists envisaged the subject of the inquiry to be an innocent witness, whose answers would be used to defend or incriminate the accused. So in *Mithridate* the king questions Monime to discover evidence against Xipharès; in *Bajazet* Roxane prompts Atalide into effectively incriminating Bajazet; and in *Athalie* the queen finds in Joas's answers further evidence of Joad's subversive religious activity. Yet to this basic situation of inquisitorial oratory Racine adds a new dimension which intensifies the audience's excitement. For all Racine's witnesses are in danger not only of incriminating a third party but also of incriminating themselves. Neither Monime nor Atalide avoid this danger. The danger is especially acute for Joas, for it is in him that Athalie is especially interested. But, by giving cautious answers, the child deprives his interrogator of the unambiguous evidence which she had sought.

If the verbal action of most confrontations between protagonists in conflict can be described as deliberative or judicial in nature, the notion of inquisitorial oratory helps to complete the picture and makes it possible to demonstrate that the dramatic interest of all such confrontations can largely be analysed in terms of the characters' specifically rhetorical behaviour.[11]

---

[11] The scene in which Bérénice persuades Antiochus to reveal Titus's shocking message (*Bérénice* III. 3) involves a small element of questioning; but the basic framework of the debate is deliberative and quite different from the inquisitorial scenes examined in this section.

III. *BÉRÉNICE*: ELEGY, VERBAL ACTION, AND CORNEILLE'S *TITE ET BÉRÉNICE*

What might be the consequences of a rhetorical analysis of *Bérénice*, a play which critics have often described as elegiac rather than dramatic? Is the verbal action of this play static rather than active, poetic rather than theatrical? The methods of analysis adopted earlier in this chapter will help to answer these questions and to make a comparison with Corneille's treatment of the same subject in *Tite et Bérénice*.

Much of the ill-will which earlier critics felt towards *Bérénice* is no doubt rooted in the belief that a tragedy ought not simply to be about the feelings of lovers. 'Un amant et une maîtresse, qui se quittent, ne sont pas, sans doute, sujet de tragédie,' said Voltaire in his commentary on the play.[12] Racine's concentration on the separation of two, or rather three, lovers led to the related criticisms of a poverty of action and an elegiac tone. 'A peine y a-t-il une action ici,' complained Racine's contemporary, the abbé de Villars,[13] who also claimed (p. 252): 'S'ils [les comédiens] s'avisent de retrancher à leur gré les madrigaux de cette pièce, ils la réduiront à peu de vers.' Michaut himself unites the two criticisms to ask (pp. 141–2): 'En quoi consiste essentiellement l'action dans *Bérénice*? Et, tout d'abord, y a-t-il même une action, ou plutôt, malgré son titre de tragédie, ne serait-elle point une idylle en dialogues?' Descotes finds that 'le ton de l'élégie est partout dans *Bérénice*'.[14] More recently and more ingeniously Pocock takes both criticisms on board only to rework them into an elegant characterization of the play as one in which 'the essential action is expressed in the poetry. At this poetic level, Antiochus, Bérénice and Titus are not characters at all: they are elements in a pattern of themes, and it is the pattern which is important.'[15]

Such views are based on the fact that the play appears to focus almost exclusively on the separation of the lovers, and consequently

---

[12] *Commentaires sur Corneille*, ed. D. Williams (Banbury, 1975), iii. 938.

[13] *La Critique de 'Bérénice'* in G. Michaut, *La 'Bérénice' de Racine* (Paris, 1907), 254.

[14] *Les Grands Rôles du théâtre de Jean Racine* (Paris, 1957), 86. C. L. Walton in the introduction to his edn. of the play lists many of the elegiac interpretations (p. 33 n. 5).

[15] *Corneille and Racine* (Cambridge, 1973), 205.

depicts, first and foremost, the passion of love. Yet, when the play itself and the terms in which these criticisms are couched are examined more closely, it seems that these are perhaps misleading formulations of a response to *Bérénice*. For they all suggest, if not boredom, certainly a peculiar absence of dramatic interest.

Such are the implications of the view which sees the play as 'un tissu galant de madrigaux et d'élégies'.[16] But to see in *Bérénice* a succession of free-standing elegiac poems is radically to call into question its dramatic unity and dramatic momentum. It is to suggest that Racine falls into the trap against which theoreticians had frequently warned, that of making characters slip out of their roles to deliver to the audience only tenuously relevant poems or orations.[17]

Is there any substance in this view of *Bérénice*? Furetière, in his dictionary of 1690, defines *élégie* as follows: 'Espece de poësie qui s'emploie dans les sujets tristes & plaintifs. Les amans font des Elegies pour se plaindre de leurs maistresses. Les Elegies Françoises se font de vers Alexandrins & en rime plate.' The speeches of the lamenting Antiochus and Bérénice and all those in which the separation of the lovers is discussed might well recall the elegy if this definition were to be used. The rhyme scheme too is appropriate. It is rather harder to see the relevance of the *madrigal*, which Furetière defines thus: 'Petite Poësie amoureuse composée d'un petit nombre de vers libres & inégaux, qui n'a ni la gesne d'un sonnet, ni la subtilité d'une Epigramme, mais qui se contente d'une pensée tendre et agreable.' There is more than a hint of contempt in this definition, and it is a contempt which the abbé de Villars no doubt shares, when he specifically describes as a madrigal Bérénice's last speech, in which she accepts that Titus loves her and resolves that she, Titus, and Antiochus should go their separate ways (p. 251). *Madrigal* seems an eminently unsuitable description of this speech as regards both form and content. The term may well have been chosen by Villars principally for its pejorative connotations. For Furetière's definition continues: 'Les petits genies qui n'ont pas la force de faire de grands Ouvrages se retranchent sur les *Madrigaux*.'

---

[16] Villars in Michaut, *Bérénice*, 253.
[17] P. Corneille, *Writings on the Theatre*, ed. H. T. Barnwell (Oxford, 1965), 19; d'Aubignac, *La Pratique du théâtre*, ed. P. Martino (Algiers, 1927), 243, 282.

If *madrigal* is an inappropriate term, *élégie* seems to have some relevance to the speeches in *Bérénice*. But what is the relevance? It does not lie in the idea of distinct poems detachable from their dramatic contexts. It is not only the spiteful abbé who suggested this, but more recent critics as well. J. D. Biard, in a study of the elegiac aspects of *Bérénice*, sees well-organized speeches *almost* capable of being autonomous poems.[18] *Bérénice* is elegiac only in that there is in this play, more perhaps than in Racine's others, a greater concentration of thematic elements which can be found in elegiac poetry: love, sadness, absence, separation. But this feature has no detrimental effect on the dramatic quality of the verbal action of the play. Biard criticizes the action of Corneille's *Tite et Bérénice* for being too rhetorical (p. 3): 'Ces plaidoyers découragent la contemplation des valeurs fondamentales engagées dans la pièce; ils nuisent au recueillement poétique tandis que la rhétorique, au service de la logique, souligne et amplifie le discours au détriment du chant.' Yet Racine's characters are rhetoricians too. They are not elegiac poets. This point is not unconnected with the charge that *Bérénice* suffers from a poverty of action, or incident. Certainly *Bérénice* is unusual in having no external events which impinge substantially on the movement of the play. But this is hardly an enormous departure from Racine's general practice. Rather it is an exploration by the dramatist of a latent tendency to reduce the amount of external action in his plays. The critic must avoid the temptation to think that, for the audience, the action is simply the sum total of what has happened by the end of the play. It is true that from this perspective the action of *Bérénice* might seem rather slight: Antiochus and Titus in turn pluck up courage to speak to Bérénice; the three characters eventually agree to leave each other. But the action as perceived by the spectators is also that which is happening in front of them at any given moment. And this, for the most part, is verbal action, a series of persuasive acts, which, as elsewhere, Racine needs to present in such a way as to make his audience attend keenly to the rhetorical strategies of his characters. Even those critics who venture doubts about *Bérénice* readily admit that Racine succeeded in doing this. 'Racine trouva le secret', said Voltaire in the dedicatory epistle to his *Oreste*, 'd'intéresser pendant cinq actes, sans autre fonds que ces

---

[18] 'Le Ton élégiaque dans *Bérénice*', *FS* 19 (1965), 6.

paroles: "Je vous aime et je vous quitte".[19] Racine himself in his preface to the play triumphantly relates the response of his critics to questions about the play (p. 325): 'Je m'informai s'ils se plaignaient qu'elle [la pièce] les eût ennuyés. On me dit qu'ils avouaient tous qu'elle n'ennuyait point, qu'elle les touchait même en plusieurs endroits et qu'ils la verraient encore avec plaisir. Que veulent-ils davantage?'

In implying that characters step out of their roles to address lyrical passages to the audience as poets or orators might, the elegiac view is perhaps unfair to the play. Yet the characters are of course orators in the way they try to achieve verbal domination over those to whom they speak.

Here, however, lies an important difference between *Bérénice* and Racine's earlier plays. For previously all the main characters knew more or less what the aims of the others were. There are the significant exceptions of Créon, Narcisse, and later Atalide, and there are examples of characters who wear a temporary mask as part of a persuasive strategy. But in *Bérénice* only the aims of Bérénice are known for certain by the other major characters. She wishes to marry Titus, but because she does not know that, despite his love for her, he wants to reject her, she is unaware that her aim needs to be fought for. Titus's aim is to persuade Bérénice that she must leave, but it is only in the second half of the play that he can summon up enough courage to broach the subject with her. Consequently, only in Act IV do these two orators clash in open conflict, aware of each other's intentions. To compensate for this lack of open conflict earlier in the play Racine invents the unhistorical Antiochus, whose real aim throughout is to leave Rome and take Bérénice with him. Titus, however, does not realize this until the end of the play.

The characters of *Bérénice*, then, cannot have such compelling aims as their predecessors.[20] They cannot have a specific aim on which they expend all their energies in conflicts with other characters. This state of affairs may well have helped to reinforce the

---

[19] *Œuvres complètes*, v, ed. L. Moland (Paris, 1877), v. 83.

[20] J. Scherer makes a related observation: 'L'usage courant au XVIIe siècle est de présenter des personnages dont la volonté est tendue vers certains buts; ils en sont séparés par des obstacles qui peuvent consister en la volonté d'autrui. Ce schéma ne s'applique guère ici qu'à Bérénice: elle veut épouser Titus et n'y parvient pas' (in edn. of *Bérénice* (Paris, 1973), 9–10).

elegiac view of the play. Yet it is a state of affairs which Racine deliberately exploits to theatrical effect in his later plays: Roxane, Acomat, Mithridate, Clytemnestre, and Thésée are all deprived of the knowledge which would help them in some of their earlier arguments.

Racine engineers scenes in such a way that characters, even though they may not be in full knowledge of the situation, do seem to have rhetorical missions. Antiochus persuades himself to reveal to Bérénice his continuing love for her (I. 2). He attempts to persuade her to regard him sympathetically, but fails (I. 4). Bérénice accuses Titus of neglecting her (II. 4). In these and other of the rhetorical activities characters seem to miss the point in their arguments because they do not know where the root of the obstacle to their desires lies (or even that there is an obstacle). Yet Racine still makes his characters behave like urgent orators, while at the same time playing games of irony with the audience and allowing the tension to mount before the flood-gates open in IV. 5. For both Titus and Bérénice are orators whom the audience sees practising their rhetoric before going on to deploy their freshly rehearsed skills when necessity demands it in Act IV.

It is instructive to take stock of the extent of the persuasive confrontations between the three protagonists in the play.

In I. 4 Antiochus relies heavily on *mores* and *narratio* in an attempt to secure Bérénice's sympathy before his departure. But Bérénice will admit to no feelings of sympathy in front of him.

Act II, Scene 4 contains a piece of judicial oratory developed by the dramatist for ironic purposes. Bérénice accuses Titus of neglecting her, adduces the evidence, and pronounces him guilty. It is ironic because it can achieve no purpose; she does not yet know the extent of her real rhetorical task. Titus, who is supposedly in command of the situation, tries to adopt the more suitable deliberative mode in order to persuade Bérénice that she must leave. He had rehearsed the arguments with Paulin earlier, but now his *actio* fails him.

When Antiochus acts as Titus's spokesman to Bérénice in III. 3, he fails to effect persuasion, but not because his rhetoric is weak. Indeed he again exploits *narratio* (853–6) and *mores* (861–70) to try and forestall any objections that his own desires might interfere with the request which he is making on Titus's behalf. Bérénice, however, knows the orator's own wishes too well not to take account of them in assessing his arguments:

> Vous le souhaitez trop pour me persuader.
>
> (*Bérénice* 914)

In both v. 5 and v. 6 Titus and Bérénice use their rhetoric on each other. It is rare to have this type of confrontation so late in the play, and is a consequence of the absence of deaths in *Bérénice*: a denouement has to be negotiated. In the first of these scenes, in a curious reversal, Titus tries to persuade Bérénice to stay, while she pleads with him to let her leave. The reason becomes clear when Titus discovers her letter explaining her intention to die. This prompts him to speak to her in a way in which he had previously been unable to do. He attempts to explain why she must leave, while also trying to prevent her from dying. The trump card is the ultimate appeal to *affectus*, the threat of suicide. Since being told of his wish that she should leave, Bérénice has been unable to see that Titus still loves her; his playing this card now helps her to realize this. It is this vital discovery which allows her to instigate the bloodless denouement (1481–2):

> J'ai cru que votre amour allait finir son cours.
> Je connais mon erreur, et vous m'aimez toujours.

Had Titus been a more competent orator in front of Bérénice earlier, the play would have ended rather sooner. Racine builds up the play by insisting on Titus's rhetorical weakness when he is with Bérénice. 'Tragédie de l'aphasie' may be an exaggerated description of *Bérénice*,[21] but it is helpfully suggestive if understood in the context of Titus's timid oratory.

Act IV, Scene 5 remains to be commented upon. This scene is the second of the three occasions on which Titus and Bérénice meet during the play. On the first (II. 4) he is unable to speak. On the third (v. 6) he speaks successfully. In IV. 5 he manages to speak, but he does not have on Bérénice the effect that he desires. This is a rhetorical confrontation that the audience has been waiting to see from early in the play, and analysis reveals Titus

---

[21] R. Barthes, *Sur Racine* (Paris, 1973), 97.

and Bérénice to be just as dramatically interesting in their oratory as the protagonists of Racine's other plays.

Both characters deploy rhetoric to defend their position and neither is prepared to yield an inch. Their attempts at persuasion are gripping. Bérénice begins by establishing the subject of the debate (1043–4):

> Eh bien? il est donc vrai que Titus m'abandonne?
> Il nous faut séparer; et c'est lui qui l'ordonne!

In Bérénice's mouth this is to all intents and purposes an accusation. Titus launches into self-defence using all three parts of *inventio* in a speech which, though short, clearly contains an *exordium*, a *narratio*, and a *peroratio*. His attempt to prevent, or at least soften, Bérénice's verdict on him relies on his creating sympathy for himself as a sufferer, on his expression of sympathy for Bérénice in her grief, and on an appeal to the abstract concepts of *devoir*, *gloire*, and *raison*. But he does not produce substantial arguments to defend his position.

This fact, coupled with Titus's lack of a *refutatio*, allows Bérénice to leap in. The dramatic effect of a speech of response is referred to by Le Gras: 'L'exorde de celuy qui parle apres un autre est merveilleux, lorsqu'il est fondé sur le discours de celuy qui a parlé le premier; & il n'y a rien qui plaise davantage que la facilité et la promptitude.'[22] Bérénice's speech is strikingly forceful, though she has neither time nor need for an *exordium*; for she is interested in reasoned arguments based on facts, in which Titus's speech had been noticeably lacking. In a *narratio* she produces all the evidence to convict Titus of having made a cruel decision and she goes through it point by point: he could have told her long before; he had always known Roman Law; he waited until just the moment when she thought that all her hopes were to be fulfilled; she had means of consolation before, she has none now. This final point is expanded with an exploitation of the *locus partium enumerationis* (1076–80):

> Je pouvais de ma mort accuser votre père,
> Le peuple, le sénat, tout l'empire romain,
> Tout l'univers, plutôt qu'une si chère main.

---

[22] *La Réthorique [sic] française* (Paris, 1671), 110.

> Leur haine, dès longtemps contre moi déclarée,
> M'avait à mon malheur dès longtemps préparée.

This is followed by material from the *locus speciei*, singling out Titus as the sole cause of her grief (1081–6):

> Je n'aurais pas, Seigneur, reçu ce coup cruel
> Dans le temps que j'espère un bonheur immortel,
> Quand votre heureux amour peut tout ce qu'il désire,
> Lorsque Rome se tait, quand votre père expire,
> Lorsque tout l'univers fléchit à vos genoux,
> Enfin quand je n'ai plus à redouter que vous.

How does the accused deal with these facts and arguments? Still wanting to soften Bérénice's verdict, he does not meet her head-on and dispute the facts, but tries to arouse her sympathy by giving a favourable impression of his character in the past. So much was he in love with her that he deluded himself into ignoring the inevitable problem. He repeats his appeal to *gloire* in order to explain the cause of his decision and uses the *locus dissimilitudinis* to distinguish between his former self and his present imperial status (1087–98). He tries to make his argument more convincing by presenting Bérénice's departure as the start of his own suffering and so draws on *affectus* (1099–1102):

> Je sais tous les tourments où ce dessein me livre,
> Je sens bien que sans vous je ne saurais plus vivre,
> Que mon cœur de moi-même est prêt à s'éloigner,
> Mais il ne s'agit plus de vivre, il faut régner.

Bérénice's accusation remains unchanged (1103):

> Eh bien! régnez, cruel, contentez votre gloire.

This present speech assumes the air of a *peroratio* to balance the *confirmatio* which constituted her previous speech. The appeal to the passions rather than to the reason of the listener is supposed to dominate the *peroratio*. So, instead of using facts to prove Titus's cruelty, she imitates Titus's appeal to *affectus* and evokes the future suffering that his untimely decision will cause her. She rubs in the salt by suggesting that Titus will remain untouched by such suffering.

The emperor does not admit defeat. He tries to claim that he too will suffer and cannot therefore be gratuitously cruel. But

Bérénice (and this suggests that her judicial rhetoric was but a pose, that she was not entirely sincere in her condemnation of Titus) jumps in at the suggestion that Titus will suffer too. She has been persuaded by less powerful rhetoric than she herself was using. Her willingness to cease her accusation changes the rhetorical situation into a deliberative one (1126):

> Ah Seigneur! s'il est vrai, pourquoi nous séparer?

She will try to persuade Titus to allow her to stay. After two very brief arguments supporting Bérénice's case (one based on *probatio inartificialis*: no law forbids her simply remaining in Rome; the other an appeal for Titus's sympathy), Titus surprisingly concedes ('Demeurez' (1130)), or rather he appears to concede. For, in his ensuing utterances, he so refutes Bérénice's arguments as to make it clear that his concession was only momentary weakness. Bérénice cannot stay in Rome, as the consequences would be dangerous (*locus consequentium*). Nor can Titus alter the law to permit the marriage: three *probationes inartificiales* support this argument. The abbé de Villars expresses indignation at Titus's arguments (p. 246): 'Il n'ose parler à ce qu'il aime, et quand il ose lui parler, il n'a point de bonnes raisons à lui dire; il allègue des exemples odieux à l'amante, peu agréables aux spectateurs, et mal propres à excuser son inconstance et ses parjures.' The abbé may well intend to criticize Racine here, but his comment provides an interesting glimpse into the way in which persuasive action can stir the audience to weigh up Titus's arguments and find them wanting. Will Bérénice, however, succeed, with her better arguments, in persuading Titus of her case?

In the final speech of the scene she is left to give up deliberative oratory as useless and she returns to the judicial kind, with which she opened the scene. It is also possible that, like Clytemnestre in *Iphigénie* IV. 4, she uses judicial oratory as an ultimate resource, a way of bullying Titus to act on her wishes. She plays both plaintiff and judge, again accusing him of cruelty (and indeed of her own threatened death (1188–90)) and meting out his punishment: the future regrets with which he will have to live.

The only progress made in this scene towards the solution of the problem is Bérénice's intention to commit suicide, stated at the very end of the scene. She could just as easily have said the same thing earlier. The reason that she did not do so is that for the dramatist and his spectators the theatrical interest lies less in the action eventually taken than in the discussions that lead to its being taken, which are in themselves action.

The evidence of this analysis suggests a different view of *Bérénice* from the elegiac one. The characters do not simply lament to each other; even less do they lament directly to the audience. They struggle desperately to make their point of view prevail over that of their interlocutor.

This bitter verbal battling aligns *Bérénice* with Racine's other tragedies, but distinguishes it from Corneille's *Tite et Bérénice*, first performed in the same month as Racine's play and evidently designed to rival it. One scene in particular invites comparison with *Bérénice* IV. 5. In *Tite et Bérénice* III. 5 the two principal protagonists meet for the second time in the play and, as in *Bérénice* IV. 5, their discussion focuses on the course of action which each is about to take. There are, of course, differences of situation. In Racine's play Bérénice, unable to understand why the emperor will not marry her and wants her to leave, accuses him of cruelty, while also attempting to persuade him that he should marry her. In Corneille's play Bérénice had already left Rome and has returned apparently to make a final attempt to prevent the politically arranged marriage between Tite and Domitie. As in Racine's play, so in Corneille's, Bérénice's first attempt to tackle the emperor fails in a dramatic way. In *Bérénice* Titus has to leave, speechless (II. 4); in *Tite et Bérénice* the emperor, surprised by the unexpected return of Bérénice, dismisses her hastily and coolly (II. 5). So, like Racine's audience, Corneille's looks forward to the occasion when emperor and queen will confront each other at length.

Yet, when this happens in III. 5, their debate is arguably less gripping, less pressing than the equivalent debate in Racine's play. It moves curiously into and out of focus, and the audience is unable to understand the point of some of the arguments.

A major cause of the problem lies in the uncertain way in which the audience has been prepared to understand Bérénice's motivation. It is clear from what has happened up to this point that Bérénice wishes to stop the marriage to Domitie. Albin, who arranged her return, spells this out in I. 3:

> Et si je vous disais que déjà Bérénice
> Est dans Rome, inconnue, et par mon artifice?
> Qu'elle surprendra Tite, et qu'elle y vient exprès,
> Pour de ce grand Hymen renverser les apprêts?
> (*Tite et Bérénice* 343–6)

What is less clear, because never stated explicitly and unambiguously, is whether or not it is also Bérénice's intention to win the hand of the emperor for herself. Some remarks suggest that this is her aim. When Domitian, taking up Tite's suggestion, offers marriage to Bérénice and is refused, he gives her advice which presupposes that her aim may well be to do more than confound Domitie. Speaking of the emperor's suggestion, he says (743–50):

> Mais à peine il le veut, qu'il craint pour moi la haine
> Que Rome concevrait pour l'époux d'une Reine.
> C'est à vous de juger d'où part ce sentiment:
> En vain par Politique il fait ailleurs l'Amant,
> Il s'y réduit en vain par grandeur de courage,
> A ces fausses clartés opposez quelque ombrage,
> Et je renonce au jour, s'il ne revient à vous,
> Pour peu que vous penchiez à le rendre jaloux.

There is also a hint in Bérénice's ironical discussion with Domitie that she would like Tite for herself (857–8):

> J'ai vu Tite se rendre au peu que j'ai d'appas,
> Je ne l'espère plus, et n'y renonce pas.

In the scene immediately before her confrontation with Tite she addresses her confidant and seems to weigh herself in the balance against Domitie and long for Tite's continued devotion to her (883–9):

> Ainsi tout est égal, s'il me chasse, il la quitte,
> Mais ce peu qu'il m'a dit ne peut qu'il ne m'irrite,
> Il marque trop pour moi son infidélité,
> Vois de ses derniers mots quelle est la dureté.
> 'Qu'on la serve, a-t-il dit, comme elle fut servie
> Alors qu'elle faisait le bonheur de ma vie.'
> Je ne le fais donc plus! Voilà ce que j'ai craint.

So when her confidant sees Tite approaching and reminds her of some unspecified rhetorical strategy to be used against him, the audience may well think that Bérénice will be arguing not only for the cancellation of the marriage to Domitie, but also for her own reinstatement as the object of Tite's affections and even, perhaps, for her marriage to him, though this has not been explicitly mentioned. Bérénice has not stated clearly for the audience what her plans are, and spectators who have recently seen Racine's *Bérénice* might well think that the enigmatic statements of Corneille's Bérénice allude to a possible marriage between her and Tite. The haziness of her intentions obstructs the audience's direct enjoyment of her oratory addressed to Tite and contributes to the lack of focus with which some of her arguments are viewed.[23]

Like Racine's Bérénice, Corneille's queen starts the confrontation with judicial oratory, criticizing Tite for his behaviour towards her. Tite tries to forestall the attack (904–6):

> Vous avez su mieux lire au fond de ma pensée,
> Madame; et votre cœur connaît assez le mien,
> Pour me justifier, sans que j'explique rien.

But Bérénice can refute the claim that she can be assured instinctively of his love, by giving evidence against this view in a *narratio* (907–12). For her, his attempt to marry her to Domitian is the equivalent of rejection. Tite's response is again sparing in rhetorical complexity: 'Le croyez-vous, Madame?' (912). Yet this seems an adequate defence, for Bérénice drops the accusation (918):

> Que de crimes! Un mot les a tous effacés.

Here is the first loss of dramatic momentum, the first lack of focus in the debate. Bérénice's ostensible aim has been achieved: she has accused Tite of not loving her and has been rapidly satisfied by his meagre defence. Will she capitalize on this to start to propose herself as his bride, if indeed that is what she has in mind? Or will she simply make a plea that he should not marry Domitie? The audience's uncertainty and inability to read the situation clearly are not dispelled by her next words (919–26):

---

[23] Critics generally comment on the motivation of Corneille's Bérénice on the basis of what they have learnt by the end of the play. But such comments do not take account of the audience's gradually developing acquaintance with the characters. P. J. Yarrow is too categorical in asserting of Bérénice that 'her only aim had been to stop the marriage of Tite with Domitie' (*Corneille* (London, 1963), 134). O. Nadal is no doubt right to give more positive expression to her love for Tite, but he does not articulate the problem for the audience of establishing her intentions precisely: 'Bérénice vient à Rome en ambassade amoureuse et non politique' (*Le Sentiment de l'amour dans l'œuvre de Pierre Corneille* (Paris, 1948), 258).

> Faut-il, Seigneur, faut-il que je ne vous accuse,
> Que pour dire aussitôt que c'est moi qui m'abuse,
> Que pour me voir forcée à répondre pour vous?
> Épargnez cette honte à mon dépit jaloux,
> Sauvez-moi du désordre où ma bonté m'expose:
> Et du moins par pitié dites-moi quelque chose;
> Accusez-moi plutôt, Seigneur, à votre tour,
> Et m'imputez pour crime un trop parfait amour.

She has already excused him, but she seems to want him to supply oral testimony that she was right to do so. Her request that he should accuse her of excessive love would, if carried out, produce a sterile and uninteresting debate. The audience can only be grateful that Corneille did not allow Tite to pursue this judicial oratory.

It is curious, however, that Tite does not say anything at all at this juncture, and even more curious that Bérénice should forget her request for him to speak his love, as she suddenly seems to start on a new and apparently unrelated topic (927–30):

> Vos chimères d'État, vos indignes scrupules
> Ne pourront-ils jamais passer pour ridicules?
> En souffrez-vous encore la tyrannique loi?
> Ont-ils encor sur vous plus de pouvoir que moi?

Bérénice appears to have launched into deliberative oratory: this is an argument from the *locus comparationis maiorum*. Surely, Bérénice is saying, she deserves to have much more influence over him than mere laws and traditions? But as Bérénice has not introduced the subject of her deliberative oratory, since she has not said what her argument is intended to support, it is difficult for the audience, and no doubt for Tite, to assess its force or indeed to attribute any force to it at all: why is she invoking Roman laws and traditions? It is only after her argument that her aim is specified (933–4):

> Pourrez-vous l'épouser dans quatre jours? O Cieux!
> Dans quatre jours!

She is to argue against the marriage to Domitie and with this knowledge her arguments come into focus for the audience. She appeals to *affectus* by conjuring up a picture of her own distress at having to witness Tite's wedding (934–42).

This prompts Tite to speak, but he does not engage with her

arguments. He neither agrees with what she is saying, nor opposes it. He simply laments his predicament in a speech which smacks very much of elegy (943–55):

> Hélas, Madame, hélas, pourquoi vous ai-je vue,
> Et dans quel contretemps êtes-vous revenue?
> Ce qu'on fit d'injustice à de si chers appas
> M'avait assez coûté pour ne l'envier pas,
> Votre absence et le temps m'avaient fait quelque grâce
> J'en craignais un peu moins les malheurs où je passe,
> Je souffrais Domitie, et d'assidus efforts
> M'avaient malgré l'amour fait maître du dehors,
> La contrainte semblait tourner en habitude,
> Le joug que je prenais m'en paraissait moins rude;
> Et j'allais être heureux, du moins aux yeux de tous,
> Autant qu'on le peut être en n'étant point à vous,
> J'allais ...

This is a longwinded development, the purpose of which seems to be simply to evoke sympathy for Tite in Bérénice, but it is not clear what Tite hopes the point of such sympathy would be.

Bérénice interrupts him with what promises to be a real engagement between the two characters: 'N'achevez point, c'est là ce qui me tue' (955). The appearance of engagement is specious, however, as Tite has produced no genuinely provocative argument. Bérénice takes advantage of her interruption to develop a new argument of her own based on the *locus speciei* (956–74). It builds on her earlier exploitation of *affectus* in an attempt to forestall the marriage to Domitie. She would accept any ordinary woman as his wife, but Domitie is a special sort of woman, the sort that would make a beautiful and worthy empress. Bérénice would be content only if Tite married an ordinary and unworthy woman. At this point the audience might well reflect on the passages from earlier scenes when Bérénice had seemed to suggest that she wanted Tite all to herself: there is at least an apparent inconsistency in the presentation of her wishes.

At last Tite makes an attempt at a persuasive reply, using the evidence of Domitie's character to assure Bérénice that Domitie is not her rival for his affection (975–78). Bérénice fails to take up Tite's persuasive point about Domitie's character and simply makes a slender appeal for his pity (979):

> N'importe, ayez pitié, Seigneur, de ma foiblesse.

It is true that Bérénice supports this persistent claim that he should not marry Domitie with evidence of his known infidelity (980–2):

> Vous avez un cœur fait à changer de maîtresse,
> Vous ne savez que trop l'art de manquer de foi,
> Ne l'exercerez-vous jamais que contre moi?

But this general evidence is not really suitable to support her particular claim against the marriage to Domitie.

Tite ignores the argument based on his infidelity and produces a new argument for the marriage based on *probatio inartificialis*: it is the will of Rome and his father (982–8). Corneille now shows a sense of *enchaînement* in Bérénice's reply. She seizes upon Tite's reference to Rome to draw, using the *locus dissimilitudinis*, a distinction between the emperor and the empire, suggesting that the former should not let the latter dictate to him (989–96).

The heat then leaves the debate as Tite, rather than fighting back, solemnly assures Bérénice that the empire does indeed dictate to the emperor (997–8). He then curiously relates to this assertion a statement of Rome's hostility to royal rank. This is a curious statement because it does not really belong in the debate according to the terms which Bérénice has appeared to establish. Rome's position on royalty has nothing to do with whether or not Tite should marry Domitie. It is as if in a fit of amnesia Tite has left the present debate to revert to the sort of discussion which had occurred before Bérénice was first persuaded to leave Rome. Tite's sudden and unexpected move to argue against marriage to Bérénice must confuse even further an audience already uncertain about Bérénice's current ambitions. He then, no doubt to show the extent of his devotion, hints hypothetically at a suicide pact, at which point Bérénice interrupts to discourse in a leisurely way on the inappropriateness of suicide pacts for people of their rank (1009–14):

> Non, Seigneur, ce n'est pas aux Reines comme moi
> A hasarder leurs jours pour signaler leur foi.
> La plus illustre ardeur de périr l'un pour l'autre
> N'a rien de glorieux pour mon rang et le vôtre,
> L'amour de nos pareils la traite de fureur,
> Et ces vertus d'Amant ne sont pas d'Empereur.

Once again the course of the debate seems to have gone astray. Are Tite's objections to a marriage with Bérénice and Bérénice's engagement with Tite's arguments (especially her regret at not possessing him as her lover in Judaea (1015–25)) not confirmation that what Bérénice would really like is to marry Tite, for which her prevention of the marriage to Domitie is only a pretext?

Tite clearly interprets Bérénice's utterances in this way, for he now states that he has been persuaded to leave Rome, go away with her, and marry her (1027–34). Perhaps surprisingly, Bérénice argues against his abdication on the grounds of the danger involved. Two *probationes inartificiales* support her case (1040–2):

> Ce fut par là qu'Othon se traita de coupable,
> Par là Vitellius mérita le trépas,
> Et vous n'auriez partout qu'assassins sur vos pas.

Tite seems to have no counter-argument, as he asks Bérénice the question which the audience must have wanted to ask her throughout the scene: 'Que faire donc, Madame?' (1043). For the first time in the play Bérénice says something which seems to offer a means of understanding her motivation (1043–6):

> Assurer votre vie,
> Et s'il y faut enfin la main de Domitie...
> Mais, Adieu, sur ce point si vous pouvez doutez,
> Ce n'est pas moi, Seigneur, qu'il en faut consulter.

Bérénice's wish seems, after all, principally to be to prevent Tite marrying Domitie, though it is strange that she now expresses so cautiously what, earlier in the confrontation, she had argued about so lengthily. Tite can finally understand Bérénice's desire and is instantly persuaded (1047–8):

> Non, Madame, et dût-il m'en coûter trône et vie,
> Vous ne me verrez point épouser Domitie.

It is only at the end of the play, when she voluntarily decides to leave Tite and Rome, that Bérénice clearly explains her motivation (1714, 1717–20):

> Votre cœur est à moi, j'y règne, c'est assez.

> Ne me renvoyez pas, mais laissez-moi partir.
> Ma gloire ne peut croître, et peut se démentir.

> Elle passe aujourd'hui celle du plus grand homme,
> Puisque enfin je triomphe, et dans Rome, et de Rome.

It could be that this criticism of Corneille's scene stems from an attempt to appreciate him on inappropriate grounds. In this confrontation between Tite and Bérénice with all its meanderings and inconsistencies, Corneille may be trying to portray the way in which he thought lovers might behave. The uncertain course of their debate might exemplify the general observation of Racine's Titus that 'un amant sait mal ce qu'il désire' (435). None the less it was usually recognized in the period that the audience had to be able to appreciate the *intérêts* and the *sentiments* of the characters in order to take an interest in their discussions. For example, d'Aubignac says (p. 272):

Le Poëte ne doit mettre aucun Acteur sur son Theatre qui ne soit aussitost connû des Spectateurs, non seulement en son nom et en sa qualité; mais encore au sentiment qu'il apporte sur la Scéne: autrement le Spectateur est en peine, et tous les beaux discours qui se font lors au Theatre sont perdus; parce que ceux qui les écoutent, ne sçavent à qui les appliquer.

The audience's appreciation of the oratory of Tite and Bérénice in III. 5 is impaired by Corneille's uncertain presentation of Bérénice's motivation in the first half of the play, all the more striking in contrast to the starkly delineated motivation of the characters in Racine's play. Moreover, the oratory itself is without any of that relentless fighting and sharp-witted point-scoring that makes the parallel scene in Racine's play such gripping theatre. Corneille's characters seem sometimes unsure what precisely they are arguing about; sometimes, unexpectedly and with no apparent provocation, they change the course of the debate; sometimes they omit to argue and instead indulge in lamentation or leisurely discourse. They are half-hearted orators, lacking the clearsightedness and urgency of their Racinian counterparts.[24]

Rhetoric, and particularly *inventio*, provides a useful tool for exploring the various ways in which Racine sets protagonists against each other in acts of persuasion. Rhetorical analysis offers

---

[24] This view of Corneille recalls Racine's criticism of his rivals (and he clearly had Corneille in mind) in his first preface to *Britannicus*. By implication he criticizes plays which contain 'une infinité de déclamations où l'on ferait dire aux acteurs tout le contraire de ce qu'ils devraient dire' (p. 256).

a framework in which to discuss differences between Racine's use of persuasive action and that of other dramatists, at times allowing the critic to point with a sure finger to those features which makes Racine's verbal action solidly theatrical, when that of a Quinault or a Pierre Corneille may be less direct in its appeal to the audience. Moreover rhetorical analysis goes some way to questioning the traditional critical view of *Bérénice* as elegy rather than drama. Relentless oratory is the hallmark of *Bérénice* no less than of Racine's other tragedies, and this hallmark is all the more visible when the play is contrasted with Corneille's *Tite et Bérénice*.

4

Informal Oratory: The Confidants

Il est banal, mais il est juste de dire que les rôles de confidents
sont une des parties les plus faibles du théâtre classique, que
ces personnages n'ont rien à faire de bien intéressant, qu'ils
n'ont qu'à écouter et à dire à leurs maîtres qu'ils ont raison.

(J. Scherer, *Racine: 'Bajazet'*, 153)

The depiction of characters in conflict with one another is a potent
source of theatricality, as Chapters 2 and 3 have demonstrated. It
is not always the case, however, that characters are in conflict
with their interlocutors. Sometimes they are very much in agreement. This chapter focuses on the most obvious occurrences of apparent agreement between characters, namely discussions between
protagonists and the much maligned confidants. While it is not my
aim to give full consideration to the role of the confidant in
Racinian tragedy, I shall suggest that some common views of their
role require modification in the light of a rhetorical analysis of
their encounters with their principal partners. I shall argue that
Racine's use of persuasive interaction in these encounters contributes to their theatrical impact and allows these scenes too to be
seen as instances of informal oratory, even though the oratory
may be of a different tenor from that of protagonists who are in
disagreement.

A confidant is someone in whom one confides, an 'ami intime, à
qui on confie tous ses secrets', according to Furetière's *Dictionnaire universel* of 1690. To many the confidant is also a rather
embarrassing type of dramatic character with which the world of
French classical tragedy is all too thickly peopled. J. Scherer is not
the only critic to feel embarrassment at these characters, who, he
thinks, have nothing interesting to do other than listen to their
partners and tell them that they are right.[1] Other critics express
the same sense of embarrassment at witnessing characters who
appear to do nothing but agree with their interlocutors: 'Lorsque

---

[1] *Racine: 'Bajazet'* (Paris, n.d.), 153, quoted as the epigraph to this chapter.

le personnage parlant n'est pas seul devant nous, lorsqu'il parle à un confident, le texte est conçu comme un monologue, et les répliques du confident ou de la confidente ne servent en somme qu'à ponctuer un discours où toute la lumière se concentre sur le protagoniste.'[2] Whereas the seventeenth-century dictionaries of Furetière and the Académie Française see the confidant as a figure from real life, with no mention of its manifestations in works of drama, today's *Petit Robert* gives the word *confident* a secondary, theatrical definition: 'Personnage secondaire qui reçoit les confidences des principaux personnages pour que le public soit instruit des desseins et des événements.' The confidant, then, is an awkward dramatic artifice.

Hence C. J. Gossip's need to apologize to his English readers for these embarrassing characters, while attempting valiantly to show them in a positive light:

> These persons can be misunderstood by English-speaking audiences. Derived from Latin and indeed Greek tragedy, they fulfil an often vital rôle as consciences to the main characters, providing them with an opportunity to speak in circumstances not too far removed from the natural ones which imitative drama might require. They are essentially listeners, allowing the protagonists to unburden themselves in scenes which, but for the presence of the confidant, would be monologues. Their questions and interjections help to break up lengthy *récits*, especially exposition narratives, and move the action in a new direction. They also act as message-bearers.[3]

Gossip seems to be aware that any defence of the confidants must point out the many dramatic functions which they are required to fulfil. They are, for instance, the frequently unacknowledged source of much of the audience's pleasure, particularly in their role as message-bearers. It is Panope who, in *Phèdre* I. 4 and V. 5, makes reports which renew the audience's interest in the dramatic situation. First, she tells Phèdre that Thésée is dead, and later she starts to prompt Thésée to realize his error of judgement, by relating the suicide of Œnone. Even when defended, however, the confidants seem to remain for Gossip 'essentially listeners'.

It is true that Racine's confidants have sometimes been singled out as representing a theatrically successful renewal of a tired

[2] E. Vinaver, *Entretiens sur Racine* (Paris, 1984), 101.
[3] *An Introduction to French Classical Tragedy* (London, 1981), 117.

convention. According to M. M. Olga, 'de la même manière qu'il a renouvelé la convention des unités . . . Racine a renouvelé le confident'.[4] Olga's defence of Racine's confidants lies largely in her belief that (p. 10) 'par ses questions et ses commentaires, le confident devient le spectateur idéal, notre délégué sur la scène'. Yet this view of the confidant as the ideal spectator seems once again to put the focus of interest on what the protagonist is saying and to play down the theatrical interaction of the two characters. All that the confidant seems to do, according to this view, is to prompt the protagonist to say interesting things. I would suggest that, if these scenes are to work in the theatre, the audience, as in scenes of informal oratory between protagonists, needs to be interested in what both parties have to say. Olga implies that, with the exception of Racine's two best-known confidants, this does not usually happen in his plays (p. 8): 'S'il a créé un Narcisse et une Œnone avec des personnalités bien marquées, il a également compris l'importance d'une Cléone et d'un Paulin complètement effacés.' It is Narcisse whom Scherer mentions in *La Dramaturgie classique* to suggest the potential vitality of the role of the confidant (pp. 49–50), but the crowd of other confidants are said to have little of interest to say (p. 46): 'Le confident ne se borne pas à écouter. Il faut bien qu'il parle quelquefois. Quand il est en scène avec le héros auquel il est attaché, il n'a rien de bien intéressant à dire; c'est sur le héros, à juste titre, qu'est concentrée la lumière.'

Are the confidants of seventeenth-century tragedy, and of Racine's tragedies in particular, as passive and theatrically dull, when they meet their principal partners, as is usually suggested? What light can rhetorical analysis throw on the question?

1. CORNEILLE'S *SOPHONISBE*: THE DANGERS ILLUSTRATED

A useful starting-point is P. Corneille's *Sophonisbe*, which was performed without much success in 1663, the year before Racine's first tragedy. Like so many plays of the period, *Sophonisbe* provoked a controversy.[5] It must perhaps be assumed that the con-

---

[4] 'Vers une esthétique du confident racinien', *JR* (1964), 12.
[5] For a sketch of the controversy and of its main documents see P. Corneille, *Œuvres complètes*, ed. G. Couton (Paris, 1987), iii, 1461–4.

tribution of the abbé d'Aubignac to the debate[6] is to some extent fuelled by the personal enmity between the abbé and Corneille which had been provoked by the latter's refusal, in his own theoretical writings (1660), to acknowledge, other than by implicit disagreement, the abbé's own *Pratique du théâtre* (1657).[7] What d'Aubignac says about the female confidants in *Sophonisbe* is, however, of great interest. Referring to them as *suivantes*,[8] d'Aubignac makes the observation that the scenes in which Herminie and Barcée meet their partners, the two rival queens Sophonisbe and Éryxe, are boring. He speculates as to why this is so (pp. 140−1). Such roles are generally played by

mauvaises Actrices qui déplaisent aussitôt qu'elles ouvrent la bouche: De sorte que soit par le peu d'intérêt qu'elles ont au Théâtre, par la froideur de leurs sentimens, ou par le dégoût de leur récit, on ne les écoute point; c'est le temps que les Spectateurs prennent pour s'entretenir de ce qui s'est passé, pour reposer leur attention, ou pour manger leurs confitures...le Théâtre tombe dans une langueur manifeste.

This criticism is ambiguous, though d'Aubignac is not usually a man to hedge his bets. He does not say specifically that the roles of Herminie and Barcée were played by bad actresses, but that is very much the implication. Nor does he imply that the fault of the scenes in question lies exclusively in the weakness of the actresses. 'Le peu d'intérêt qu'elles ont au théâtre' and 'la froideur de leurs sentimens' can also be the fault of the dramatist. It is clear from a later remark that d'Aubignac believes Corneille to be at least as responsible as the actresses for the weakness of these scenes. For he claims the worst problem to be this: that the confidants already

---

[6] *Remarques sur la tragédie de Sophonisbe de M. Corneille envoyées à Mme la duchesse de R.* (Paris, 1663). I refer to the text as reproduced in Granet's *Recueil*, i. 134−53.

[7] The enmity between Corneille and d'Aubignac is traced by G. Couton in *La Vieillesse de Corneille* (Paris, 1949), 46−57.

[8] Not every confidant was described in the list of characters as a 'confident(e)'. There was also the 'suivant(e)', the 'ami(e)', the 'lieutenant', the 'esclave', the 'gouverneur', and, as is the case for the two female confidants in *Sophonisbe*, the 'dame d'honneur'. On this varied terminology see J. Scherer, *La Dramaturgie classique en France* (Paris, 1950), 47 and J. C. Lapp, *Aspects of Racinian Tragedy* (Toronto, 1955), 85. The social status of the confidant can vary and this fact in itself allows for a variety of types of relationship between the confidants and those characters whom, for convenience, I shall call their partners, those who confide in them.

know what the queens tell them and the queens already know
what the confidants say in reply (p. 141). In other words the
characters do nothing interesting in these scenes other than deliver
information exclusively for the benefit of the audience. While the
audience is ready to be informed, especially at the beginning of the
play,[9] it would seem that to be informed in too obvious a way is
not acceptable, because it induces boredom.

The play begins with a lively account, heard by Sophonisbe, of
how Syphax and the Romans have ceased fighting and are about
to discuss terms for peace. Corneille then finds himself in the
second scene with much information still to be conveyed to the
audience about Sophonisbe's relationship with Syphax, her strong
sense of devotion to her native Carthage, her hostility to Rome,
her former, and continuing, love for Massinisse, now fighting on
the side of Rome, and finally her jealousy of Éryxe, Syphax's
captive, who, as well as admiring Massinisse, would probably
marry him if peace were struck with the Romans.

In order to convey this information to the spectators Corneille
makes Sophonisbe tell it to her confidant, Herminie. D'Aubignac
is no doubt right to point out that the audience will feel that
Herminie knows everything she is hearing. This, of course, is a
common problem for any dramatist in an expository scene, as
Corneille himself was aware.[10] So, does Corneille adopt any
strategy to prevent the spectators from feeling that this diet of
information is being fed too obviously and directly into their own
mouths? Scrutiny of the scene suggests that d'Aubignac is right to
criticize Corneille for not providing sufficient dramatic interest,
for not masking with dramatic artifice, or, as d'Aubignac would
say, *couleur*, the scene's informative function.

In Corneille's favour is the fact that the first scene of the play,
which has announced a possible peace, should allow Sophonisbe
to speak to Herminie with passion, for she is strongly opposed to
peace. But any hint of passion is overwhelmed by the weight of
the information being conveyed. For Corneille's strategy is simply
to let Herminie, by means of explicit and implicit questions to
which she must already know the answers, prompt Sophonisbe to

---

[9] See d'Aubignac, *La Pratique du théâtre*, ed. P. Martino (Algiers, 1927),
293–4.
[10] See the first *Discours* (*Writings on the Theatre*, ed. H. T. Barnwell (Oxford,
1965) 21–5) and the *examen* of *Rodogune* (ibid. 132–3).

describe her recent past, and her current attitude towards the other characters. Herminie's first question and Sophonisbe's first answer illustrate Corneille's failure to focus attention on Sophonisbe's potentially interesting passion, as a mechanism for conveying the expository information in a less obvious way.

Sophonisbe has given a cool reception to a possibly imminent peace:

> Le roi m'honore trop d'une amour si parfaite.
> Dites-lui que j'aspire à la paix qu'il souhaite,
> Mais que je le conjure, en cet illustre jour,
> De penser à sa gloire encor plus qu'à l'amour.
> (*Sophonisbe* 31–4)

The news-bearer Bocchar leaves and Herminie comments on Sophonisbe's coolness (35–7):

> Madame ou j'entends mal une telle prière
> Ou vos vœux pour la paix n'ont pas votre âme entière;
> Vous devez pourtant craindre un vainqueur irrité.

What the audience wants to know is why Sophonisbe does not want peace and Herminie's comment seems to invite an explanation from her mistress. Sophonisbe's reply, however, must strike the audience as gratuitous. For what she says is in the form of a narrative which does not provide an immediate explanation of her coolness towards a peace treaty. By the end of her story the reasons for her opposition to peace with Rome have started to emerge, but they have been expressed in a strangely detached and indifferent way (38–54):

> J'ai fait à Massinisse une infidélité.
> Accepté par mon père, et nourri dans Carthage,
> Tu vis en tous les deux l'amour croître avec l'âge.
> Il porta dans l'Espagne et mon cœur et ma foi;
> Mais durant cette absence on disposa de moi.
> J'immolai ma tendresse au bien de ma patrie:
> Pour lui gagner Syphax j'eusse immolé ma vie.
> Il était aux Romains, et je l'en détachai;
> J'étais à Massinisse et je m'en arrachai;
> J'en eus de la douleur, j'en sentis de la gêne;
> Mais je servais Carthage, et m'en revoyais reine;
> Car, afin que le change eût pour moi quelque appas,

Syphax de Massinisse envahit les États,
Et mettait à mes pieds l'une et l'autre couronne,
Quand l'autre était réduit à sa seule personne.
Ainsi contre Carthage et contre ma grandeur
Tu me vis n'écouter ni ma foi ni mon cœur.

Sophonisbe's first line is disorientating in its mention of Massinisse, whose name the audience has not heard before. This line suggests that Sophonisbe is not replying directly to Herminie's comments and the impression that Sophonisbe is speaking for the benefit of the audience rather than that of her interlocutor is maintained throughout the speech. It is with a similar gratuitousness that Herminie interrupts and prompts Sophonisbe to move on to the next stage of her exposition. Corneille seems to be at a loss for a means of making these two characters speak to each other in a plausible and dramatically interesting way. It is of some importance to my argument to note the negative fact that this scene is not susceptible of the sort of rhetorical analysis that I have practised on scenes of formal and informal oratory between protagonists. Sophonisbe exploits the *locus repugnantium* to show that she would not be afraid of Massinisse if he and the Romans were victorious: for his love for her would quell any resentment he might feel (59–74). But there are no other persuasive devices in the scene, because there is no persuasion. Genuine interaction between Sophonisbe and her confidant is absent. Herminie is a confidant who bears out the standard critical view of this role. She is essentially a listener who has nothing interesting to say. This does not make for an exciting scene.

The passivity of the confidants in *Sophonisbe* is even more striking when viewed from a different, statistical perspective. There are four confidants in the play. Bocchar, 'lieutenant de Syphax', is only a potential confidant, appearing in just two scenes, silent in one of them, and never engaging in conversation with Syphax.[11] Mézétulle, 'lieutenant de Massinisse', appears in eleven scenes, but speaks in only four.[12] He has just one interview with his partner Massinisse (III. 1). Herminie, 'dame d'honneur de Sophonisbe', appears in sixteen scenes, but speaks in only three, all three being

[11] He speaks in I. 1 and is silent in I. 4.
[12] He appears in II. 3–4; III. 1, 3–5; IV. 3–5; V. 2–3. He speaks in III. 1; IV. 5; and V. 2–3, though in IV. 5 he has just one line.

discussions with Sophonisbe.[13] Finally, Barcée appears in eleven scenes, but speaks in only one.[14] Out of a total of twenty-eight scenes confidants appear in twenty-five. But of the twenty-five scenes in which they appear they speak in only nine. They are a largely silent presence.

Their silence is something of which d'Aubignac seems to approve, regretting that the female confidants are allowed to speak in even four scenes. He refers to the Ancients, in whose plays there are often royal followers, but who decline to give these followers any dialogue, because it could not be dramatically interesting:

> On leur [aux suivants] fait des commandemens qu'ils vont exécuter, mais sans répondre, pour ne leur pas mettre en la bouche de mauvais vers, & des complimens inutiles, ainsi que nous le remarquons souvent sur nos Théatres: & le meilleur avis que l'on pourrait donner à nos Poëtes, ce seroit de suivre en cela l'exemple des anciens, & de ne point faire parler leurs Suivantes, si elles ne se trouvent engagées dans les affaires de la Scéne, & qu'elles ne soient des Actrices nécessaires (*Dissertation sur Sophonisbe*, 141).

D'Aubignac's view, then, is that in order to prevent any loss of attention among the spectators, to keep their minds off the distractions of their confectionery, the dramatist should silence his confidants.

ii. RACINE'S PERSUASIVE CONFIDANTS: THE EXAMPLE OF ALBINE

Racine may well have learnt some aspects of his dramatic art from the recommendations of the abbé,[15] but his treatment of confidants is in clear defiance of d'Aubignac's strictures. Most of his tragedies seem to prove both that d'Aubignac's theoretical recommendations are unnecessary or misguided and that Corneille's practice can be improved upon.

---

[13] She appears in I. 1–4; II. 3–5; III. 3–6; IV. 5; V. 1–4. She speaks in I. 2; II. 5; and V. 1.

[14] She appears in I. 3; II. 1–3; III. 2–3; V. 3–7. She speaks in II. 1.

[15] In *The Tragic Drama of Corneille and Racine* (Oxford, 1982), H. T. Barnwell suggests some of the things which Racine may have learnt from d'Aubignac: e.g. ch. 5 suggests how Racine attempts to 'take up the challenge offered by hostile criticisms of Corneille [by d'Aubignac] by dramatizing simple actions characterized by "peu d'incidents", "peu de matière"' (p. 143).

The statistics suggest that, far from silencing his confidants, Racine tends to reduce the number of scenes in which they appear without anything to say, and substantially increases the number of scenes in which they actually speak. His first two tragedies and *Athalie* are exceptions to this generalization. *Athalie* has only one confidant, Nabal, who appears in five, and speaks in three, of the thirty-five scenes. One reason for the virtual disappearance of the confidant from *Athalie* is the relatively large number of protagonists who confide in each other. In *La Thébaïde* the confidants appear in sixteen of the twenty-five scenes and speak in nine of them, while in *Alexandre* there are no confidants at all. It may be that in his first two plays Racine is experimenting and that, in particular, he is testing out d'Aubignac's theories on confidants. From *Andromaque* to *Esther*, however, Racine gives his confidants a significant role. It is, for instance, usual for a confidant to speak in at least half of the scenes in which he or she appears.[16] Consequently, the confidants each have rather more private interviews with their principal partners than their quieter counterparts in *Sophonisbe*.

Racine seems deliberately to exploit a technique which had been criticized as undramatic. How does he set about creating interest in a confrontation between a confidant and his or her partner, when it would seem that the confidant has nothing more interesting to say than that his or her interlocutor is right? Rhetorical analysis suggests an answer.

Racine's practice is to engineer a conflict between the two characters, not a deep-rooted conflict, but one which lasts usually just for the duration of the scene. This element of conflict allows him to base the discussion between confidant and protagonist on judicial or deliberative oratory. The two characters then use the recommendations of *inventio* and, to a lesser extent, of *dispositio* as persuasive tools. By engineering a momentary conflict, which, however, is not at the heart of the plot, Racine is able to give to scenes between characters who might at first appear to be in

---

[16] The exceptions are Albine (*Britannicus*), who speaks in 3 of her 7 scenes; Aegine (*Iphigénie*) in 2 out of 11; Doris (*Iphigénie*) in 3 out of 13; Théramène (*Phèdre*) in 4 out of 10; Ismène (*Phèdre*) in 1 out of 5; Hydaspe (who is to all intents and purposes Aman's confidant in *Esther*) in 2 out of 5 scenes; and Élise (*Esther*) in 4 out of 12.

agreement a dramatic momentum similar to, if ultimately less compelling than, scenes of genuine conflict.

Racine's use of persuasion in scenes between confidants and protagonists is not generally noticed, even by those who speak in positive ways about Racine's confidants.[17] Yet the point emerges clearly from a comparison between the expository scene in Corneille's *Sophonisbe* involving Sophonisbe and Herminie (I. 2) and the expository scene in *Britannicus* with Agrippine and Albine (I. 1). B. Weinberg's comment on the role of Albine is simply an application to her confrontations with Agrippine of the traditional critical view of confidants: 'Albine, as a confidante [*sic*], really has no part in the action, largely serving only to provide Agrippine with the occasion to express her feelings.'[18] Such a comment might well suit Herminie, whose sometimes gratuitous questions prompt Sophonisbe to explain herself for the benefit of the audience. But for the expository scene of *Britannicus*, although Albine does serve an informative function, Racine has deployed a more complex and dramatically more interesting means of conveying the information to the spectators.

The audience needs to know where the action takes place, who the main characters are, that Agrippine has schemed to put her son Néron on to the throne, that Néron is no longer showing any gratitude to his mother, that his half-brother Britannicus has a claim to the throne and has some supporters, that Néron has just kidnapped the woman Britannicus loves, and finally that Agrippine intends to do all she can to restore her own control over her son.

Wearing a cap different from that as critic of *Sophonisbe*, d'Aubignac admits that at the beginning of a play the audience will tolerate informative narrations as long as their length is kept under control and they do not become too cluttered with unnecessary details.[19] In *Britannicus* I. 1 Racine goes one better, concealing the informative nature of his narrations beneath a veil of persuasion and conflict. All the information required by the audience is conveyed, as if incidentally, in a scene which has as its

---

[17] e.g. J. Delon and B. Girard in J. Truchet (ed.), *Recherches de thématique théâtrale* (Paris, 1981), 133–7.

[18] *The Art of Jean Racine* (Chicago, 1963), 125.

[19] *La Pratique*, 293–5.

predominant dramatic focus an opposition of views between the protagonist and the confidant.

The situation is based on a combination of deliberative and judicial oratory. The deliberative element, with which the scene opens and closes, lies in Albine's initial wish to persuade her mistress not to wait at Néron's door at so early an hour of the morning, but to return to her own apartment (1−5). Once the deliberative element has provided an impetus, it gives way to judicial oratory. For whether or not Agrippine waits to see Néron depends largely upon the degree of seriousness of any change in his character. The two women put Néron on trial, Albine defending and Agrippine attacking.

Agrippine's first speech serves as an *exordium*, in which the emperor's mother refutes Albine's urgent plea that she go back to her own apartment and, at the same time, makes the transition into judicial oratory:

> Albine, il ne faut pas s'éloigner un moment.
> Je veux l'attendre ici. Les chagrins qu'il me cause
> M'occuperont assez tout le temps qu'il repose.
> Tout ce que j'ai prédit n'est que trop assuré:
> Contre Britannicus Néron s'est déclaré.
> L'impatient Néron cesse de se contraindre;
> Las de se faire aimer, il veut se faire craindre.
> Britannicus le gêne, Albine, et chaque jour
> Je sens que je deviens importune à mon tour.
>
> (*Britannicus* 6−14)

Agrippine must wait for him, because he is such a changed character that she cannot rest until she has spoken to him. This comment could simply be Agrippine's response to Albine's request. It need not be an *exordium* to a further development. But that is what it turns out to be. For Agrippine's announcement of her distrust of Néron's character has both stimulated Albine's interest and moves her to disagree in an early, and therefore dramatically exciting, piece of *refutatio* (15−20):

> Quoi? vous à qui Néron doit le jour qu'il respire,
> Qui l'avez appelé de si loin à l'empire?
> Vous qui, déshéritant le fils de Claudius,
> Avez nommé César l'heureux Domitius?
> Tout lui parle, Madame, en faveur d'Agrippine:
> Il vous doit son amour.

The evidence which she uses to refute Agrippine is less argument than narration. By pointing out that Agrippine not only gave birth to Néron, but also saw to it that he became Roman emperor, Albine casts doubts on the case that the mother had started to make against her son. As well as being informed of some basic facts of the situation, the audience is kept interested by the developing disagreement between these two women.

Albine's *refutatio* prompts Agrippine to clarify her charge against the emperor. It is a charge of ingratitude (20–2):

> Il me le doit [son amour], Albine;
> Tout, s'il est généreux, lui prescrit cette loi;
> Mais tout, s'il est ingrat, lui parle contre moi.

Agrippine focuses on a charge which will form the basis of her major confrontation with her son in IV. 2. The opening scene of the play is in some ways a rehearsal for the later one, a rehearsal for the benefit of Agrippine, but also for the benefit of the audience, which is being apprised of the main facts of the case, the better to appreciate the later conflict. The way in which Agrippine frames her charge prepares the audience both for the evidence that she will produce to substantiate it and for an explanation of what she herself may have done to prompt Néron's ingratitude. In other words, Agrippine provides a hint of what the rhetoricians call a *divisio*, that part of a speech which can follow an *exordium* and sets out how the subject will be treated.

Agrippine does not, however, continue immediately with her charge. For Albine interrupts yet again with another *refutatio*, this time refuting specifically the charge of ingratitude with recourse to a narration suggesting the qualities already demonstrated by Néron (23–9). This narrative evidence is supported by the *locus comparationis minorum*: Augustus was already old before he became a good emperor; the current emperor is showing great qualities while still young (29–30). Albine's present argument is not so convincing as her former one. For she has not perceived that Agrippine's charge is that Néron is behaving in a way which shows ingratitude to her, his mother. Albine's defence of him in this speech is simply a defence of him as a promising emperor.

This relatively weak *refutatio* allows Racine to make Agrippine's reply seem all the more forceful. She first takes up and crushes Albine's argument that Néron is likely to make a good emperor, before going on to argue for his ingratitude towards her and suggest reasons for it. All this she does in lines 31–70, interrupted once for just half a line by Albine. These lines constitute her combined *narratio* and *confirmatio*.

The initial force of her reply comes from the way in which she seizes on Albine's *comparatio minorum* and twists it into a *comparatio maiorum* so as to argue the very opposite from Albine. The apparently concessive nature of the opening two lines is merely cosmetic (31–4):

> Non, non, mon intérêt ne me rend point injuste:
> Il commence, il est vrai, par où finit Auguste;
> Mais crains que l'avenir détruisant le passé,
> Il ne finisse ainsi qu'Auguste a commencé.

She then draws on the *locus generis* to suggest that Néron's nature is likely to turn out for the worse (35–8) and she adduces the *probatio inartificialis* of Caligula to show that a reign can start off well before turning sour (39–41).

Having crushed Albine's defence of Néron as a promising emperor by exploiting a wider range of *loci* in a greater number of arguments, Agrippine returns to her original charge that Néron is ungrateful to herself. A transitional passage (43–8) draws on the *locus dissimilitudinis*, allowing Agrippine to distinguish between herself and everybody else. It is she herself in whom she is interested, a point which will be driven home to the audience throughout the play.

Then follows a *narratio*, in which she produces the most striking piece of evidence against her son's character: he has kidnapped Junie, the beloved of his potential political rival, Britannicus (49–54). A *confirmatio* explores the *locus causarum* in such a way as to suggest that Néron's criminal act against Junie is actually caused by his desire to suppress his mother (55–8):

> Que veut-il? Est-ce haine, est-ce amour qui l'inspire?
> Cherche-t-il seulement le plaisir de leur nuire?
> Ou plutôt n'est-ce point que sa malignité
> Punit sur eux l'appui que je leur ai prêté?

The audience must take stock of both the kidnap and the reason that Agrippine should think herself to have been in some sense its cause. To signal the importance of these points for his spectators

Racine makes Albine express surprise at Agrippine's argument: 'Vous, leur appui, Madame?' (59). Albine's surprise renders plausible Agrippine's fuller explanation of her rather elliptical argument, an explanation which comes in the form of a *narratio* (59–70). That Agrippine explains the extent of her support for her son's rival is essential for the audience. But it is also necessary to add persuasive force to her charge of her son's ingratitude, of which she is trying to persuade Albine.

Albine deploys further narrative evidence with which to calm Agrippine's fears about her son (75–87), but the determined mother has more counter-evidence (88–114) and it is Albine who, in the end, makes some concession to her interlocutor (115–17):

> Ah! si de ce soupçon votre âme est prévenue,
> Pourquoi nourrissez-vous le venin qui vous tue?
> Daignez avec César vous éclaircir du moins.

Albine does not actually concede the judicial point that Néron's character has turned bad. She is prepared, however, not to pursue the point related to the deliberative aspect of their oratory, which would be to persuade Agrippine to go back to her own apartment. She seems to suggest that allowing Agrippine to wait and see Néron is the best way of making Agrippine realize that her charge against his character is mistaken. In retrospect, of course, the audience will see that it is Albine's defence that is mistaken.

The main point to emerge from this analysis of *Britannicus* I. I is that Racine has engineered a dramatically interesting framework in which to convey expository information to the audience. This framework is a combination of deliberative and judicial oratory, made possible by the contrivance of a momentary, but theatrically urgent, conflict between Agrippine and her confidant. What the characters say is not restricted to the range of information required by the audience. They produce a variety of arguments with which to attack each other's opinions, and the vital information is contained in some of those arguments, indeed is shaped as argument. The sense of awkwardness in the expository scene of *Sophonisbe* is absent from the confrontation between Agrippine and Albine. Albine is no mere listener. She plays an actively persuasive role in this scene.

The introduction of an element of persuasion into a confrontation between a protagonist and a confidant is Racine's favourite method of conveying expository information to the audience. It occurs with Jocaste and Olympe in *La Thébaïde* (I. I), with Oreste and Pylade in *Andromaque* (I. I), with Xipharès and Arbate in *Mithridate* (I. I),[20] with Agamemnon and Arcas in *Iphigénie* (I. I), and with Hippolyte and Théramène in *Phèdre* (I. I). All these scenes can be analysed along similar lines to those followed in the analysis of *Britannicus* I. I. Hippolyte tries to persuade Théramène that he (Hippolyte) must leave the palace, and Théramène consistently refutes his arguments. Xipharès justifies his love for Monime and his intention to secure the Bosphorus, and Arbate is persuaded to remain loyal to him. When characters tell each other news, Racine tries to make sure that they are plausibly in need of the information and he generally tries to draw attention away from the narrative nature of their speeches, dramatizing it with some degree of persuasion.[21]

III. WHEN CONFIDANTS MEET THEIR PARTNERS AFTER THE EXPOSITION: *ANDROMAQUE* AND *PHÈDRE*

The examples of meetings between confidants and partners have all, so far, been taken from expository scenes. Confidants, however, meet their partners throughout the play and the purpose of such meetings is, according to the conventional view, to allow the protagonists to express their reactions to the twists and turns of the plot. The confidants are no more than a means of allowing this to happen in a plausible way, preventing the dramatist from having recourse to too many monologues. In fact Racine puts more into these scenes than the protagonists' expression of emotion or opinion. Here too Racine injects theatrical interest in the form of a disagreement engineered between the characters.

This procedure can be found working in a tentative way in Racine's first play when Créon speaks to his confidant, Attale, in *La Thébaïde* III. 6. Créon has just appeared to Attale and to the

---

[20] This is an unusual variation, as Arbate is of course Mithridate's confidant, not that of Xipharès.

[21] A notable exception is the exposition to *Bajazet* (I. I). Racine, unusually, presents both Acomat and the confidant Osmin as self-conscious narrators (6–7, 11–16). It is less by the introduction of a note of disagreement than by the creation of a sense of mystery that Racine seeks to interest his audience in this exposition.

audience to perform a volte-face. Far from inflaming the rivalry of the two brothers as might have been expected, he has seemed to encourage Étéocle to look favourably on Polynice. In the present scene Créon explains his motives. But the explanation is given theatrical impetus by the way in which Racine frames it as a piece of persuasion. Attale is made to raise a number of objections to Créon's strategy (855–9, 891–2). So Créon has not only to explain his motivation, but also to convince Attale that it is justifiable.

In the scene in *La Thébaïde* it seems not to matter very much what Attale thinks of Créon's explanation and arguments. From *Andromaque* on, however, Racine makes more vigorous use of this technique by involving the confidants in discussions about decisions which are of central importance to the characters and he does so in such a way as to make it appear that the confidants play an active role in the reaching of important decisions. Créon simply attempts to justify himself to Attale after the event. But in *Andromaque* Phoenix is instrumental in II. 5 in taking Pyrrhus's mind away from the eponymous heroine and focusing it, if only momentarily, on his duty and promise to Hermione. Phoenix actually persuades a weak Pyrrhus to go and see the Greek princess. In a scene similarly based on deliberative oratory Pylade tries to deter Oreste from kidnapping Hermione, but in the end Oreste's persistent refusal to acknowledge the weight of any of his friend's arguments leads Pylade to give way and promise to help the ambassador (III. 1).

There is equally impassioned debate in III. 8 and IV. 1 between Andromaque and Céphise. Céphise says relatively little in these scenes in comparison with Pylade and Phoenix in their scenes, but what she does say establishes her as a determined character, ready with arguments to put up against any of Andromaque's threats of suicide. When, for instance, Andromaque expresses her horror at the thought of saving her son by making Pyrrhus Hector's successor, Céphise produces a forceful argument with which she tries to counteract Andromaque's horror:

> Ainsi le veut son fils, que les Grecs vous ravissent.
> Pensez-vous qu'après tout ses mânes en rougissent?
> Qu'il méprisât, Madame, un roi victorieux
> Qui vous fait remonter au rang de vos aïeux,
> Qui foule aux pieds pour vous vos vainqueurs en colère,

Qui ne se souvient plus qu'Achille était son père,
Qui dément ses exploits et les rend superflus?

(*Andromaque* 985–91)

The force of this argument lies in the way in which it should appeal to Andromaque on a number of fronts. Mention of Astyanax and of his possible loss to the Greeks is based on *affectus* and appeals to Andromaque's strong sense of maternal affection. Reference to the shade of Hector, coupled with a long and favourable *definitio* of Pyrrhus, suggests that the dead husband would regard her marriage to Pyrrhus as quite excusable. Meanwhile, the *definitio* is in its own right designed to clear Pyrrhus in the eyes of Andromaque of his former crimes against Troy, drawing on *mores*. Céphise's argument is unsuccessful, but it has a twofold importance for the audience. The words of the confidant lend dramatic momentum to a scene which would otherwise be simply an expression of despair and uncertainty by Andromaque. Not only, however, do Céphise's words give movement to the scene. They also, by dint of being a plausible and forceful argument, allow the audience to appreciate the real difficulty of Andromaque's dilemma. By opposing her mistress in a credible way Céphise increases the audience's sympathy for Andromaque.

The fourth confidant in *Andromaque* is Cléone, who is as persuasive in her dealings with her partner, Hermione, as the other confidants are with theirs. In II. 1, for example, she argues against Hermione that the princess must see Oreste and must return to Greece if Astyanax is not handed over. But, as an instance of the dramatic inventiveness with which Racine is beginning to treat his persuasive confidants, it is Cléone's deliberative speech in IV. 2 that stands out as particularly striking.

Racine's aim in this scene seems to be to let the audience see Hermione containing a seething fury, which is likely to boil over at any moment. The theatrical effect should be primarily visual, but the means with which the effect is created is verbal. For Racine gives Cléone a deliberative speech in which she attempts to persuade Hermione to break silence (1130–42):

Non, je ne puis assez admirer ce silence.
Vous vous taisez, Madame, et ce cruel mépris
N'a pas du moindre trouble agité vos esprits!
Vous soutenez en paix une si rude attaque,

Vous qu'on voyait frémir au seul nom d'Andromaque!
Vous qui sans désespoir ne pouviez endurer
Que Pyrrhus d'un regard la voulût honorer!
Il l'épouse, il lui donne, avec son diadème,
La foi que vous venez de recevoir vous-même,
Et votre bouche encor, muette à tant d'ennui,
N'a pas daigné s'ouvrir pour se plaindre de lui?
Ah! que je crains, Madame, un calme si funeste,
Et qu'il vaudrait bien mieux . . .

Cléone has barely started the *confirmatio* when she is interrupted by Hermione's abrupt request to see Oreste. The audience has heard enough of Cléone's speech to take stock of Hermione's mood. For persuasion in its own right is of less importance here than in the other scenes from *Andromaque* discussed above. What matters here is the conveying of silence through words.[22]

With *Andromaque* Racine has discovered how to inject dramatic excitement into encounters between protagonists and their confidants. He does so largely by making the confidant into a persuasive force. It is a technique which he practises to particular effect in scenes between desperate young women and their confidants. Atalide and Zaïre (*Bajazet* IV. 1 and V. 12), Monime and Phœdime (*Mithridate* IV. 1 and V. 1), Ériphile and Doris (*Iphigénie* II. 1 and IV. 1) are all in this category. In each case the confidant exercises a vigorous restraining influence on the protagonist and in each case the situation is an oratorical one.

This is even so for a short scene such as that between Bérénice and Phénice in *Bérénice* IV. 2. This scene might at first be dismissed solely as a functional scene designed to clarify for the audience the reasons for the movements of the characters on and off stage. But this function is fulfilled through largely deliberative oratory, which gives the scene momentum. The subject of the debate is slight. Phénice attempts to persuade Bérénice to retire to her own apartment and restore her appearance before, on the queen's request, Titus comes to see her. The conclusion to be drawn from her premises, though she does not spell it out, is that it would not help Bérénice's case if Titus saw her in a dishevelled state. Bérénice perceives the unstated conclusion and replies

---

[22] For a commentary on the dramatic effect of Hermione's silence see R. Parish, '"Un calme si funeste": Some Types of Silence in Racine', *FS* 34 (1980), 397–9.

directly, using the same *locus effectorum* to reach the opposite conclusion: her persuasion of Titus would be all the more effective if accompanied by the visual signs of her distress. She then considers the other side of the same argument by suggesting that Titus is, in any case, no longer moved by her beauty. Phénice starts to reply to this argument with a defence of Titus and so a move into judicial oratory, but she is interrupted by the arrival of Titus, Paulin, and other courtiers. This arrival puts an end to their debate, as Phénice ushers her mistress out. Bérénice leaves without further argument, no doubt because Titus is accompanied. She had been expecting to confront him by himself. The rhetorical framework creates excitement in a scene which, in less skilful hands, might have been lacking in that quality.

The most thoroughgoing piece of persuasion executed by a female confidant on her mistress occurs in *Phèdre* when, in III. 1 and III. 3, Œnone comes to verbal blows with Phèdre. Close analysis highlights a feature of confrontations between confidants and protagonists which has already begun to emerge. In contrast to scenes of formal oratory or scenes of informal oratory based on genuine conflict between protagonists, Racine, in the present type of scene, uses rhetorical procedures in a highly elastic way. The main subject and direction of the debate can change more frequently and characters, if they employ the recommendations for *dispositio*, do so in an idiosyncratic fashion, as Agrippine does in *Britannicus* I. 1, but in a fashion which, none the less, suits their persuasive aims.

Racine's compensation for the absence of dramatic irony and compelling urgency in confrontations between a protagonist and a confidant is to make the debate fast-moving (by treating the characters' oratory flexibly), to make the outcome seem important, and to increase the element of conflict by giving both characters weighty arguments. Racine achieves all this in the scenes between Œnone and Phèdre in Act III of *Phèdre*.

Unusually for such a scene, there is in III. 1 a degree of dramatic irony, but not in the sense that one character has superior knowledge to another. Here both characters are victims of the irony. For neither Phèdre nor Œnone seems to have heard the rumour reported by Théramène at the end of the previous act that Thésée might have returned. Their discussion of Hippolyte in III. 1 is based on the assumption that Thésée is dead, which increases the audience's sense of pity for the wishful imaginings of Phèdre.

Phèdre begins the scene with a speech which is deliberative in intention. She attempts to persuade Œnone to leave her alone and prevent her from being seen in public. The reason which she alleges, based on *affectus* and appealing to Œnone's pity, is that she is too troubled a soul. This is reinforced by a *narratio* of her encounter with Hippolyte in II. 5 and of his insensitivity to her.

Œnone responds to Phèdre's speech, putting the opposite view that she must carry out her royal duties. She supports her view with two arguments. The first is a perceptive undermining of Phèdre's appeal for her confidant's pity:

> Ainsi, dans vos malheurs, ne songeant qu'à vous plaindre,
> Vous nourrissez un feu qu'il vous faudrait éteindre.
> (Phèdre 753–4)

Phèdre is too full of self-pity, suggests Œnone, who refuses to be moved by it. Her second argument exploits the *locus generis* (755–8):

> Ne vaudrait-il pas mieux, digne sang de Minos,
> Dans de plus nobles soins chercher votre repos,
> Contre un ingrat qui plaît recourir à la fuite,
> Régner, et de l'État embrasser la conduite.

A noble lineage demands noble action.

To these arguments Phèdre replies with yet another, based yet again on *affectus*: a woman as weak, as filled with guilt, and as bereft of reason as she is cannot surely be expected to reign.

Perhaps showing a sign of impatience with Phèdre's continuing self-pity, Œnone suddenly changes the course of her deliberative oratory and expresses her new recommendation in one word: 'Fuyez' (763). Phèdre gives a similarly concise response by way of refutation: 'Je ne le puis quitter' (763), appealing for a third time for Œnone's pity. But Œnone is in fighting form and tersely exploits the *locus comparationis maiorum*: 'Vous l'osâtes bannir, vous n'osez l'éviter?' (764).

This prompts Phèdre to use a different, more aggressive type of argument. Flight, she claims, is too late an option, for she has declared her love and formed too strong an affection for Hippolyte to be able to leave him. Here is still an element of *affectus*. But lest she be sharply reproached once again by Œnone, she exploits the *locus causarum* and introduces a hint of judicial oratory, attacking her confidant as the root cause of her plight (769–72):

> Toi-même rappelant ma force défaillante,
> Et mon âme déjà sur mes lèvres errante,
> Par tes conseils flatteurs tu m'as su ranimer;
> Tu m'as fait entrevoir que je pouvais l'aimer.

Thus Phèdre initiates the accusations against Œnone which culminate in her condemnation of her confidant at the end of Act IV. Refusing to enter properly into the judicial mode and defend herself, Œnone persists in fighting Phèdre's self-pity and vain hopes by giving a *narratio* of Hippolyte's reaction to Phèdre's declaration of love. It is a *narratio* the details of which Phèdre knows only too well already (773–80):

> Hélas! de vos malheurs innocente ou coupable,
> De quoi pour vous sauver n'étais-je point capable?
> Mais si jamais l'offense irrita vos esprits,
> Pouvez-vous d'un superbe oublier les mépris?
> Avec quels yeux cruels sa rigueur obstinée
> Vous laissait à ses pieds peu s'en faut prosternée!
> Que son farouche orgueil le rendait odieux!
> Que Phèdre en ce moment n'avait-elle mes yeux!

These details tally with Phèdre's own account of Hippolyte's re-action given in her first speech of the present scene. But they are clearly details which, despite Œnone's insistent repetition of them, Phèdre prefers to forget or excuse, as her following speeches in the scene make clear.

The debate is one of predominantly deliberative oratory. Phèdre's persuasive aim, however, seems to be a rather negative one. Put at its most positive, it is to persuade Œnone not to trouble her. Œnone, on the other hand, has attempted to persuade Phèdre to look at her situation constructively and either to reign, as if nothing had happened between her and Hippolyte, or to flee. She has tried to crush Phèdre's continuing interest in her stepson. Yet ironically it is Œnone's attempt to crush such interest by means of her account of Hippolyte's indifference that actually renews Phèdre's interest in him in a constructive way. For Phèdre now draws on the *locus causarum* to explain away the young man's surprise at her declaration (781–6) and this leads her, despite Œnone's objections (787, 789), to adopt a new, positive plan. She will send Œnone to plead with Hippolyte on her behalf and she tells Œnone the arguments that she is to use on him (790–812). The deliberative oratory comes to an end when Phèdre asserts her authority over Œnone (791–2):

> Enfin, tous ces conseils ne sont plus de saison:
> Sers ma fureur, Œnone, et non point ma raison.

Mistress and confidant can engage in persuasion and counter-persuasion, but when the mistress gives a command, the persuasion ceases and the confidant has to obey. Phèdre wins the debate by social rank rather than by argument. She simply refuses to listen to Œnone's reasons.

Œnone goes away to execute Phèdre's order, but promptly returns with the news that the outlook has changed so completely as to have forestalled Phèdre's designs. Thésée has returned. The scene which ensues is a reversal of III. 1. The latter scene had closed with an order issued by Phèdre to Œnone. Act III, Scene 3, surprisingly and exceptionally, opens with an order issued by the confidant to her mistress (825–6):

> Il faut d'un vain amour étouffer la pensée,
> Madame. Rappelez votre vertu passée.

It is true that the order is fleshed out by a persuasive *narratio* of Thésée's return. But Phèdre recognizes the force of the order and does not need any further arguments in order to be persuaded that her intended course of action can no longer be pursued (832).

Another reversal is apparent by the end of the scene. In the earlier scene Phèdre had started with weak arguments and finished with a determined plan which she ordered her confidant to carry out. In the present scene she starts with a determined judicial oration accusing herself and pronouncing her death sentence. But she finishes by giving way to Œnone, who plans to keep her alive by making a false accusation against Hippolyte to the newly returned husband. One of Œnone's arguments which contributes to her successful persuasion is based on *affectus*: Phèdre's children would be very much to be pitied if their mother died (869–70). It is the sort of argument which Phèdre had used unsuccessfully in

the earlier scene. Her confused mental state is underlined at the
end of the scene by her renunciation of debate (911–12):

> Fais ce que tu voudras, je m'abandonne à toi.
> Dans le trouble où je suis, je ne puis rien pour moi.

Throughout these scenes Œnone has her mistress's interests at
heart. She is on her side against the forces of a cruel and confusing
world. But, in persuasive confrontation, she is her opponent, producing and refuting arguments, which frequently take off in new
directions. It is with this opposition of two orators that Racine
seeks to hold the attention of his audience. It is with Phèdre's
dependence on *affectus* as a source of argument and her recourse
to self-accusation that he hopes to move the audience to pity for
his heroine. Such pity is reinforced by the reversal in the second
scene of the course taken by the debate in the first scene. The
oratory of Phèdre and Œnone is a strikingly successful instance of
Racine's treatment of scenes between a protagonist and a confidant. Phèdre and Œnone are far removed from Sophonisbe and
Herminie, and amply justify Racine's not heeding d'Aubignac's
strictures against confidants.

5
Self-Persuasion: Monologues

Le monologue n'a pas de rôle à jouer tant qu'il n'est pas action.

(J. A. McF. Moravcevich, 'Monologue et action', 8)

If it is the persuasive interaction of characters that constitutes the theatricality of Racinian discourse, what becomes of verbal action if characters speak when they are alone, or accompanied by silent and anonymous followers? When d'Aubignac says that in seventeenth-century French tragedy to speak is to act, he gives the example of Émilie's monologue at the beginning of *Cinna* (*La Pratique*, p. 282). If persuasion is central to an understanding of verbal action involving two or more characters, can it not be useful in appreciating monologues? Does the definition of verbal action have to change to incorporate any features that might be peculiar to monologues? This chapter explores answers to these questions.

The generally accepted view is that the monologue has a type of action peculiar to itself. G. Pocock focuses on the lyrical and poetic nature of Racine's monologues: 'The archaic use of *stances* and soliloquies points to a concern less with forwarding the plot than with lyricism and the poetic development of a theme.'[1] C. J. Gossip reinforces this view of the poetic nature of Racine's mono- logues when he suggests why Racine might have wished to revive the monologue at a time when his immediate contemporaries were using it very sparingly, if at all: 'Le monologue tombe victime des théoriciens dramatiques qui le jugent invraisemblable. Seul Racine y reviendra dans la deuxième moitié du siècle, et cela à des fins poétiques.'[2] Both these critics seem to echo the view of J. Scherer that: 'La fonction essentielle du monologue est de permettre l'expression lyrique d'un sentiment . . . Le monologue permet au

[1] *Corneille and Racine* (Cambridge, 1973), 170.
[2] C. J. Gossip in his edn. of Cyrano de Bergerac's *La Mort d'Agrippine* (Exeter, 1982), xvi, n. 30.

dramaturge, non seulement de faire connaître les sentiments de son héros—facilité que lui offre tout dialogue—mais de les chanter.'[3] To the view of the monologue as a moment of lyricism and poetry is added the view of it as an expression of passion and a demonstration of a character's tragic solitude. This is the contribution of J. C. Lapp:

> In Racine, the monologue that is pronounced by an actor alone upon the stage ... permits us that glimpse of the workings of his tormented soul that can only be revealed in solitude.
>
> Indeed one of the monologue's chief purposes is to stress the terrible solitude of the Racinian tragic character.[4]

Critical tradition tends to invite the spectator to admire the monologue as a piece of poetry or as an opportunity to step aside from the plot and indulge in some close character-analysis. I shall argue that, in the case of Racine's monologues at least, such an invitation might lead the spectator away from the essentially dramatic nature of this form.

It is right to mistrust these traditional critical judgements, for, on monologues in particular, many critics are demonstrably unreliable. The term 'monologue' has been used in a loose way to describe Hermione's verbally violent condemnation of Pyrrhus, addressed directly to the king himself, in *Andromaque* IV. 5,[5] as well as Agrippine's attempt in *Britannicus* IV. 2 to persuade Néron that he ought to do as his mother wishes.[6] If both these speeches are monologues, surely most of the speeches in Racine's plays can be so described. Such freedom in the use of a critical term is no doubt the cause of critics' inability to agree on the number of monologues to be found in certain of Racine's plays. Pocock counts three monologues in *Bajazet*,[7] but Scherer[8] and Vinaver[9] count seven. Pocock counts five in *Phèdre*,[10] where J. P. Short can count only four.[11]

---

[3] *La Dramaturgie classique en France* (Paris, 1950), 246.
[4] *Aspects of Racinian Tragedy* (Toronto, 1955), 111.
[5] E. Vinaver, *Racine et la poésie tragique* (Paris, 1963), 141.
[6] C. Venesoen, 'Le Néron de Racine', *IL* 33 (1981), 134.
[7] *Corneille and Racine*, 192.
[8] *La Dramaturgie classique*, 260.
[9] *Entretiens sur Racine* (Paris, 1984), 100.
[10] *Corneille and Racine*, 192.
[11] *Racine: 'Phèdre'* (London, 1983), 32.

Clearly it is time to look afresh at the monologue, and not only because the views of modern critics invite scepticism. Theoretical debate about monologues in the seventeenth century and the history of the use of this dramatic form in the period suggest that its nature in Racine's tragedies might be more complex than is often supposed. As Scherer points out,[12] the monologue experienced a startling change of fortune in the seventeenth century. Towards the beginning of the century the form occupied a quantitatively important place in most plays. In Théophile's *Pyrame et Thisbé* (1623) the whole of the last act is composed of monologues. Scherer (p. 256) counts as many as nineteen examples of the form in Racan's *Bergeries* (1625) and in Mareschal's *La Sœur Valeureuse* (1634), and fourteen in Corneille's *Clitandre* (1632), which account for 34.5 per cent of the total number of lines in the play. The table below, based on figures taken from the thesis by J. A. McF. Moravcevich,[13] shows the decline into which the monologue gradually fell in the serious plays of Pierre Corneille after *Le Cid*. These figures suggest that in the middle of the century the monologue started to become much less frequent and much shorter. The figures for Pierre Corneille can be supported by those for other dramatists. For instance, none of the last four tragedies of Quinault contains a monologue.[14]

A remark made by the abbé d'Aubignac suggests why audiences liked the frequent and long monologues of the first half of the century, while also pointing out why such monologues had to be employed with caution:

J'avoüe qu'il est quelquefois bien agréable sur le Theatre de voir un homme seul ouvrir le fond de son ame, et de l'entendre parler hardiment de toutes ses plus secrettes pensées, expliquer tous ses sentimens, et dire tout ce que la violence de sa passion lui suggère; mais certes il n'est pas toujoürs bien facile de le faire avec vraisemblance.[15]

Rather like Lapp, d'Aubignac sees the monologue as an expression of passion, an outpouring of the soul, not simply as a lyrical interlude. He makes it clear that it is the concern with illusionist

[12] *La Dramaturgie classique*, 256–60.
[13] 'Monologue et action dans les trois premières tragédies de Racine et dans le théâtre de son temps' (Ph.D. thesis, Univ. of Wisconsin, 1970), 32.
[14] *Agrippa* (1662), *Astrate* (1664), *Pausanias* (1668), *Bellérophon* (1670–1).
[15] *La Pratique du théâtre*, ed. P. Martino (Algiers, 1927), 250.

Play	First performance	Number of monologues	Lines of monologue
Le Cid	1637	7	$160\frac{3}{4}$
Horace	1640	3	115
Cinna	1640–1	5	$206\frac{1}{2}$
Polyeucte	1641–2	2	98
Pompée	1642–3	0	0
Rodogune	1644–5	7	193
Théodore	1645	3	$20\frac{3}{4}$
Héraclius	1646–7	1	44
Nicomède	1650–1	1	12
Pertharite	1651–2	2	$44\frac{1}{2}$
Œdipe	1659	1	50
Sertorius	1662	1	4
Sophonisbe	1663	0	0
Othon	1664	2	9
Agésilas	1666	0	0
Attila	1667	1	16
Tite et Bérénice	1670	1	2
Pulchérie	1672	3	$7\frac{1}{2}$
Suréna	1674	2	3

theatre which must deprive audiences of the pleasure of the monologue. Indeed the bulk of his chapter on monologues is composed of warnings about those offences against *vraisemblance* which the careless writer of monologues might all too easily commit: the character must not be made to address the audience directly; it must be the sort of character who might reasonably speak alone; and the time, place, and other circumstances must conspire to make the monologue plausible. 'En un mot par tout il faut se laisser conduire à la Vraysemblance comme à la seule lumière du Theatre' (p. 253). The audience will be more than compensated for the decline in the monologue by the more effective illusion of reality in the theatre. D'Aubignac is not, of course, necessarily a reliable guide to understanding Racine's monologues, because d'Aubignac has in mind plays from the first half of the century and Racine's monologues can be very different from monologues in earlier plays.

Corneille's theoretical writing moves in the same direction as d'Aubignac's. When Corneille comments in 1660 on his early play *Clitandre* he is critical of the monologues and adds a new perspective on their earlier popularity, suggesting that they responded to the actors' desire to show off: 'Les monologues sont trop longs et trop fréquents en cette pièce; c'était une beauté en ce temps-là: les comédiens les souhaitaient, et croyaient y paraître avec plus d'avantage.'[16]

Yet when the monologue appeared to be playing a minimal role in serious drama, Racine started to make it a more important feature of his plays. There are substantial monologues in all his tragedies except *Britannicus* and *Athalie*. It is not my aim to speculate as to why Racine made this move. Rather I shall examine a number of monologues in order to suggest that Racine was not, as is sometimes supposed,[17] simply reviving an old-fashioned form in which poetry and passion takes over temporarily from dramatic conflict. Rhetorical analysis shows that, in Racine's tragedies, scenes of monologue are, like scenes of dialogue, instances of persuasive action.[18]

The monologues I shall consider are those speeches of some length (usually more than ten lines) delivered either by a character who is alone on stage, or by a character who is accompanied but who, as he speaks, is evidently not addressing his companion directly and is not, however, afraid of being overheard by this companion.[19] This perspective excludes from my analysis a number of short speeches which others might rightly consider as monologues. There are, for instance, Antigone's prayer for the safekeeping of Hémon (*La Thébaïde* I. 6), Narcisse's revelation of his self-seeking desires (*Britannicus* 757–60), and Burrhus's concern for Néron's behaviour (*Britannicus* 800–8). These monologues fulfil an important dramatic function, informing the audience unambiguously about a character's real desires. But they are not the sort of speeches which have been described as lyrical expressions

---

[16] *Writings on the Theatre*, ed. H. T. Barnwell (Oxford, 1965), 85.

[17] e.g. Scherer, *La Dramaturgie classique*, 260.

[18] The thesis of Moravcevich, cited in n. 13, suggests that monologues are active if they relate in a necessary way to the plot.

[19] This last qualification distinguishes the monologue from the much shorter aside, of which there are very few examples in Racine's tragedies. The best known is perhaps Monime's 'O ciel! me serais-je abusée?' in *Mithridate* (1116).

of passion. It is this latter type of monologue which rhetorical analysis can help the critic to view afresh.[20]

1. LYRICISM VERSUS PERSUASION: ANTIGONE, ANTIOCHUS, AND ATALIDE

If the monologue is a moment of poetic stasis, Antigone's *stances* in *La Thébaïde* v. 1 must be an undoubted candidate for consideration as a lyrical pause from the surrounding action. But Antigone's monologue is certainly not a lyrical pause. For on close inspection the speech turns out to be a piece of deliberative oratory closely related to the dramatic action as a whole.

The rhetorical task which Antigone has to perform is to persuade herself for or against suicide. She has to determine what her action is to be and she has to act quickly:

> A quoi te résous-tu, princesse infortunée?
> Ta mère vient de mourir dans tes bras;
>   Ne saurais-tu suivre ses pas,
> Et finir en mourant ta triste destinée?
> A de nouveaux malheurs te veux-tu réserver?
> Tes frères sont aux mains, rien ne les peut sauver
>   De leurs cruelles armes.
> Leur exemple t'anime à te percer le flanc;
>   Et toi seule verses des larmes,
>   Tous les autres versent du sang.
>
> Quelle est de mes malheurs l'extrémité mortelle?
>   Où ma douleur doit-elle recourir?
>   Dois-je vivre? dois-je mourir?
> Un amant me retient, une mère m'appelle:
> Dans la nuit du tombeau je la vois qui m'attend;
> Ce que veut la raison, l'amour me le défend
>   Et m'en ôte l'envie.
> Que vois-je de sujets d'abandonner le jour!
>   Mais, hélas! qu'on tient à la vie,
>   Quand on tient si fort à l'amour!

[20] It will be evident from my comments so far that the definition of the monologue is a thorny problem. One approach might be to take the cue from Racine's stage direction 'seul(e)', but this would discount, for instance, what critics would generally agree to be monologues in *Mithridate* III. 4, III. 6, and IV. 5. Although Mithridate is the only named character in these scenes, he is not alone.

Oui, tu retiens, Amour, mon âme fugitive;
  Je reconnais la voix de mon vainqueur:
    L'espérance est morte en mon cœur,
Et cependant tu vis, et tu veux que je vive;
Tu dis que mon amant me suivrait au tombeau,
Que je dois de mes jours conserver le flambeau
    Pour sauver ce que j'aime.
Hémon, vois le pouvoir que l'amour a sur moi:
    Je ne vivrais pas pour moi-même,
    Et je veux bien vivre pour toi.

Si jamais tu doutas de ma flamme fidèle...
Mais voici du combat la funeste nouvelle.
                (*La Thébaïde* 1203–34)

It is a measure of the non-lyrical quality of this monologue that it can readily be analysed according to the conventions of persuasive oratory. The question is identified immediately: 'A quoi te résous-tu?' (1203). This later becomes more specific: 'Dois-je vivre? dois-je mourir?' (1215). It is noteworthy that she begins by addressing her oratory to herself as if she were a different person, before changing at 1213 to the first person.

After the first introductory line, which announces the question to be decided and serves as a brief *exordium*, the monologue has an unusual *dispositio*. Instead of presenting a *narratio* followed by a more substantial *confirmatio*, Antigone proceeds by considering elements of *narratio*, each followed by its own relevant *confirmatio*. Two facts are introduced, both of which are important pieces of news for the audience. The first is that her mother has just committed suicide (1204). Antigone uses *inductio* to conclude from this that she should do likewise (1205–6) and exploits the *locus consequentium* to conjure up briefly the wretched future which would await her if she were to remain alive (1207). The second fact is that her brothers are at this moment fighting (1208–9). Again Antigone uses *inductio* to conclude that she should commit suicide (1210). This is developed by a brief exploitation of the *locus generis* (1211–12):

        Et toi seule verses des larmes,
        Tous les autres versent du sang.

By considering the *genus* to which she belongs (mother and brothers), she realizes that she is the odd one out. These lines are expressed in the form of an enthymeme. The conclusion is taken for granted: namely that she too should be shedding blood.

If Antigone were arguing determinedly for one course as opposed to another, what would follow would be a refutation of the rejected course. But she is arguing for two conflicting courses with the aim of adopting whichever seems to have been more persuasively promoted. So the second stanza introduces the fact of her love for Hémon (1216) which her argument in the first stanza had neglected. Antigone does not proceed to argue. Rather she amplifies the dilemma contained in these contradictory circumstances. Hence she exploits the *locus repugnantium* to paint a picture of love and reason pulling in opposite directions. By evoking the irresistibility of love against all the claims of reason, Antigone paves the way to the next stage, in which she will put the case for remaining alive for Hémon. In doing this she is appealing to her own sense of pity, and indirectly, of course, to that of the audience.

With pity thus aroused for her predicament, she can put the case for living and make it seem acceptable even though it is a weaker case. For she makes just one point, based on the *locus consequentium* (1227–9):

> Tu dis que mon amant me suivrait au tombeau,
> Que je dois de mes jours conserver le flambeau
> Pour sauver ce que j'aime.

Convinced by this enthymeme, Antigone expresses, in a sort of *peroratio*, the result of her persuasion. She has decided not to commit suicide; instead she will remain alive, but not for her own sake, only for that of Hémon (1230–2). This final qualification is an attempt to do some justice to the claims that she has made for her suicide. For she has not been able entirely to dismiss these.

The first line of another stanza follows this (1233), but it is left as an incomplete sentence because of the arrival of Olympe. In rhetorical terms this line is redundant. Antigone completes her rhetorical task when she reaches a decision on the question under discussion. The function of the extra line seems to be to avoid the charge of *invraisemblance* that could be levelled against a dramatist who has new characters coming on stage at exactly the right moment.

How does the audience react to Antigone's oratory? The spectators can identify and weigh the arguments. They can also, and perhaps simultaneously, be carried along by her persuasion, putting themselves in the position of her notional addressee. Above all, the spectators are interested in the movement of her speech and in the way she seems to be responding to her own arguments. They want to know whether or not she is going to die. Indirectly Antigone's rhetoric generates pity and fear in the audience.

Nor is the dramatic interest of the monologue at an end when the decision to stay alive has been taken. The arguments have to be remembered later in the act when Racine will exploit them for a specific dramatic effect. At the end of v. 3 Antigone leaves the stage without telling Créon if she will accept the throne. Equipped with the knowledge of her earlier arguments, the attentive audience realizes that, now that Hémon is dead, Antigone will conclude that she has nothing to live for and will die too. Créon, who does not have the privilege of having witnessed her earlier debate (v. 1), cannot know this and believes that it is only a matter of time before he can persuade her to accept his point of view and marry him (v. 4). This scene of dramatic irony functions only in so far as the audience remembers the precise nature of Antigone's argument in her monologue.

In drawing up arguments for one course of action and then for another, Antigone makes of the monologue a piece of persuasion. Instead of hearing the rhetoric used by one character against another, as happens most of the time, the audience hears the rhetoric used by Antigone against herself.

This is very different from the monologue, also in *stances*, in Pierre Corneille's Theban play *Œdipe*, of 1659. In III. 1, a character of Corneille's invention, Dircé, daughter of Laïus and Jocaste, delivers a fifty-line monologue (779–828), a monologue of exceptional length for Corneille's dramatic writing at this date. In the preceding act Dircé arrives at the conclusion that she must be the original cause of Laïus's murder (II. 3) and that she must therefore die in order to fulfil the oracle and rid Thebes of the plague. Even though she was hoping to marry Thésée, and despite Thésée's own suicide threats (II. 4), she intends to die. So much has been decided by the end of Act II. In the monologue which opens Act III she expresses no further doubts about this course of action. There is no judicial oratory, no self-accusation. Her speech is a statement of her intention to die and a poetic elaboration of the theme of the sacrifice of love for personal glory. The first two stanzas are addressed to her thirst for glory and invite the audience to consider the whole speech as a lyrical interlude:

> . . . souffre qu'en ce triste et favorable jour,
> Avant que te donner ma vie,
> Je donne un soupir à l'amour.
>
> (*Œdipe* 786–8)

The third stanza paints a generalized picture of her glory at odds with love, an exploitation of the *locus repugnantium*. Then the final two stanzas are addressed to Thésée in his absence, assuring him that for all her intention to die her love remains strong. If this is oratory at all, it is demonstrative oratory, painting a portrait of two opposing feelings. But it is not even demonstrative oratory in the usual sense of a speech of praise or blame. And certainly it is not judicial or deliberative oratory. For there is no attempt at persuasion. The monologue is best seen as a poetic pause in which a character engages in an elegiac reflection on her unfortunate situation. This is the way in which Corneille here seeks to appeal to the audience's sense of pity.

Critics have often assumed that Racine conceives his monologues in the same way. But the example of Antigone's *stances* suggests that Racine engages the pity of the audience by showing the character in the throes of self-persuasion rather than lamentation. Analysis of another Racinian monologue, which has been explicitly called 'lyrical',[21] will reinforce this view of self-persuasion as an important feature.

Far from being a moment of dramatic stasis like the *stances* of Dircé in *Œdipe*, the monologue of Antiochus in *Bérénice* I. 2 (19–50) is an act of persuasion, reminiscent, in its *dispositio*, of a miniature classical oration. It has an *exordium* (19–22), a *narratio* (23–6), a *confirmatio* (27–34), a *refutatio* (35–47), and a *peroratio* (48–50):

> Eh bien, Antiochus, es-tu toujours le même?   (19)
> Pourrai-je, sans trembler, lui dire: 'Je vous aime?'
> Mais quoi? déjà je tremble, et mon cœur agité
> Craint autant ce moment que je l'ai souhaité.

[21] Pocock, *Corneille and Racine*, 198.

Bérénice autrefois m'ôta toute espérance; (23)
Elle m'imposa même un éternel silence.
Je me suis tu cinq ans, et jusques à ce jour,
D'un voile d'amitié j'ai couvert mon amour.
Dois-je croire qu'au rang où Titus la destine (27)
Elle m'écoute mieux que dans la Palestine?
Il l'épouse. Ai-je donc attendu ce moment
Pour me venir encor déclarer son amant?
Quel fruit me reviendra d'un aveu téméraire?
Ah! puisqu'il faut partir, partons sans lui déplaire.
Retirons-nous, sortons, et sans nous découvrir,
Allons loin de ses yeux l'oublier, ou mourir.
Hé quoi? souffrir toujours un tourment qu'elle ignore? (35)
Toujours verser des pleurs qu'il faut que je dévore?
Quoi? même en la perdant redouter son courroux?
Belle reine, et pourquoi vous offenseriez-vous?
Viens-je vous demander que vous quittiez l'empire?
Que vous m'aimiez? Hélas! je ne viens que vous dire
Qu'après m'être longtemps flatté que mon rival
Trouverait à ses vœux quelque obstacle fatal,
Aujourd'hui qu'il peut tout, que votre hymen s'avance,
Exemple infortuné d'une longue constance,
Après cinq ans d'amour et d'espoir superflus,
Je pars, fidèle encor, quand je n'espère plus.
Au lieu de s'offenser, elle pourra me plaindre.
Quoi qu'il en soit, parlons: c'est assez nous contraindre. (48)
Et que peut craindre, hélas! un amant sans espoir
Qui peut bien se résoudre à ne la jamais voir?

It is clear from the first line that Antiochus, like Antigone, is both the orator and his own immediate audience. For he addresses himself as 'tu', though thereafter the persuader and the listener merge into the same 'je', as also happens in the case of Antigone.

His subject is the question as to whether or not, before leaving, he should tell Bérénice that he has continued to love her for the previous five years. It is a subject whose arguments allow Racine to convey important expository information to the audience. But it is not simply an expository monologue. For the action of Antiochus as orator addressing himself is of much interest in its own right. The audience wants to know for which of the two alternatives the orator in Antiochus will make a case, and whether or not the listener in him will be persuaded by the case put forward.

In the *exordium* the orator should normally win his hearer's goodwill and make him tractable. In attempting to achieve the first of these two aims Antiochus has a peculiar advantage. He knows his listener intimately. The mention of his paradoxical hoping and fearing is a way of saying that he will be honest with himself. Tractability, or *docilité*, according to Le Gras, needs a good 'sommaire de la cause'.[22] This Antiochus supplies in line 20.

The *narratio*, though not always necessary in deliberative oratory, here serves to convey some expository material to the audience. Whilst this is indeed expository, it is far from being divorced from its rhetorical context. It is there 'pour éclaircir quelque particularité... pour expliquer quelque raison importante' (Le Gras, *La Réthorique française*, 113). If the issue is the possibility of Antiochus's declaring his love to Bérénice, an event of the utmost importance to be taken into consideration is Bérénice's former rejection of his love and her establishment of a purely friendly relationship between them.

There follows the *confirmatio*, where the arguments of the speaker are presented, and after that the *refutatio*, where the arguments for the opposite cause are reviewed and, traditionally, rejected. This speech, however, follows an unusual course, unusual, that is, for a classical oration, not unusual for a dramatic monologue. The persuader had started in the *exordium* by implying that he was inclining towards not declaring his love (because of fear). The *narratio* supports this attitude with reference to the significant past event, and the *confirmatio* leads to the firm conclusion that Bérénice should not be told of Antiochus's continuing love. Material is drawn from three *loci* to support this view: *comparatio maiorum* (Bérénice will be less likely to listen to him now as a Roman empress-to-be than before as queen), *adiuncta* (with the wedding imminent, this is the wrong moment to speak to Bérénice), and *effecta* (there can be no fruitful outcome). The *refutatio*, however, does not so much dismiss the objections that might be made to this case as actually espouse them and argue eloquently for them, so that the *peroratio*, such as it is, exhorts in the opposite direction from the *confirmatio*. The listener in Antio-

---

[22] *La Réthorique* [*sic*] *française* (Paris, 1671), 102.

chus suddenly gets the better of the persuader and so changes the course of the persuasion. The objections raised are also drawn from three *loci*: *consequentia* (not declaring love would leave Antiochus suffering in silence, an argument which also draws upon *affectus* as Antiochus appeals to his own self-pity), *dissimilitudo* (Antiochus distinguishes the projected declaration from a request that his love be returned), and *definitio* (he defines specifically the content of his projected address to Bérénice). The *peroratio* summarizes the thrust of these arguments and concludes in favour of a meeting with the queen.

It is an unquestioned assumption throughout this speech that Bérénice will certainly marry Titus. By allowing a character to accept this assumption as the basis for a series of arguments, Racine manages to persuade his audience to accept it too. In this way he occasions greater surprise when, at the beginning of Act II, the assumption is revealed to be false.

By 1670 the expository monologue was even more unfashionable than the monologue *tout court*. Yet by creating an act of persuasion in which the expository material finds an apparently natural place, Racine succeeds in conveying necessary information to the spectators while also attracting their attention more generally to the persuasive activities of his characters.

The expository monologue delivered by the eponymous hero of Rotrou's *Hercule mourant* (1634) shows how different monologues earlier in the century could be from those of Racine (I. 1). For all its length, this sixty-line speech conveys relatively little information to the audience other than the fact that Hercule is an exceptional hero whose one weakness is his love for Iole, which remains unsatisfied. The information about Iole emerges only in lines 53–60, which means that most of the speech is an elaboration of Hercule's heroism. It is clearly not a speech of self-persuasion. It begins rather as a prayer addressed to Jupiter and it seems momentarily that this demonstrative speech in praise of Hercule's deeds might become a deliberative speech persuading Jupiter to allow Hercule into heaven. Such deliberative potential, however, remains unfulfilled. For it is with a tone of defiance that Hercule sings his own praises before, oddly (given his defiance and the address to Jupiter), admitting his weakness for Iole. Poetic elaboration this speech certainly is, though less so than the speech in Seneca's *Hercules Oetaeus* on which it is based.[23] Yet the laudatory lines and the personal revelation sit uneasily together. Rotrou, unlike Racine and Corneille in the examples discussed above, has not provided a plausible addressee for Hercule's rhetoric. His speech is poetic and static rather than persuasive and dynamic.

Another Racinian monologue has lent support to the traditional view of Racine's use of the form. That is Atalide's speech in *Bajazet* v. 1. For M. M. McGowan, this is a scene 'which contributes nothing to the action, but which allows the free flow of emotion'.[24] Of the last act of *Bajazet* P. France writes that 'the first scene is a monologue. As such it lacks the interest of conflicting characters'.[25] It is true that Atalide's monologue differs from those of Antigone and Antiochus in that she is not attempting to persuade herself to adopt or to reject a course of action. Indeed the speech opens and closes with lines whose purpose is not persuasive at all, but which aim to lend verbal support to two instances of physical action. Those actions are Atalide's desperate search for the lost and incriminating letter, and the arrival of her captor, Roxane. The speech is composed largely of a *narratio* as she recalls the events which led to her losing Bajazet's letter. This narrative account, however, is framed as a criticism first of Atalide herself (1431), then of heaven (1432–5), and finally of Roxane's female servants (1443–5). This judicial aspect is not dominant, but it serves the important function of making the speech both plausible and forceful. The judicial connotations of the speech allow Racine to focus Atalide's account in a way in which, for instance, Rotrou fails to do for Hercule's list of deeds. Atalide's monologue also serves to prepare the audience for the more thoroughgoing act of self-accusation with which Atalide will close the play and end her life.

Rhetorical analysis of the monologues of Antigone, Antiochus, and Atalide suggests that these speeches, though often used to exemplify the view of Racine's monologues as lyrical pauses from the main course of the dramatic action, are in fact integral to the

---

[23] Rotrou's adaptation of this speech is based on *Hercules Oetaeus* 1–15, 42–78. He omits a long catalogue of Hercule's works. See the edn. of *Hercule mourant* by D. A. Watts (Exeter, 1971), 77.

[24] *Bajazet*, ed. M. M. McGowan (London, 1968), 135.

[25] *Racine's Rhetoric* (Oxford, 1965), 104.

action and function dramatically in a similar way to scenes of dialogue. Racine's monologues are persuasive actions and the outcome of the persuasion is, or should be, of vital importance to the audience. Will Antigone commit suicide? Will Antiochus reveal his continuing love to Bérénice? Whom will Atalide ultimately blame for the possible demise of Bajazet and how will she act on her judgement? These types of question keep the audience interested in the acts of self-persuasion of Racine's soliloquizing characters. Yet the audience can ask no such questions during the monologues of Dircé and Hercule, which demand appreciation along more traditional lines as moments of lyricism and mood-painting.

11. DELIBERATIVE AND JUDICIAL ORATORY IN RACINE'S MONOLOGUES

Not all critics, it must be admitted, have described Racine's monologues as simply lyrical effusions. Le Bidois recognizes that such monologues would not be as dramatic as Racine's clearly are:

> Pour être vraiment dramatique, le monologue doit offrir de certains caractères. Il est évident qu'il ne servirait pas à l'action s'il n'était qu'une doublure des confidences ordinaires, ou s'il se réduisait à une pure effusion lyrique ... un bon monologue doit être au fond un dialogue débordant de vie et ... ce moment consacré en apparence à la pure réflexion est en réalité un haut période de l'action.[26]

Le Bidois's attempt to identify the dramatic in Racine's monologues leads him to suggest that the action in a monologue is the character's struggle to arrive at a decision.[27] This approach has induced some to see monologues as deliberative speeches[28] and the phrase 'monologue de délibération' has been adopted.[29] The *stances* of Antigone and the monologue of Antiochus are both examples of deliberative monologues.

With its judicial overtones, however, the example of Atalide's monologue at the beginning of Act V of *Bajazet* should alert critics to the fact that not all monologues in which persuasion

---

[26] *De l'action dans la tragédie de Racine* (Paris, 1900), 233.

[27] He also says that, while Corneille's characters do reach a decision, Racine's fail to do so (ibid. 233–5).

[28] e.g. Scherer, *La Dramaturgie classique*, 248–51.

[29] J. Morel, 'Rhétorique et tragédie au XVIIᵉ siècle', *DSS* 80–1 (1968), 101.

takes place are instances of deliberative oratory. While some
commentators have perceived the persuasive nature of the action
in some of Racine's monologues, the kind of oratory involved has
not always been accurately identified. Careful scrutiny of the kind
of oratory contained in monologues promotes a better understanding of how these speeches work in their dramatic context
and in the theatre.

The monologue of Hermione which begins the last act of
Andromaque is a case in point. Hermione has already dispatched
Oreste to murder Pyrrhus (IV. 3) and has had her desire for the
king's death confirmed by her subsequent meeting with him (IV.
5), in which Pyrrhus failed to show even the slightest understanding of her rejected love. She is now alone, awaiting the outcome of
Oreste's mission (1393–1429):

> Où suis-je? Qu'ai-je fait? Que dois-je faire encore?   (1393)
> Quel transport me saisit? Quel chagrin me dévore?
> Errante et sans dessein je cours dans ce palais.
> Ah! ne puis-je savoir si j'aime ou si je hais?
> Le cruel! de quel œil il m'a congédiée!   (1397)
> Sans pitié, sans douleur au moins étudiée!
> L'ai-je vu se troubler et me plaindre un moment?
> En ai-je pu tirer un seul gémissement?
> Muet à mes soupirs, tranquille à mes alarmes,
> Semblait-il seulement qu'il eût part à mes larmes?
> Et je le plains encore! Et pour comble d'ennui,   (1403)
> Mon cœur, mon lâche cœur s'intéresse pour lui!
> Je tremble au seul penser du coup qui le menace!
> Et prête à me venger, je lui fais déjà grâce!
> Non, ne révoquons point l'arrêt de mon courroux: (1407)
> Qu'il périsse! aussi bien il ne vit plus pour nous.
> Le perfide triomphe et se rit de ma rage:
> Il pense voir en pleurs dissiper cet orage;
> Il croit que toujours faible et d'un cœur incertain,
> Je parerai d'un bras les coups de l'autre main.
> Il juge encor de moi par mes bontés passées.
> Mais plutôt le perfide a bien d'autres pensées:
> Triomphant dans le temple, il ne s'informe pas
> Si l'on souhaite ailleurs sa vie ou son trépas.
> Il me laisse, l'ingrat, cet embarras funeste.
> Non, non, encore un coup, laissons agir Oreste.
> Qu'il meure, puisqu'enfin il a dû le prévoir,

Et puisqu'il m'a forcée enfin à le vouloir . . .
A le vouloir? Hé quoi? c'est donc moi qui l'ordonne?   (1421)
Sa mort sera l'effet de l'amour d'Hermione?
Ce prince, dont mon cœur se faisait autrefois
Avec tant de plaisir redire les exploits,
A qui même en secret je m'étais destinée
Avant qu'on eût conclu ce fatal hyménée,
Je n'ai donc traversé tant de mers, tant d'États,
Que pour venir si loin préparer son trépas?
L'assassiner? le perdre? Ah! devant qu'il expire . . .

Jean Cousin has no doubt that the second hemistich 'Que dois-je faire encore?' (1393) signals a deliberative speech.[30] Morel evidently agrees, examining this speech in his paragraph on deliberative monologues.[31] Barnwell, on the other hand, seizes on the rhetorical question 'Qu'ai-je fait?' (1393) to explore the judicial characteristics of the speech,[32] and concludes that 'far from being deliberative, Hermione's soliloquy and succeeding scenes, while bearing many of the marks of judicial rhetoric, are a form of dramatic action in which, thanks to the imperious impulses of her passion, she leaps to conclusions on incomplete evidence and without reasoned argument' (p. 201).

Barnwell's description of the speech is very helpful in pointing out that it is not simply a deliberative or judicial speech. Normally the conclusions of most deliberative or judicial speeches in tragedies, whether monologues or not, have some effect on the development of the dramatic action as a whole. Antigone's deliberative speech leads to her taking her own life. Hermione's speech, however, can have no such effect on the action of the play. For although she seems to be judging Pyrrhus, she has really judged him previously and found him guilty. And although she appears to be deciding how to act on this judgement, she has in fact decided previously and sent Oreste to mete out punishment on Pyrrhus. When she utters her monologue, it is too late to recall Oreste. Hermione's speech is neither deliberative nor judicial in the usual way.

What then is the point of her speech? First, it fulfils the function

---

[30] 'Rhétorique latine et classicisme français', *Revue des cours et conférences*, 1932–3: article iv. 'Rhétorique et tragédie; suite', 166.
[31] 'Rhétorique et tragédie', 101–2.
[32] *The Tragic Drama of Corneille and Racine* (Oxford, 1982), 195–201.

of informing the audience of a fact necessary for the appreciation of Hermione's imminent meeting with Oreste: namely that she is not at all certain that she wants to see Pyrrhus die. A framework of deliberative and judicial elements in which this information is conveyed to the audience provides a means of creating persuasive action out of dramatic necessity.

Secondly, the speech shows a character who had been an impeccable orator in persuading Oreste to do as she thought she wanted in IV. 3, now using rhetoric inappropriately and incompetently. This use of rhetoric suggests a character losing control of herself and so secures sympathy for Hermione. The rhetoric is inappropriate because the issues raised by her initial questions (What have I done? What am I going to do?) have already been dealt with in the previous act. Though she does not acknowledge the fact, further discussion can be of no consequence. It is incompetent rhetoric for two reasons. On the one hand, she does not deal with the different issues in sequential order, but rather in fits and starts. If the terminology of *dispositio* were applied to the speech, the analysis would run as follows: *exordium* (1393–6), *narratio* (1397–402), followed unusually and prematurely by a *refutatio* (1403–6), *confirmatio* (1407–20), in which she adduces the *probatio inartificialis* (which she can only have imagined) of Pyrrhus's present state of mind, and finally *refutatio* (1421–9). On the other hand, a symptom of this fitful *dispositio* is Hermione's inability to bring together into one argument the conflicting facts of Pyrrhus's guilt and her continuing love for him.

Hermione makes improper use of the deliberative and judicial framework, and in this way temporary rhetorical incompetence becomes a tool with which the dramatist can arouse pity for the orator he is representing. By putting Hermione in a rhetorical situation but disrupting the expected pattern, Racine shows a character in emotional turmoil.

Another monologue which combines deliberative and judicial oratory is that of Titus in *Bérénice* IV. 4. Titus has been unable, despite the encouragement of his adviser Paulin, to summon up enough courage to approach Bérénice and ask her to leave Rome. Barnwell suggests that Titus's monologue is a judicial speech in which the emperor passes judgement on his own conduct.[33] In

---

[33] Ibid. 205.

fact the speech combines self-judgement with deliberation. Self-judgement leads Titus to consider the cruelty involved in explaining to Bérénice the need for separation (987–94). This results in deliberative oratory, making the case for allowing Bérénice to remain and become his queen. Two *loci* are exploited. First, *consequentia*: the consequence of trying to confront Bérénice would be an inability to explain such as he has experienced before (995–9). Then, *causae*: the main reason for making Bérénice depart is his own sense of public duty. If he were to forget this, there would be no reason for her to leave; for the public has not formally requested her to do so. Titus is not convinced by this argument. Indeed he had already dismissed it when it occurred in his earlier discussion with Paulin (II. 2). He then delivers a brief judgement on his own oratory, with a suggestion that he is blindly failing to take the appropriate circumstances into account:

> Titus, ouvre les yeux.
> Quel air respires-tu? N'es-tu pas dans ces lieux,
> Où la haine des rois avec le lait sucée,
> Par crainte, ou par amour, ne peut être effacée?
> (*Bérénice* 1013–16)

There follow arguments making the opposite case, in favour of speaking to Bérénice (1017–38). Titus is concluding when Bérénice bursts into the room, so allowing him to act immediately (1039–40):

> Ne tardons plus. Faisons ce que l'honneur exige.
> Rompons le seul lien...

So Titus, who has been unable to perform rhetorically in front of Bérénice, proves himself to be a perfectly competent orator when he is his own audience. His monologue is an act of persuasion in which judicial and deliberative rhetoric combine to urge the execution of a further specific act of persuasion.

The persuasive nature of this monologue is vital in revealing in Titus a basically determined man, an aspect of his character often forgotten in favour of his weakness and vacillation elsewhere. When alone, he reaches a decision which he starts immediately to put into effect.[34] Rhetorical analysis permits the critic to highlight

---

[34] This is evidence against Le Bidois's view of Racine's indecisive soliloquizing characters. See *De l'action*, 233–5.

the theatrically striking contrast between a thoughtful but determined Titus (when he is alone in IV. 4) and an indecisive Titus
(when he is faced with Bérénice in IV. 5).

In two other monologues deliberative and judicial elements are
powerfully combined; both occur towards the end of the fourth
act of their respective plays. In *Mithridate* IV. 5 the ageing king
takes stock of the evidence he has now collected against his wife-
to-be and his son, and attempts to reach a verdict. But although
Mithridate is here a judge, he is very much a deliberating judge,
looking for a course of action which will least inconvenience him
personally. The audience is interested in his argument precisely
because the decision is a difficult one and, moreover, a matter of
life or death. Can Mithridate sacrifice a son whose military skills
he sorely needs? Can he punish Monime whom he deeply loves? A
decision is prompted only by Arbate's announcement that Pharnace
and apparently Xipharès have rebelled and joined the Romans.
The act ends with threats against both sons (1445–6) and the
fiancée (1451–2).

Agamemnon is in a similar position to Mithridate in his monologue in *Iphigénie* IV. 7–9. Like Mithridate, Agamemnon has the
power to make a decision affecting the life of another character,
but, unlike Mithridate, Agamemnon manages to decide on a course
of action by the end of his monologue. The decision-making
process is made more interesting dramatically by the injection of a
judicial element. Agamemnon's decision is not now as straightforward as it had been earlier in the play. It is no longer simply a
question of balancing the sacrifice of his daughter against the loss
of political security. For Agamemnon's confrontation with Achille
in IV. 6 has provoked him to pass judgement on the young
warrior. A desire to punish Achille for his insolent threats is now a
force in Agamemnon's reasoning, and the decision reached bears
witness not only to Agamemnon's wish to save his daughter, but
also to his need to pass a verdict on the offensive behaviour of
Achille. Iphigénie will live, but Achille will not be allowed to
marry her (1450–6). In the case of Agamemnon, as in that of
Hermione, Titus, and Mithridate, the judicial and the deliberative
combine to make their options more complex and hence the
outcome of their debates more uncertain and more interesting for
the audience.

Judicial oratory can, for all that, be used by itself in monologues to powerful effect, as the speech of Axiane in *Alexandre* IV. 1 reveals. Wishing to have no involvement in any peace treaties, Axiane has sent Porus to fight against Alexandre (674), without, however, having told him unambiguously of her love for him. Rather she has suggested her love only cryptically:

> La victoire est à vous, si ce fameux vainqueur
> Ne se défend pas mieux contre vous que mon cœur.
>
> (*Alexandre* 675–6)

In Act III she has heard from Taxile, Porus's rival for her affections, that Porus has fled (747–52). Alone at the beginning of Act IV, Axiane considers her part in Porus's downfall and possible death (957–1004):

> N'entendrons-nous jamais que des cris de victoire,
> Qui de mes ennemis me reprochent la gloire?
> Et ne pourrai-je au moins, en de si grands malheurs,
> M'entretenir moi seule avecque mes douleurs?
> D'un odieux amant sans cesse poursuivie,   (961)
> On prétend malgré moi m'attacher à la vie:
> On m'observe, on me suit. Mais, Porus, ne crois pas
> Qu'on me puisse empêcher de courir sur tes pas.
> Sans doute à nos malheurs ton cœur n'a pu survivre.
> En vain tant de soldats s'arment pour te poursuivre:
> On te découvrirait au bruit de tes efforts,
> Et s'il te faut chercher, ce n'est qu'entre les morts.
> Hélas! en me quittant ton ardeur redoublée   (969)
> Semblait prévoir les maux dont je suis accablée,
> Lorsque tes yeux, aux miens découvrant ta langueur,
> Me demandaient quel rang tu tenais dans mon cœur,
> Que sans t'inquiéter du succès de tes armes,
> Le soin de ton amour te causait tant d'alarmes.
> Et pourquoi te cachais-je avec tant de détours
> Un secret si fatal au repos de tes jours?   (975)
> Combien de fois, tes yeux forçant ma résistance,
> Mon cœur s'est-il vu près de rompre le silence!
> Combien de fois, sensible à tes ardents désirs,
> M'est-il, en ta présence, échappé des soupirs!
> Mais je voulais encor douter de ta victoire:
> J'expliquais mes soupirs en faveur de la gloire,
> Je croyais n'aimer qu'elle. Ah! pardonne, grand roi,
> Je sens bien aujourd'hui que je n'aimais que toi.
> J'avouerai que la gloire eut sur moi quelque empire;

Je te l'ai dit cent fois. Mais je devais te dire
Que toi seul en effet m'engageas sous ses lois.
J'appris à la connaître en voyant tes exploits,
Et de quelque beau feu qu'elle m'eût enflammée,
En un autre que toi je l'aurais moins aimée.
Mais que sert de pousser des soupirs superflus   (991)
Qui se perdent en l'air et que tu n'entends plus?
Il est temps que mon âme, au tombeau descendue,
Te jure une amitié si longtemps attendue;
Il est temps que mon cœur, pour gage de sa foi,
Montre qu'il n'a pu vivre un moment après toi.
Aussi bien, penses-tu que je voulusse vivre   (997)
Sous les lois d'un vainqueur à qui ta mort nous livre?
Je sais qu'il se dispose à me venir parler,
Qu'en me rendant mon sceptre il veut me consoler.
Il croit peut-être, il croit que ma haine étouffée
A sa fausse douceur servira de trophée.
Qu'il vienne. Il me verra, toujours digne de toi,   (1003)
Mourir en reine, ainsi que tu mourus en roi.

This monologue has been criticized by B. Weinberg on the grounds that it is useless to the plot: 'The reader wonders about the usefulness of the monologue; for the sentiments expressed are already well known to him, and since Axiane will not ultimately die, her resolution establishes no probability. There is no change in our attitude towards her.'[35] This criticism, however, seems not to attend to the monologue's theatrical qualities. Axiane's monologue is not as dramatically useless as Weinberg suggests. First, Axiane's feelings are not already well-known. This is the first time that the audience hears unequivocally of her love for Porus. Secondly, the belief which Axiane encourages, namely that Porus is probably dead, contributes to the surprise of the audience when, at the end of the act, his reappearance is announced. Thirdly, her resolution to die, to which the monologue gives rise, casts an ironic shadow over the ensuing scene, in which Alexandre tries to persuade her to accept Taxile. And finally the monologue is a persuasive action which interests the audience at the time of its delivery. As a piece of judicial oratory in which Axiane accuses herself of having behaved short-sightedly towards Porus and condemns herself to follow him in death, its effect on the audience is

---

[35] *The Art of Jean Racine* (Chicago, 1963), 57.

to arouse curiosity as to how she will proceed in her accusation, to prompt feelings of pity for Axiane, and to promote apprehension as to her fate. For at this moment the audience has no reason to suppose that Axiane will not commit suicide after seeing Alexandre.

A brief analysis reveals how Axiane draws on the resources of *inventio* and *dispositio* to conduct her case. The first four lines constitute an *exordium*, but a dramatic rather than a rhetorical one. These lines provide the dramatic excuse for the monologue. The rest of the speech is framed as an address to the supposedly deceased Porus. Axiane accuses herself of having neglected Porus's love and pleads with him to forgive her. Her speech has an *exordium* (961–8), in which she secures the attention of her addressee and of the theatre audience by describing her present plight, and she captures Porus's goodwill by expressing sympathy with him. A *narratio* follows (969–74), in which she relates the occasions of her neglect of Porus's affection. Then comes a *confirmatio* (975–90), in which she explains this neglect as self-deceit: she thought her love had been only for Porus the imminent victor, when all along it had been for Porus the man. Exploitation of the *locus dissimilitudinis* allows her to express her disillusionment by contrasting love of *gloire* with love of man (975–90). While accusing herself, Axiane is also attempting to *excuse* herself and restore her good image in Porus's eyes. The *peroratio* depends particularly upon the exploitation of *mores* and *affectus*. Her resolution to die (991–6) is offered as a token of her sincerity, and her dismissal of Alexandre (997–1003) appeals to Porus's hatred of his enemy while, at the same time, aligning Axiane with Porus, an alignment which is reinforced by the culminating exploitation of the *locus similitudinis* (1003–4).

Axiane's monologue is a piece of special pleading veiled as a confession, self-defence veiled as self-accusation. Axiane's aim is to arouse pity for herself in her notional addressee, the shade of Porus. No less than Hermione in *Andromaque* v. 1, but by using a different rhetorical framework, Axiane also arouses the pity of the audience.

Indeed monologues based partly or wholly on a judicial situation seem particularly appropriate for the arousal of pity. For Racine employs them at, or towards, the end of three of his tragedies: for Créon in *La Thébaïde* v. 6, for Oreste in *Andromaque* v. 4–5, and for Atalide in *Bajazet* v. 12.

In the last scene of *La Thébaïde* Créon delivers a long monologue in which he decides to follow Antigone, who has escaped his
advances by committing suicide. His speech is an accusation of
himself and an attempt to persuade the gods to punish him for his
crimes. His main persuasive strategy is *mores*. Preceded by a
narratio of Antigone's escape (1479–92), the judicial speech
proper has an *exordium* (1495–8) and a *confirmatio* with an
element of *narratio* (1499–1512). Then, dramatically, just as the
peroratio is about to start ('Arrêtez...' (1513)), Créon's persuasion appears to be successful as he claims to sense the onset
of divine vengeance:

> La foudre va tomber, la terre est entr'ouverte,
> Je ressens à la fois mille tourments divers,
> Et je m'en vais chercher du repos aux enfers.
>   (*La Thébaïde* 1514–16)

At this point Créon falls, mad or dead,[36] into the arms of the
guards, his persuasion accomplished successfully, it might seem.

Oreste's last speeches are also preoccupied with the cruelty of
the woman he loves, with the vengeance of heaven, and with a
description of his bizarre vision. Yet, while Créon's last speech is
forgotten territory in the Racinian corpus, Oreste's is one of the
most sought-after landmarks: 'Un mot de Mme de Staël résume
bien la question: "Les grands acteurs se sont presque toujours
essayés dans les fureurs d'Oreste". Et non seulement les grands. La
remarque de Mme de Staël a en particulier le mérite de bien fixer
les limites de cette attirance: les *fureurs* d'Oreste beaucoup plus
que le rôle.'[37] As regards *inventio* and *dispositio*, there is no
substantial difference between the speech of Créon and those of
Oreste.[38] Racine seems to use the framework of Créon's speech as

---

[36] The text does not make it plain whether Créon dies or not. T. Cave clearly
believes that he does (*Recognitions* (Oxford, 1988), 327). B. Weinberg also assumes
that he dies, and thinks his death unconvincing (*Art*, 25). P. Yarrow assumes that
he simply goes mad or approaches madness (*Racine* (Oxford, 1978), 29). The hint
of physical action in lines 1493–4 and 1513 suggests that Créon tries to stab
himself. But the text leaves ambiguous the reason for Créon's fall into the arms of
the guards. Whatever is supposed to happen to him at the end of the play, it is
clear that he attributes it to the success of his judicial oratory directed against
himself to the gods.

[37] M. Descotes, *Les Grands Rôles du théâtre de Jean Racine* (Paris, 1957), 30.

[38] *Dispositio* in Oreste's speeches is analysed by France in *Racine's Rhetoric*,
227–8.

a foundation for those of Oreste. But the differences that he introduces are all-important in accounting for the particular favour
with which posterity has received Oreste's last words. To be sure,
Oreste's description of his vision is longer, more detailed, and
offers an actor more scope for the portrayal of various degrees of
fear and horror:

> Mais quelle épaisse nuit tout à coup m'environne?
> De quel côté sortir? D'où vient que je frissonne?
> Quelle horreur me saisit! Grâce au ciel j'entrevoi...
> Dieux! quels ruisseaux de sang coulent autour de moi!
> (Andromaque 1625–8)

The implied physical movement and trembling give Oreste's
speeches a more varied visual interest than that of Créon. Oreste's
address to the gods is also rather different from that of Créon. The
latter demands punishment which both he and the audience know
he deserves. With Oreste, however, the invocation of the gods is
bitterly ironic. He has blamed them throughout the play for all his
misfortunes. If Oreste has committed a crime, he sees it as the
fault of the gods. Their punishment of him is presented as very
unjust. Oreste's address to heaven, then, is dramatically richer
than that of Créon, largely because Oreste does not accept the
judicial case against himself.

Another feature common to these two monologues is the use of
judicial oratory to convey recognition by a character of the horror
of what he has done. Indeed if the audience feels any sympathy for
Créon at all it must be owed entirely to this tragic act of recognition on his part. There is a similar hint of recognition in the
judicial elements of Hermione's monologue, though the full horror
of Pyrrhus's murder strikes her only after it has taken place and
then, ironically, she is not prepared to recognize her involvement.

It is perhaps in Atalide's speech in *Bajazet* v. 12 that monologue, judicial oratory, and recognition combine most successfully
to prompt feelings of pity in the audience. Coming after what has
been a very busy denouement, Atalide's monologue gives the audience time to take in what has happened and to focus on the plight
of the only surviving protagonist (Acomat excepted).

Atalide has just learnt of the deaths of Bajazet and Roxane and
of the imminent re-establishment by the sultan of the old order.
Acomat has expressed his intention to flee by sea and has offered

to take her with him. He hurries off, leaving her to decide what to do. The question in the mind of the audience must be: will Atalide flee with Acomat or not? And if not, what will she do? The audience, however, is presented not with a deliberative but with a judicial speech (*Bajazet* 1722–47):

> Enfin, c'en est donc fait; et par mes artifices,   (1722)
> Mes injustes soupçons, mes funestes caprices,
> Je suis donc arrivée au douloureux moment
> Où je vois par mon crime expirer mon amant!
> N'était-ce pas assez, cruelle destinée,   (1726)
> Qu'à lui survivre, hélas! je fusse condamnée?
> Et fallait-il encor que pour comble d'horreurs,
> Je ne puisse imputer sa mort qu'à mes fureurs?
> Oui, c'est moi, cher amant, qui t'arrache la vie: (1730)
> Roxane, ou le sultan, ne te l'ont point ravie;
> Moi seule, j'ai tissu le lien malheureux
> Dont tu viens d'éprouver les détestables nœuds.
> Et je puis, sans mourir, en souffrir la pensée,   (1734)
> Moi qui n'ai pu tantôt, de ta mort menacée,
> Retenir mes esprits prompts à m'abandonner?
> Ah! n'ai-je eu de l'amour que pour t'assassiner?
> Mais c'en est trop: il faut, par un prompt sacrifice,   (1738)
> Que ma fidèle main te venge et me punisse.
> Vous, de qui j'ai troublé la gloire et le repos,
> Héros qui deviez tous revivre en ce héros,
> Toi, mère malheureuse, et qui dès notre enfance
> Me confias son cœur dans une autre espérance,
> Infortuné vizir, amis désespérés,
> Roxane, venez tous, contre moi conjurés,
> Tourmenter à la fois une amante éperdue,
> Et prenez la vengeance enfin qui vous est due.

Though Zaïre is present, Atalide acknowledges her at no point during the speech, and, though the monologue is ostensibly directed to a variety of different addressees at different moments (destiny (1726), Bajazet (1730), royal ancestors (1741), Atalide's mother (1742), Acomat (1744), Bajazet's supporters (1744), Roxane (1745)), these apostrophes do not in fact indicate that Atalide's oratory is aimed at these addressees. They are rather part of the persuasive strategy which she uses on herself. Atalide's choice of judicial oratory suggests that she has leapt far ahead of Acomat's offer. For she knows that she will not flee with the vizier. What she needs to know is whether or not she can pass the death sentence on herself.

She begins with an *exordium* (1722–5), which introduces the accusation that she is going to pursue against herself, namely her part in bringing about the death of her lover. It is important to realize that in developing this judgement Atalide is not utterly vindictive towards herself. She will certainly claim that she deserves to die, but she will also claim that she cannot bear to live. In other words Atalide as speaker will try to appeal to Atalide as listener by presenting herself in a sympathetic light. This she does in the *exordium* by mentioning the pain which the outcome of events has inflicted on her ('douloureux moment'). This exploitation of *mores* prepares the path for further references to her awareness of present pain (1726–9, 1735).

Judicial speeches do not require a distinction between *narratio* and *confirmatio*. Nor does Atalide make such a distinction. These two aspects of her speech run in parallel from 1726 to 1737. In this part of her speech she draws on a number of *loci*, all of which point to her criminality first suggested in 1725. First, *comparatio minorum*: surviving Bajazet would be difficult; surviving him in the knowledge that she caused his death would be even harder (1726–9). This is followed by *species*: Atalide singles herself out from others who might be thought to be implicated in Bajazet's death, in such a way as to bring the onus of blame on to herself (1730–3). Next comes an exploitation of *definitio*, in which there is a narrative allusion to Atalide's revelatory faint (1734–7). By defining herself as the fainter, she points to the action which gave Roxane good ground for distrusting her and Bajazet. Atalide's final *locus* is *repugnantia*: 'Ah! n'ai-je eu de l'amour que pour t'assassiner?' (1737). She desperately contrasts her love with what she unquestioningly assumes to have been her murderous action.

Atalide's monologue is unlike most others and certainly unlike those of Roxane in III. 7 and IV. 4, where *confirmatio* and *refutatio* intertwine. Her monologue is unusual in that she argues unswervingly towards one decision. Her arguments and her vocabulary ('crime' (1725), 'assassiner' (1737)) make this plain. There is the suggestion of a *refutatio* at 1731: 'Roxane, ou le sultan, ne te l'ont point ravie [la vie]'. But it is always clear that

Atalide herself is never likely to accord any weight to this possible objection.

So when she begins her *peroratio* (1738–47), the audience is in no doubt about the decision that she will reach. She gives her verdict promptly and briefly (1738–9) before invoking all those whom she wishes to taste vengeance in her suicide. At this point she stabs herself.

Usually monologues interest the audience to some extent because there is uncertainty until a final decision has been reached (if indeed one is reached at all). Analysis of Atalide's final monologue suggests that there is no uncertainty as to the outcome of this instance of self-persuasion. How, then, does her oratory appeal to the audience? I would suggest that it does so on two levels. First, suspense is aroused by the presence of Zaïre throughout the speech. For although Atalide does not address her directly, there is always the possibility that Zaïre might interrupt her mistress and deflect her from her suicidal intention. This possibility must be felt particularly towards the end of the *peroratio*. In this respect the presence of Zaïre fulfils an important dramatic function. On a second level, the audience is made to pity Atalide as she persuades herself that she is guilty of Bajazet's murder and deserves her own death sentence. The audience might well be more inclined to blame Roxane for Bajazet's death and take pity on Atalide for her harsh verdict on herself. It is instructive to ask why Atalide is so harsh. She sees her uncontrollable lapse in her manœuvring between Roxane and Bajazet as the main factor in his downfall. That she condemns herself for such a lapse is evidence of the excessive trust she had put in rhetoric as a means of bringing about her happiness. The dramatist allows the audience to stand back from the events depicted and see that rhetoric is not a reliable means of achieving happiness. Atalide deserves pity for recognizing her part in Bajazet's demise. But she deserves as much pity for not recognizing that other characters and factors were at least as responsible. The enlightened audience pities the un-enlightened Atalide.

III. ACCOMPANIED MONOLOGUES: *PHÈDRE*, RACINE, AND PRADON

Not poetic interludes amid the surrounding dialogue, Racine's monologues are usually instances of deliberative and/or judicial oratory. They can be probed rhetorically from one further angle: do they vary depending upon whether a character is alone or accompanied?

In a monologue a character addresses his oratory either to himself or to a notional audience, which may be an absent character, a dead character, ancestors, or gods. The speech is a monologue precisely because the addressee is also the orator, or because the addressee is not there to reply. This is why a speech can still be called a monologue even if there is a second character present and listening, as long as this character plays no part in the rhetorical situation on which the monologue is based (that would be the beginning of dialogue). Hence Atalide's final speech delivered in the presence of her confidant is a monologue. So are Oreste's final speeches and that of Créon. And so is Agamemnon's monologue extending over three scenes in *Iphigénie* VI. 7–9, even though Eurybate is present in Scene 8 and guards are present in Scenes 8 and 9. A similar status might be claimed for Clytemnestre's tirade against Ériphile, delivered in the presence of only Aegine in *Iphigénie* V. 4. Furthermore, there are speeches in which a confidant who is present might be named, but in which the soliloquizing character is essentially addressing himself and does so at some length. Such are the speeches of Bérénice which close the first two acts of *Bérénice*, when the eponymous heroine persuades herself first that Titus is about to marry her, then that he is, at least, very much in love with her.

It would be wrong to think that the confidant, not being involved in the rhetorical situation of these accompanied monologues, is therefore useless from a dramatic perspective. I have suggested that Zaïre's presence at the end of *Bajazet* creates suspense: will she attempt to stop Atalide's imminent suicide? Similarly, the presence of Eurybate and the guards in Agamemnon's monologue adds visual impact to the movement of the speaker's argument. Just as Agamemnon seems to have resolved to go ahead with the sacrifice of his daughter and expresses his resolve by summoning Eurybate and other guards, other arguments present themselves and he leaves the men standing uncertainly while these arguments are weighed in the balance. His new resolve, to save Iphigénie, is marked by his request that Eurybate go and fetch Iphigénie and her mother. Bérénice's ability to delude herself about Titus's intentions is all the more remarkable when she does this in front of Phénice, whom, to all intents and purposes, she ignores, carried away by her delusion. It seems that Lapp's observation[39] that Racine uses monologues to reveal the solitary status of his protagonists is particularly convincing when it is related to instances of accompanied monologue. A character's loneliness is more striking when he or she speaks oblivious of the people around.

Lapp's observation is, however, even more convincing when related to a different type of accompanied monologue, a type which Racine uses in a number of plays, but most effectively in *Phèdre*. This is the use of monologue in the very midst of dialogue. It happens when a character suddenly ignores his interlocutor and addresses his oratory elsewhere, and suggests a degree of mental abstraction. This type of monologue is not to be confused with the more straightforward device of invocation or apostrophe occurring in the course of a dialogue,[40] nor with the occasional failure of a character to reply to a point made by an interlocutor.[41]

One example of what I shall call monologue-within-dialogue is Atalide's reply to Zaïre in *Bajazet* III. 1. Zaïre has informed her mistress of the apparent reconciliation between Bajazet and Roxane. The prospect of a marriage between them clearly shocks Atalide and this shock prompts Zaïre to ask if Atalide regrets having saved Bajazet's life by asking him to make amends with Roxane. Atalide replies:

> Non, non; il ne fera que ce qu'il a dû faire.
> Sentiments trop jaloux, c'est à vous de vous taire;   (818)
> Si Bajazet l'épouse, il suit mes volontés;
> Respectez ma vertu qui vous a surmontés;
> A ces nobles conseils ne mêlez point le vôtre,

---

[39] *Aspects*, 111.

[40] e.g. Agamemnon's reply to Arcas in *Iphigénie* I. 1 apostrophizes Iphigénie: 'Non, tu ne mourras point; je n'y puis consentir' (40).

[41] e.g. in *Bajazet* IV. 5 Roxane does not respond to Zatime's argument that Amurat is more to be feared than Bajazet (1283–95). Roxane is too obsessed by her jealousy and intent on vengeance.

Et loin de me le peindre entre les bras d'une autre,
Laissez-moi sans regret me le représenter
Au trône où mon amour l'a forcé de monter.
Oui, je me reconnais, je suis toujours la même.   (825)
Je voulais qu'il m'aimât, chère Zaïre: il m'aime;
Et du moins cet espoir me console aujourd'hui
Que je vais mourir digne et contente de lui.

The first line is a direct response to Zaïre. But lines 818–24 are addressed to her own feelings of jealousy, in other words to herself, and form a deliberative monologue as she persuades herself not to give way to jealousy. The last four lines continue her reply to Zaïre's question and show that her momentary self-persuasion has been successful. Atalide's loneliness, her need to depend entirely on her own resources when external support is removed, comes across clearly in her resort to monologue-within-dialogue.

The same sense of loss is conveyed in Monime's use of this technique in *Mithridate* v. 1, when she believes Xipharès, the object of her affections, to be dead. To Phœdime, who advises her to wait until she has had confirmation (1464–73), Monime replies that she is sure he is dead because the Romans have wanted his blood for so long (1474–81). Then, like Atalide, but at greater length, she veers into monologue (1482), delivering a judicial speech accusing herself of bringing about Xipharès's presumed death. Narration of her crimes gives way to her own death sentence, which in turn gives way to two invocations. First (1497–9)—and these are three lines of potential dialogue—she addresses the servants who prevent her from rushing off to administer her death sentence. Then (1500–8) she blames and throws away the diadem with which she has earlier tried in vain to strangle herself. No less than Atalide Monime arouses pity in the audience for her solitary plight, which is reinforced by the use of monologue-within-dialogue, as well as by the wilful and, it turns out inappropriate, self-accusation.

It is, however, with Phèdre that Racine's use of this technique achieves special effects. There are, of course, monologues of the standard type in *Phèdre*: Phèdre's deliberative address to Venus persuading the goddess to make Hippolyte love his stepmother (III. 2); Thésée's judicial speech against Hippolyte in which the son's death sentence is passed (IV. 3); Phèdre's ironic, because retrospective, deliberative monologue in which she persuades herself that she should not defend Hippolyte before Thésée (IV. 5—she has reached the same conclusion on impulse in the preceding scene); and finally Thésée's monologue in V. 4, not a persuasive speech, but an imaginative verbal representation of the mental steps which start to lead him to the discovery of the truth about Phèdre. But it is the use of monologue-within-dialogue in this play that is particularly striking. For Phèdre has recourse to it on three occasions.

The first and most interesting of these is her first appearance on stage when the technique is used to convey her extreme mental distress (I. 3). Her words, moreover, are reinforced by a visual effect, for Phèdre walks on stage looking physically weak and trembling (153–7). She sits down and gestures tiresomely at her carefully prepared dress and hair (158–61). To Œnone's comments criticizing her for a new lapse into indifference to the world around her (163–8) and encouraging her to be more positive (173–5), Phèdre makes no direct reply, but, instead, addresses first the Sun-god:

> Noble et brillant auteur d'une triste famille,
> Toi, dont ma mère osait se vanter d'être fille,
> Qui peut-être rougis du trouble où tu me vois,
> Soleil, je te viens voir pour la dernière fois!
>
> (*Phèdre* 169–72)

and then the gods in general (176–8):

> Dieux! que ne suis-je assise à l'ombre des forêts!
> Quand pourrai-je, au travers d'une noble poussière,
> Suivre de l'œil un char fuyant dans la carrière?

Aware that Phèdre is mentally astray, Œnone recalls her with the sharp question 'Quoi, Madame?' (179) and Phèdre's response articulates verbally her inability to focus intelligently on dialogue (179–81):

> Insensée, où suis-je? et qu'ai-je dit?
> Où laissé-je égarer mes vœux et mon esprit?
> Je l'ai perdu: les dieux m'en ont ravi l'usage.

In this scene Racine has found a specifically theatrical way of representing Phèdre's distress and madness. In addition to the visual effect, he uses the technique of monologue-within-dialogue that he had used in earlier plays, but he uses it in a new way. He interweaves, as he did not in the case of Atalide or Monime, the confidant's attempts at dialogue and the protagonist's persistent monologue, and thereby makes the solitude of the protagonist all the more forceful. And whereas Atalide's and Monime's monologues-within-dialogue had been persuasive speeches like most of Racine's monologues, Phèdre's utterances are simply an elaborated statement and an expression of a wish. Finally, that Phèdre has two speeches which are quite unrelated in thought intensifies the impression of her madness. In using this technique in a novel way Racine produces two short monologues which, ironically, suit the traditional description of all his monologues. For Phèdre's two monologues here do represent a lyrical pause from the dialogue which Œnone is attempting to provoke, and they are poetically elaborated statements which reveal the workings of a tormented soul. Yet these monologues are very much the exception to Racine's rule. The special effect which he achieves in this scene is suggested by a sonnet written in 1677 to attack Racine's play. The opening lines seem to describe Phèdre's first exchanges with Œnone:

> Dans un fauteuil doré, Phèdre tremblante et blême
> Dit des vers où d'abord personne n'entend rien.[42]

The suggestion is that Phèdre's words are so obscure that neither Œnone nor the audience can understand them. This may well have been intended to be a criticism of Racine, but in fact it shows how striking is his use of monologue-within-dialogue in this scene.

Phèdre's later uses of monologue-within-dialogue, when she confronts Hippolyte in II. 5 (especially 645−62)[43] and Œnone in IV. 6 (especially 1264−94), are formally more like Racine's earlier exploitations of the technique. The fact that Racine employs this technique three times for the same character points to his ability

---

[42] See R. Picard, *Nouveau Corpus Racinianum* (Paris, 1976), 96.

[43] It is true that she continues to address Hippolyte directly here, but she does so in a way which suggests loss of control over the dialogue, straying drastically from her proposed object of persuasion. This is of course another interesting way of conveying mental distress.

boldly to adapt conventional dramatic forms and use them in a highly suggestive way.[44]

The same cannot be said of Pradon. As in Racine's play, Pradon's Phèdre uses monologue-within-dialogue when she first appears on stage (I. 3) and confesses her love to her trusted friend (though in Pradon's play the trusted friend is ironically Aricie, Phèdre's rival). It is instructive to contrast the monologue of Pradon's Phèdre with the speeches of Racine's Phèdre examined above. In Pradon's play Phèdre's monologue begins the scene:

> Arreste, Phedre, arreste, & cours plutôt cacher
> Un secret que l'Amour commence à t'arracher;
> Et vous, cruels Tyrans, impétueuse flame,
> Gloire, dépit, raison, qui déchirez mon ame,
> Secret fardeau pesant qui me fais soûpirer,
> Helas! pour un moment laissez-moy respirer.
> Princesse, vous voyez une Reyne affligée
> Dans les plus noirs chagrins mortellement plongée,
> Qui ne peut plus se taire, & qui n'ose parler,
> Et qui cherche partout qui peut la consoler.
>
> (*Phèdre et Hippolyte* 211–20)

Only the first six lines of this speech are monologue. The visual effects which accompanied the verbal representation of mental distress in Racine are mostly absent from Pradon's scene, except that Pradon's Phèdre does stop in her tracks, though the text does not make it clear why. Her monologue is deliberative in intention: she asks her overwhelming passions to give her a chance to breathe. Pradon does not, as Racine does, employ the obvious absence of rhetorical focus to suggest Phèdre's state of mind. Nor, unlike Racine, does Pradon play off the interlocutor's common-sense remarks against Phèdre's verbalized thoughts. Pradon's Phèdre does not need to be jogged back to her senses, but returns to them easily of her own accord, spelling out her sorry state for the benefit of Aricie (216–20). It is as if Pradon cannot, or does not

---

[44] C. Abraham speaks of the 'parallel monologues' and 'simultaneous litanies' in this kind of scene (*Racine* (Boston, Mass., 1977), 130). Such remarks are unhelpful for two reasons. They are inaccurate: only Phèdre is metaphorically deaf; Œnone in I. 3 tries to engage in dialogue with her. Nor does such a remark isolate the rare occurrences of the technique, effective because of their rarity. With similar vagueness L. Goldmann speaks of II. 5 as a 'dialogue de sourds' (*Racine* (Paris, 1970), 120).

wish to, convey Phèdre's mood suggestively, and instead chooses to let the character explain it herself. Moreover, any hint of mental distress which this speech may convey soon evaporates when Phèdre gets down to business, laying bare her plans for Aricie's marriage to Phèdre's brother Deucalion. Pradon's Phèdre is business-like. Hints of any lack of control are only momentary. This could be technical incompetence or unimaginative writing on the dramatist's part, but equally he could be trying simply to do something different from Racine. Indeed it might be said that the speech of Pradon's Phèdre is the sort of monologue-within-dialogue that one of Racine's earlier heroines might have uttered. For the accompanied monologue of Racine's Phèdre is very much the exception to Racine's usual accompanied monologues.

In a study of *Bajazet*, published over twenty years after the first appearance of *La Dramaturgie classique*, J. Scherer still insists that the essential function of the monologue in Racine's tragedies is to provide a lyrical expression of emotion: 'Le monologue répond, en effet, à des nécessités dramatiques nombreuses, dont la principale est d'ordre lyrique. Ce qui constitue l'originalité du monologue, ce qui fait sa fonction essentielle chez les auteurs classiques, c'est qu'il permet l'expression lyrique du sentiment.'[45] This chapter has aimed to question this traditional view of the monologue, which, though it may be partly true of earlier dramatists, certainly misrepresents Racine.[46]

If the traditional view of Racine's monologues is accepted, it will not help the critic or the audience to distinguish between Racine's monologues and that of Corneille's Dircé or that of Rotrou's Hercule, which work in different ways from Racine's. Corneille can, of course, write monologues which have the same dramatic and persuasive interest as Racine's, as the well-known deliberative *stances* of Rodrigue bear witness (*Le Cid* I. 6). But what might usefully be recognized is that, even when they are soliloquizing, Racine's characters are almost invariably orators, entertaining the audience with their verbal action.

---

[45] *Racine: 'Bajazet'* (Paris, n.d.), 135.
[46] In 'The Dilemma Monologue in Pre-Cornelian French Tragedy (1550–1610)', in A. Howe and R. Waller (eds.), *'En marge du classicisme'* (Liverpool, 1987), Howe argues that some of the long, so-called poetic set-piece monologues of Renaissance tragedy have more dramatic impact than is usually thought.

6

Persuasive Narrations

> Je présuppose icy d'abord un Poëte instruit en la Rhétorique,
> et en tout ce que les excellens Autheurs de cét art ont écrit de
> la Narration.
>
> (D'Aubignac, *La Pratique du théâtre*, 288)

The predominant kind of verbal action in a Racinian tragedy is
the interaction between characters who are engaged in acts of
persuasion. A less frequent kind is the monologue in which a
character engages with himself in an act of self-persuasion. To
these two kinds of verbal action d'Aubignac adds a third by giving
as an illustration of '*Parler*, c'est *Agir*' 'la Narration de la mort
d'Hypolite chez Senéque' and by saying that this is 'l'Action d'un
homme effrayé d'un Monstre qu'il a veu sortir de la Mer, et de la
funeste avanture de ce Prince' (*La Pratique*, 282). On the surface,
a narration might not seem to offer the scope for persuasive action
which scenes of debate and even monologue clearly do. Moreover,
it might seem odd to find d'Aubignac recommending narration as
verbal action immediately after he has drawn the Aristotelian
distinction between the dramatic and the narrative modes of presenting an event: 'Ce poëme est nommé *Drama*, c'est à dire,
Action et non pas *Récit*' (*La Pratique*, 282). In his chapter 'Des
Narrations' (part iv, chapter 3) d'Aubignac makes it quite clear
that narrations are problematic for the dramatist, as they can all
too readily be undramatic and boring (pp. 292–3). Yet narrative
is obviously necessary to some extent in drama, for the spectators
need to be sufficiently informed about the characters' fictional
world to be able to understand what they can see and hear. The
essential question is this: how can the playwright make his narrative dramatic?

1. DRAMATIC NARRATIVE: *BAJAZET*

In a careful study and application of the principles of narratology
N. C. Ekstein attempts to show how Racine makes his narrative
passages dramatically interesting.[1] She attributes four potential
functions to the *récit*: a narrating character can inform the spectators of an event unknown to them; he can inform a second
character of a similarly unknown event; he can, while informing
this other character, also seek to move him; and he can, while
informing the spectators, also move them.[2] The narrative is least
successful dramatically when the audience feels that a character is
narrating for no other purpose than simply to convey information
to them. The best narratives are those in which all four functions
are at work.

While this, in itself, is a useful framework in which to assess
dramatic narrative, Ekstein's book loses some of its force because
the rigid application of a narratological definition of narrative
leads her to consider two very different kinds of dramatic narrative as if they were the same thing.[3] She does not distinguish
between narrative which is not problematic in drama and narrative which is problematic, the latter being the sort discussed by
d'Aubignac in his chapter 'Des Narrations'. Much of what she
considers as narrative is in effect the *narratio* section of a deliberative or judicial speech. One example is from Hermione's outburst
against Pyrrhus, who has come to apologize for breaking off their
engagement:

> J'ai dédaigné pour toi les vœux de tous nos princes;
> Je t'ai cherché moi-même au fond de tes provinces;
> J'y suis encor, malgré tes infidélités,
> Et malgré tous mes Grecs honteux de mes bontés.
> Je leur ai commandé de cacher mon injure;
> J'attendais en secret le retour d'un parjure;
> J'ai cru que tôt ou tard, à ton devoir rendu,
> Tu me rapporterais un cœur qui m'était dû.
> Je t'aimais inconstant, qu'aurais-je fait fidèle?

---

[1] *Dramatic Narrative* (New York, 1986).
[2] Ibid. 8–10.
[3] For Ekstein a narration or *récit* is any passage containing two events expressed
as inflected verbs in independent clauses forming a chronological sequence and a
significant whole (ibid. 3).

Et même en ce moment où ta bouche cruelle
Vient si tranquillement m'annoncer le trépas,
Ingrat, je doute encor si je ne t'aime pas.

(*Andromaque* 1357–68)

Hermione is here using narrative, as rhetoricians recommended, as part of her strategy to persuade Pyrrhus of the depth of her love for him and to make him feel guilty at his hasty and tactless dismissal of her love. This is not, however, the problematic sort of narrative. It is almost perverse to discuss this passage outside its obviously persuasive context. Characters very frequently use a *narratio*, the second part of an oration, as part of their persuasive technique and the best way to assess its dramatic impact is surely to consider it, as I have done in the preceding chapters, in its context of a deliberative or judicial speech.

Such *narrationes* are best treated separately from those moments at which the dramatist needs to convey a good deal of information to the audience and has no obviously persuasive framework in which to do this. These are the problematic moments which d'Aubignac discusses in his chapter 'Des Narrations', and these are the moments which can particularly tax a dramatist's ingenuity in making action out of narrative.

I have already suggested in Chapter 4 how a dramatist might cope with this problem at the beginning of his play. He can invent an isolated and short-term conflict between a protagonist and a confidant, and allow the information to emerge in the course of their discussion. I showed how Racine achieves this with some sophistication in the opening scene of *Britannicus* between Agrippine and Albine. With long narrations containing a good deal of information for the audience the dramatist has to perform a magic act: he has to make them appear as if they are instances of verbal action.

This is much easier at the beginning of the play when, according to d'Aubignac, the spectators have fresh minds and are more receptive to the information which is being transmitted to them. Later in the play, however, the spectators become less tolerant of lengthy narrations, and if the dramatist needs to have recourse to them he must introduce them in a dramatically pleasing way.

For d'Aubignac the touchstone is whether or not the narration is presented plausibly: it must be plausible that the narrator knows the event (p. 301); he must have a plausible reason for narrating it to his interlocutor (pp. 301–2); the interlocutor must have a plausible reason for being interested in the news (p. 302); the news must be told in a plausible place (p. 302) and at an appropriate moment in the play (p. 302). These are the basic criteria for ensuring plausibility of presentation. Another remark of d'Aubignac's suggests how the narration actually becomes a verbal action. He is speaking about extended narrations occurring after the exposition: 'Dans la suitte de l'Action, elles ne peuvent estre recevables... si elles ne sont fort pathétiques, et soûtenuës par le mélange des divers sentimens de celuy qui parle et de celuy qui écoute' (p. 295). In other words, he is suggesting that even the long narrations designed to inform the audience of events must, in order to be successful, be presented in such a way as to create interest in the interaction of the two characters on stage, one narrating, the other listening. The personal interests and opinions of both characters must be in some way engaged in the events being narrated. The long narration, then, for all that it is principally narrative in form, can involve a degree of persuasion or manipulation by the narrating character.

This point has been noted by G. Conesa, who notices an evolution in Molière's presentation of narrative passages: 'Elles [les tirades narratives] ne se présentent plus comme un élément statique, nécessaire à la compréhension de la situation, et qu'il faut bien placer quelque part, mais comme un argument employé par l'un des interlocuteurs dans une situation conflictuelle.'[4] In the case of Racine, Ekstein's study of the obviously persuasive *narrationes* which occur in the course of a deliberative or judicial speech has the advantage of leading her to consider a possible persuasive, or, as she calls it, 'performative' aspect in some of the longer and apparently more independent narratives, often thought to be principally narrative rather than persuasive.[5] She comments, for example, on Acomat's account of the off-stage reconciliation between Bajazet and Roxane (*Bajazet* III. 2), and decides that there is a 'performative' aspect, but only a limited one: 'Acomat, unaware of Atalide's feelings for Bajazet, tells her an essentially

[4] *Le Dialogue molièresque* (Paris, n.d.), 32.
[5] 'Both conveying ideas and establishing a vision of a context fall into the category of *informative* functions. The functions of provoking or stimulating reactions could better be designated as performative' (*Dramatic Narrative*, 20).

informative récit, performative only to the extent that he seeks to reassure himself . . . that all has been resolved' (p. 102). Ekstein's study is useful in drawing attention to the fact that more happens in the longer narratives than has often met the critics' eyes. But the notion of rhetoric or persuasion is absent from her book. With this notion she would have been better situated to comment on some of the more obviously persuasive *narrationes* occurring in the context of a deliberative or judicial speech. She would also have been able to take further her identification of 'performative' elements in some of the longer and apparently independent *récits*.

While Ekstein underplays the 'performative' aspect, thinking that Acomat's *récit* is essentially informative, this *récit* in fact has an important persuasive aim, integral to the audience's appreciation of the dramatic situation. Acomat arrives to announce what he thinks will be happy news to Atalide and he intends to use this news as a means of broaching the subject of his own claim on her. All his words in this scene have to be seen in the light of his own central aim: to see the conspiracy succeed and to ensure his own future by allying himself with Atalide in marriage. What looks very much as if it is entirely narrative can, therefore, be viewed as a persuasive narration. Atalide interrupts Acomat's speech and obliges him to take a detour. Acomat is a flexible orator and, if he has not by the end of the scene said all that he had at the beginning perhaps planned to say, he seems to believe that he has said sufficient for him to be quietly confident that his conspiratorial and matrimonial hopes will materialize.

Acomat begins by summarizing the new state of affairs (843–52). Use of the first-person-plural possessive adjective and pronoun allows him to present his *mores* favourably, associating his own response with the presumed response of Atalide: 'nos amants sont d'accord' (843), 'un calme heureux nous remet dans le port' (844). In his summary he is careful to accord himself a central role:

> Je vais de ce signal faire entendre la cause,
> Remplir tous les esprits d'une juste terreur,
> Et proclamer enfin le nouvel empereur.
> *(Bajazet* 850–2)

He assumes that his conspiratorial role will appeal to Atalide. Acomat is presenting an image of himself without saying explicitly what his persuasive aim is. His technique is one of *insinuatio*. When he thinks that he has won his interlocutor's attention and sympathy, he broaches the subject of their marriage (853–60). He does this cautiously ('Cependant permettez...' (853)) and periphrastically, exploiting the *locus definitionis* ('le prix qu'on promit à mon zèle' (854)). Another sign of his caution is the sudden introduction of an element of *refutatio* before he has spoken clearly about his claim (855–6):

> N'attendez point de moi ces doux emportements,
> Tels que j'en vois paraître au cœur de ces amants.

The careful self-image which Acomat is trying to convey in this speech at the same time as he refers to the reconciliation of Roxane and Bajazet is, of course, ironically flawed. Because he does not know of Atalide's love for Bajazet, Acomat is led into making wrong calculations about the rhetorical strategy to use on her. Before he has even mentioned his intended marriage explicitly, Atalide interrupts in order to pick up his reference to 'ces doux emportements' (862):

> Mais quels sont ces transports qu'ils vous ont fait paraître?

At the same time she attempts to deflect any talk of her wedding (860–1). Acomat answers her with an enthymeme couched in a rhetorical question (863–4):

> Madame, doutez-vous des soupirs enflammés
> De deux jeunes amants l'un de l'autre charmés?

Atalide is not satisfied with this. She wants specific details about Bajazet and Roxane, and in particular she wants to know if they are about to marry. Her next questions produce the desired narration from Acomat. But, though she has prevented him from speaking openly about his marriage to her, he is still manipulative enough to give himself a central role in his narration.

The account which Acomat supplies of recent events is in effect an expansion of his opening statement. Atalide's question and her deflection have not really caused him to doubt any aspects of his presentation. He still lays great stress on the happiness caused by the reconciliation of Roxane and Bajazet. Indeed the first part of his account contrasts his desperate departure when Roxane's patience with Bajazet had run out with his joy at being recalled to witness the scene of reconciliation. While he stresses his distant observation of this scene (883), his interpretation of the actions which he sees (885–8) and his mention of the words addressed to him by Roxane (890–4) are sufficient to convince Atalide of a fact which she had been unwilling to accept earlier in the scene, namely that Roxane and Bajazet are genuinely reconciled ('ils se vont épouser' (904)). Atalide's 'Hélas à' (889), uttered in the middle of Acomat's account, must go unheard by the narrator. He pursues his story unaware of the effect which it is having on Atalide and returns, by the end, to another cautious exploitation of *mores* (897–900):

> Trop heureux d'avoir pu, par un récit fidèle,
> De leur paix en passant vous conter la nouvelle,
> Et m'acquitter vers vous de mes respects profonds,
> Je vais le couronner, Madame, et j'en réponds.

He does not return to the subject of his own marriage, but is content with the suggestion of an imminent new order and his own expectant wait for his reward.

Acomat's use of the word 'récit' (897) draws attention to his role as narrator. Yet to lay emphasis on the narrative aspect of this scene is to fail to give a full account of the dramatic and persuasive function of Acomat's words. Throughout the scene Acomat has the aim of persuading Atalide that she should give thought to marrying him. He first narrates briefly the off-stage reconciliation, because that serves as evidence that he is ready to accept his reward. He narrates the scene in detail only when Atalide makes him take a detour from his persuasive path. Even then he is unaware of the extent to which his oratory has been deflected. For he does not know of Atalide's real interest in Bajazet, nor does he pick up any of the verbal clues which Atalide provides for him in this scene. Would-be-persuasion has simply been masquerading as narration. Acomat's speeches are verbal action not by virtue of their being narrations (the act of narrating is not in itself a dramatic act); they are verbal action by virtue of the conflicting interests of the characters that are at play in the scene, and by virtue of the manipulative and persuasive intent with which he presents his story.

His speeches are an example of the type of discourse which, on the page, looks as if it is a narrative designed to inform the audience of an off-stage event, perhaps rendered interesting by the presence of Atalide. Such discourse certainly looks very different from the short *narrationes* which characters insert regularly into their deliberative and judicial oratory. Yet, on stage and after rhetorical analysis, Acomat's discourse can be viewed as persuasive narrative. To see persuasive elements in Racine's lengthy narrations is a way of appreciating their dramatic impact. Of course the audience may be interested in learning the information being related to them. But no less than when characters are engaged in debate or monologue, the audience can also be gripped by their persuasive strategies when they are narrating.

11. THE DEATH *RÉCIT*: *ANDROMAQUE*, *BRITANNICUS*, AND *PHÈDRE*

Such a conclusion might well seem premature without consideration of the most common sort of lengthy narration after expository narrations. It is not usual for critics to appreciate the death *récits*, which occur at or towards the end of so many tragedies, as persuasive narrations. D'Aubignac was no friend of the terminal *récit*: 'Quand ces longues Narrations se trouvent à la Catastrophe pour faire le dénoüement, elles sont entierement insupportables' (*La Pratique*, 293). According to d'Aubignac, audiences are far too keen to find out how the play ends to be willing to listen to lengthy narrations. Modern critics tend to defend the death *récit*, but on poetic rather than theatrical grounds.

Speaking of the *récit* in general, J. Scherer says: 'Il faut qu'il attire l'attention par quelque ampleur, qu'il soit un morceau d'éloquence...Le récit est construit selon les règles de la rhétorique.'[6] J. C. Lapp's reading is similar: 'Those famous "set-pieces" of Racinian tragedy, the *récits*, or passages of epic description, are, like the informative speeches of the exposition, detached from the action by their very nature.'[7] In *Racine's Rhetoric* P. France confirms these readings many times over:

There are many similarities between the speeches of formal rhetoric and the long tirades which form so large a part of these tragedies...To take

---

[6] *La Dramaturgie classique en France* (Paris, 1950), 235.
[7] *Aspects of Racinian Tragedy* (Toronto, 1955), 103.

one striking example, the *récit* of classical tragedy often recalls the funeral oration (p. 2).

The *récit* corresponds to the type of oratory known as the demonstrative, its aim being not just to tell us what has happened, but also to praise . . . to blame, to impress on the hearers (as on the audience in the theatre) the horror, singularity or magnitude of the events described. (p. 217).[8]

The conventional defence of the death *récit* and description of its attributes might be summarized as follows: (i) the *récit* offers a striking example of the impact of rhetoric on dramatic composition, being constructed according to the rules of rhetoric; (ii) the *récit* is an example of demonstrative oratory and, as such, is a noble piece of descriptive writing comparable to the funeral oration; and (iii) because of its form the *récit* is inevitably detached from the surrounding action. It seems to me that there are problems with all these responses to the death *récit*.

First, the view that the *récit* is a strikingly rhetorical part of a tragedy must, in the light of my analyses in earlier chapters, be rather doubtful. For the impact of the art of persuasion is surely more obviously in evidence in other parts of these plays. There are a good many speeches, like Oreste's ambassadorial address to Pyrrhus, Éphestion's embassy to Taxile and Porus, and Esther's to Assuérus, which lend themselves readily and unambiguously to analysis according to the precepts of the rhetoricians when they discuss *inventio*, *dispositio*, *elocutio*, and *actio*. While the figures of *elocutio* and the gestures of *actio* may well find their place in the death *récit*, nobody, as far as I am aware, has suggested that *récits* draw on the means of persuasion prescribed by *inventio* or on the conventional structure of an oration prescribed by *dispositio*: *exordium, narratio, confirmatio*, and *peroratio*.

It is far from obvious, then, that the *récits* are particularly indebted to rhetoric. It is other parts of these plays that are *strikingly* rhetorical.

The second supposed characteristic of the death *récit*, related to the first, is that it is an example of demonstrative oratory and, as such, comparable to the funeral oration. This too is doubtful. Of the three kinds of oratory (judicial, deliberative, and demonstra-

---

[8] See also *Racine's Rhetoric* (Oxford, 1965), 108: 'In classical tragedy the *récit* always stands apart from the surrounding action; it is a noble piece of descriptive writing in something like epic style and often, . . . coming at the end of the tragedy, it serves as a dignified and moving funeral oration'.

tive), it is above all the deliberative and judicial kinds that are suitable for transposition into dramatic form. For these two kinds involve the interaction of often conflicting orators and can interest an audience in the uncertain and usually important outcome of the debate. Demonstrative oratory does not lend itself to dramatic situations. Concerned most often with praising a person whom the orator and his audience will usually have agreed to be worthy of praise, the demonstrative oration can arouse none of that excitement resulting from the uncertainty of the outcome of the speech; demonstrative orations usually do not have an outcome.

Demonstrative oratory is composed almost entirely of *narratio*. There is no urgency to draw on *mores* in an *exordium*, or *probationes* in a *confirmatio*; though in the case of a funeral oration the speaker might well deem it appropriate to use *mores* in giving a favourable account of the deceased and *affectus* in a *peroratio*. It might seem tempting to latch on to demonstrative oratory as a means of explaining the apparently different rhetorical nature of the death *récit* when compared to the much more common deliberative speeches of Racine's characters. And indeed to go back to the beginning of the seventeenth century is to discover a wealth of demonstrative death *récits*. An example from Montchrestien's *Hector*, first published in 1604, shows clearly how the death *récit* can be presented as a demonstrative oration. The messenger precedes his narrative with a statement of the important event:

> Il est mort cet Hector des Troyens l'asseurance.
> (*Hector* 2094)

He goes on to tell not only the story of how Hector was killed but also to demonstrate just why he had been 'des Troyens l'asseurance'. The *récit* is constructed as a hymn of praise to Hector. Similes, for instance, are developed at length in order to contribute to the bestowal of praise (2137–46):

> Comme quand un faucon soustenu de ses aisles
> Descouvre le voler des faibles Colombelles,
> Qui retournent des champs et coupent seurement
> La vague remuant du venteux élement,
> Il se laisse tomber sur la bande timide;
> La pluspart fuit legere où la crainte la guide,
> Proye à d'autres oiseaux, mais celles-là qu'il bat
> Et de bec et de mains sur terre les abat:

> Hector fondant de mesme en l'Argolique armee,
> On la void sur le champ deçà delà semée.

The laudatory tone helps to orchestrate the grief of Priam, Hecube, and Andromache for the dead warrior. In this case and in this one respect, the analogy of the death *récit* to the funeral oration is valid.

But Racine's death *récits* do not work in the same way as those of Montchrestien. Oreste's narration of the death of Pyrrhus in *Andromaque* v. 3 is obviously no hymn of praise for the deceased. Nor does Oreste wish to prompt pity for Pyrrhus in his listener, Hermione. Burrhus's narration to Agrippine in *Britannicus* v. 5 cannot be seen as a demonstrative oration with Britannicus as its focal point. In *Bajazet* v. 11 Osmin has some kind words for the heroic way in which Bajazet met his death. Yet this emerges only incidentally in the course of a speech intended also to relate the deaths of Roxane and Orcan. The *récit* at the end of *Iphigénie* is concerned with far more than the fate of Ériphile. Of all Racine's death *récits* the only candidate for consideration as a demonstrative speech might be Théramène's account of the death of Hippolyte in *Phèdre* v. 6. But I shall suggest that to consider this primarily as a demonstrative oration is to overlook a different rhetorical dimension of the speech.

I have indicated why the description of Racine's death *récits* as demonstrative speeches comparable to the funeral oration should be viewed with some scepticism. There is another reason for scepticism on this issue and it is connected with the third point often made about the death *récit*: namely that it is a set-piece inevitably detached from the surrounding action. Demonstrative oratory is, of the three kinds, the one most geared towards the production of set-pieces in which the audience can admire the linguistic and stylistic virtuosity of the performer. J. Masefield defended the Greek messenger speech in these terms when Gilbert Murray's translations were first being performed:

For the first year or so, some actors were afraid of them: they were 'story-telling on the stage'. They soon learnt what opportunities a Messenger Speech gave to anyone who had any sense. Each Messenger at once has all the attention that has been artfully prepared for him, during the preceding hour or so. He enters upon a stilled house in which few even dare to cough. He finds a sort of malleable mind in front of him that he can play with as he will. A very few years after the first of these Greek plays in London, an actor said to me, 'No one has ever known a Greek Messenger Speech to fail: they are always wild successes'.[9]

Masefield's words are quoted by Lapp in *Aspects of Racinian Tragedy* (p. 103), who extends their scope to cover the effect of the Racinian *récit* (p. 104): 'One may assume that Racine's seventeenth-century audience reacted in much the same way to his *récits* as did the Victorian spectator to the Greek Messenger speeches.' But Lapp's assumption does not attend to the fact that the workings of the *récit* are controlled by a vital aspect of seventeenth-century dramatic theory. Theorists strongly recommended that at no point in a play should an actor step out of his role and appear to become an orator or poet addressing fine words directly to the audience. When this happens the speech becomes detached from the surrounding action. This is a danger which is particularly acute in speeches which are *récits*. D'Aubignac criticizes *Les Visionnaires* (1637) of Desmarets de Saint-Sorlin on this very score: 'Nous avons veû sur nôtre Theatre un Capitan, un Poëte, & un Amant visionnaire, sans qu'ils eussent à faire les uns aux autres, & leurs Recits ressembloient proprement à des Oraisons de trois Escholiers qui montent successivement dans la méme chaire pour faire trois Discours sans aucun rapport, liaison, ny dependance.' (*La Pratique*, 243.) D'Aubignac's recommendations for the presentation of *récits* enumerated in the first section of the present chapter are specifically designed to prevent playwrights from producing undramatic, poetic interludes barely related to the surrounding action. Given contemporary critical attitudes towards the *récit*, it would be strange if Racine went on to produce messenger speeches like those described by Masefield. It is not likely that Racine's death *récits* really are set-pieces detached from the surrounding action.

So far I have indicated why conventional views of the death *récit* might be inadequate. This might seem rather negative. If the death *récit* is not a strikingly rhetorical demonstrative oration set apart from the surrounding action, what is it?

The death *récit*, no less than other narrative passages like the speeches of Acomat analysed above, can be verbal action, if, as well as using the *récit* to transmit information to either the audi-

---

[9] 'The Joy of Story-Telling', *Atlantic Monthly*, 187 (Apr. 1951), 69.

ence or a character on stage, the dramatist also introduces some persuasive or manipulative intention into the words of the narrator. For d'Aubignac it is enough that Seneca's messenger in his *Phaedra* has been so frightened by the manner of Hippolytus' death that the narrator's horror as he conveys this information to Theseus is in itself sufficient to make his account dramatic rather than merely informative. Racine, however, takes even greater steps to ensure the dramatic nature of his death *récits*, building on d'Aubignac's suggestions in his chapter 'Des Narrations' and making of the *récit* almost the sort of persuasive confrontation that characterizes most of his scenes.

Dramatic convention accorded to the death *récit* its very own structure and content. It is important to know what the conventional structure and content are so that it can be clearly shown how Racine manipulates them to make of the *récit* a persuasive action.

The structure of the death *récit* is repeated time and time again by all dramatists of the period with only minor variations.[10] The narrator usually makes a concise statement of the event. This is followed by an exclamation from the interlocutor. Then comes the *récit* proper, which may be followed by further exclamations and which may even be interrupted by exclamations.

A close reading of a number of death *récits* also reveals certain features which are regularly treated. The narrator describes the scene and the protagonist before the momentous event. He points to the actions of the protagonist immediately before the death. The death itself is related with one or more elements of concrete detail. The last words of the character who is to die are often reported. If there were witnesses, their reaction to the death is described, and then that of the narrator himself. With this knowledge, it should be easier to see how Racine's characters manipulate their *récits* to persuasive ends.

Conventional elements can readily be perceived in Oreste's narration of Pyrrhus's death in *Andromaque* v. 3. There is an initial statement of the catastrophe:

> Madame, c'en est fait, et vous êtes servie:
> Pyrrhus rend à l'autel son infidèle vie.
> (*Andromaque* 1493–4)

---

[10] Scherer has demonstrated this in *La Dramaturgie classique*, 235–9.

This statement serves Oreste as an *exordium*: by telling Hermione that she has been obeyed, he hopes to capture her goodwill. There follows an exclamatory question from the interlocutor (1495). Then comes the *récit* itself. It begins with a statement of its subject (1495–6):

> Il expire; et nos Grecs irrités
> Ont lavé dans son sang ses infidélités.

In successive stages Oreste describes how he arrived at the temple; Pyrrhus's supposed reaction when he first caught sight of Oreste and the Greeks; the wedding ceremony (he reports Pyrrhus's words directly); the attack on Pyrrhus; Oreste's own departure from the scene of the murder to announce the news to Hermione and claim his reward. Like most *récits*, this one lets the spectators know the circumstances of the death of a character in whom they have become interested. But the informative function is far from being the sole function of this particular narration.

Oreste is not merely informing Hermione of Pyrrhus's death. He is also persuading her to fulfil her promise, persuading her to come away with him. To do this, he includes in his narration details which, he hopes, will make sure that the anger of Hermione is still fuelled against Pyrrhus. In other words, he exploits *affectus*. This is the point of his description of Pyrrhus's reaction to Oreste when the king first sees him (1501–4):

> Pyrrhus m'a reconnu, mais sans changer de face:
> Il semblait que ma vue excitât son audace,
> Que tous les Grecs, bravés en leur ambassadeur,
> Dussent de son hymen relever la splendeur.

Pyrrhus, as Oreste admits (1501), does not appear to react at all. But Oreste freely interprets Pyrrhus's feelings to be those of pleasurable defiance. This interpretation helps to make his punishment seem all the more justified both in Oreste's own eyes and, he would like to think, in those of Hermione. More particularly aimed at arousing Hermione's fury are the account of the ceremony and the reporting of Pyrrhus's last words (1505–12):

> Enfin, avec transport prenant son diadème,
> Sur le front d'Andromaque il l'a posé lui-même:
> « Je vous donne, a-t-il dit, ma couronne et ma foi!
> « Andromaque, régnez sur l'Épire et sur moi,

« Je voue à votre fils une amitié de père;
« J'en atteste les dieux, je le jure à sa mère:
« Pour tous mes ennemis je déclare les siens,
« Et je le reconnais pour le roi des Troyens. »

The pleasure and confidence of Pyrrhus, the double mention of Andromaque, the calling of the gods to witness that Pyrrhus's choice has irrevocably fallen on Andromaque and not on Hermione, all the details of this report are calculated to anger Hermione.

In addition to encouraging Hermione's fury against Pyrrhus, there is another aspect of Oreste's persuasive technique in the narration. Hermione's last request to him (1268), between Acts IV and V, had been that he made it plain to Pyrrhus

Qu'on l'immole à ma haine, et non pas à l'État.

Oreste is acutely aware that he has failed to fulfil this request, so aware that, when Hermione responds to his *récit* with the ambiguous question 'Qu'ont-ils fait!' (1525), Oreste interprets this as an accusation of neglecting to carry out orders and he attempts to defend himself (1525–33). Sensitive on this point, he constructs his narration in such a way as partly to gloss over his deficiency, and partly to include a defence of it. There is no hint of it until two-thirds of the way through the account. By this point he hopes to have aroused Hermione's hatred of Pyrrhus to such a degree that, when she hears of his death, she will be satisfied no matter how it occurred. When he does finally mention it, he does so in a way which, while making his non-involvement clear for the audience, attempts to excuse it in the eyes of Hermione (1513–16):

A ces mots, qui du peuple attiraient le suffrage,
Nos Grecs n'ont répondu que par un cri de rage;
L'infidèle s'est vu partout envelopper,
Et je n'ai pu trouver de place pour frapper.

The pejorative epithet describing Pyrrhus under attack ('infidèle') evokes the ruler's infidelity to Hermione and seeks subtly to relate that to the occasion of his murder. The audience and Hermione both realize that the Greeks killed Pyrrhus not because of his infidelity to her, but because of his disloyalty to his Greek allies. Oreste's excuse for not striking first (there was no room) is rather lame, and this, coupled with Cléone's reports of his hesitancy in the previous scene and his own avowed horror at the beginning of his *récit* (1497–8), makes it easy for Hermione and the audience to conclude that Oreste is pusillanimous.

In the first edition of the play Andromaque herself was present in this scene. It is interesting to note that Oreste used her presence to help him in his persuasive aim. He used her as a witness and, in his second and third lines in the scene, invited her to speak:

> Voyez cette captive: elle peut mieux que moi
> Vous apprendre qu'Oreste a dégagé sa foi.
> (*Andromaque*, 1st edn., v. 3)

Later, he drew attention to her in a similar way in his *récit*:

> Cependant j'ai voulu qu'Andromaque aujourd'hui
> Honorât mon triomphe et répondît de lui.

Despite Andromaque's function as Oreste's witness, it is easy to appreciate why Racine subsequently removed her from the scene. The audience is too interested in the interaction between Oreste and Hermione to listen patiently to Andromaque's account of her feelings at being twice widowed.[11]

Yet, in both versions of this scene, Oreste's narration not only informs Hermione and the audience of the manner of Pyrrhus's death; it also serves as a piece of persuasion and self-defence. A consequence of this is the considerable importance and interest to the audience of Hermione's reaction throughout Oreste's speeches. Oreste thinks that, if his persuasion and self-defence work, he will obtain Hermione's hand as his promised reward. Since dispatching Oreste to do the deed, Hermione has permanently wavered between wanting Pyrrhus dead and wanting him alive. Immediately before Oreste's arrival in this scene, she is in a vengeful mood (1484–92). But will it last? The audience realizes that, although Oreste's attempt at subtle persuasion may well work, it is equally likely to fail; and not only to fail, but to have been a waste of his breath. Ironically, it is the account of Pyrrhus's death that makes Hermione realize that she wanted him to live. As soon as this realization has hit her, Oreste's self-defence becomes, in Hermione's eyes, self-accusation.

---

[11] For further discussion of the different states of this scene see I. D. McFarlane, 'Reflections on the Variants in *Andromaque*', in W. D. Howarth et al. (eds.), *Form and Meaning* (Avebury, 1982), 109–13. He concludes that 'in terms of structure the original scene was a serious anti-climax' (p. 113).

Whilst Oreste's narration contains the conventional elements of the death *récit*, the fact that it is delivered by one of the accessories to the murder as a piece of pleading to the instigator, who is about to repudiate the crime, adds a dimension which keeps the audience alert as to the intricacies of the situation being played out on stage. Far from being a demonstrative oration, Oreste's *récit* is a deliberative speech with judicial elements, the dramatic effect of which depends largely upon the audience's observation of Hermione's uncertain state of mind in the immediately preceding scene.[12]

The death *récit* in *Britannicus* is a judicial oration. Burrhus's narration of the death of Britannicus was deemed by Victor Hugo to be an unfortunate substitution for a much more exciting scene: 'Si [Racine] n'eût pas été paralysé comme il l'était par les préjugés de son siècle, s'il eût été moins souvent touché par la torpille classique, il n'eût... pas relégué dans la coulisse cette admirable scène du banquet où l'élève de Sénèque empoisonne Britannicus dans la coupe de la réconciliation.'[13] Hugo tries to make Burrhus's account seem a dull alternative to the feast itself. Le Bidois goes some way to correcting this prejudiced perspective, suggesting that in place of the off-stage spectacle of the banquet, Racine supplies a different spectacle, equally, if not more, interesting: the visible reaction of Agrippine and Junie to Burrhus's news.

Regardez Agrippine tandis que Burrhus raconte l'attentat. Tout en elle respire l'impatience et la passion. Il le faut ainsi pour que la narration ait son point d'optique, comme il convient qu'aux premiers mots de Burrhus, Junie éperdue quitte la scène... Sa narration, comprise ainsi, nous offre des spectacles d'une rare beauté théâtrale.[14]

Le Bidois is certainly right to remind the spectator and particularly the reader of the presence of Agrippine throughout Burrhus's narration. But Le Bidois seems to remove all the attention from Burrhus to Agrippine, whereas Burrhus is doing more than inform Agrippine of something to which she can react in a visually interesting way.

[12] In *Dramatic Narrative* Ekstein too draws attention to Oreste's ironical self-justification, but generally she underplays the persuasive element in the speech (pp. 90–2).

[13] *Préface de Cromwell* in *Théâtre complet*, ed. J. Thierry and J. Mélèze (Pléiade edn.; [Paris], 1963), i. 432.

[14] *De l'action dans la tragédie de Racine* (Paris, 1900), 107–8.

Burrhus's narration is almost accidental. So shocked is he by what he has seen that he wishes simply to run away. But he is stopped by Agrippine, who demands an explanation:

> Burrhus, où courez-vous? Arrêtez. Que veut dire...
> (*Britannicus* 1611)

What Burrhus goes on to say is both a confession and a justification. Burrhus is not a neutral medium through which news is conveyed to Agrippine and the audience. His own response to the murder is as significant as that of Agrippine. His narration has much of the conventional structure and content of the death *récit*, but there are important differences. He delivers the news briefly as soon as he has been prompted to do so (1612):

> Madame, c'en est fait, Britannicus expire.

This is followed by exclamations of shock and horror from Agrippine and Junie.

Then, after Junie's hasty departure, Burrhus introduces the narration proper with the words (1616–17):

> Je n'y pourrai survivre,
> Madame: il faut quitter la cour et l'empereur.

The narration which follows must be seen in the light of this statement as a justification of Burrhus's sudden decision to leave Néron and his court. In the earlier parts of the action Burrhus has always been on the defensive when facing Agrippine. He has not wished to let her know of any of his fears about Néron's encroaching criminality. It is Agrippine who appointed him Néron's adviser (144), and now, very late in the day, he must tell her that his charge has irretrievably escaped his reins; he must explain why he can no longer retain his position; and he must convince her that he is not the bad influence on Néron that she has up to this point believed him to be. In short, he has to admit that his judgement has been at fault in so far as he did not reveal his fears earlier; and that, in the mean time, others have been able to propel Agrippine's son into crime.

Burrhus's account paints the reconciliation scene at the banquet (1620–8), and describes Britannicus's sip from the drinking cup and his collapse (1629–32). He dwells for some time on the reactions of those present (1633–42), before ending with a suggestion of his own reaction (1643–6). On the surface this looks simply like the transmission of conventional information. But in fact the young man who dies has relatively few lines devoted to him. Burrhus's stress throughout is on the horrific calm of Néron and Narcisse as they execute their plan. By stressing the collusion of the emperor with Narcisse, Burrhus clears himself, in the eyes of Agrippine, of the charge of corrupting her son. By lingering on Néron's coolness in crime, and in particular on his dismissal of the death as an epileptic fit (1637–40), he amply justifies his overwhelming grief and his desire to get away from Néron and the court. As a piece of oratory, in which *mores* are especially prominent as an indication of his good character, it proves to be very persuasive. Agrippine doubts no part of Burrhus's presentation, and makes it clear two scenes later (v. 7) that she has corrected her judgement of him (1695–6):

> Ah ciel! de mes soupçons quelle était l'injustice!
> Je condamnais Burrhus pour écouter Narcisse.

This makes it clear that in the mouth of Burrhus the death *récit* is a piece of judicial oratory.

It is possible to extend this observation about the way in which the death *récit* works as persuasive action to instances in others of Racine's plays. Though dramatically one of the least engaging *récits* (because it concerns a character of whom the audience has scarcely any knowledge), Antigone's narration of the death of Ménécée in *La Thébaïde* (III. 3) is presented as a deliberative speech. Ménécée's death is evidence that the oracle has been fulfilled and now Jocaste, Antigone's interlocutor, can be more hopeful. In the same play, Créon so exploits *mores* in his account to Antigone of the deaths of Hémon, Étéocle, and Polynice as to attempt to present himself in a good light and make his offer of marriage more acceptable (v. 3). Though, in the penultimate scene, Olympe's aim is simply to inform Créon and the audience of Antigone's suicide, the dramatic effect arises from the juxtaposition of Créon's shock on hearing the news with his immediately preceding confidence that Antigone would agree to marry him. In *Alexandre* v. 3 the ambassador Éphestion reports Taxile's death in such a way as to present Porus, then Alexandre's captive awaiting judgement, in a favourable light and so rehabilitate him in Alexandre's eyes. There is no time for expansive demonstrative oratory at the end of *Bajazet* (v. 11), when three deaths are summarily recounted in a single *récit* which, with the unexpected mention of Bajazet's death, is engineered to create surprise and shock both for those listening on stage (Atalide and Acomat) and for the audience. The lengthy *récit* at the end of *Iphigénie* (v. 6) certainly fulfils an important informative function. But it is a speech with judicial connotations. Just as Burrhus developed his narration so as to restore his good image in Agrippine's eyes, Ulysse does the same before Clytemnestre; narration and self-defence intermingle.

It is also from the angle of judicial oratory that the *récit* of Théramène in *Phèdre* v. 6 deserves to be approached. Though Racine was often accused of writing a long narrative poem for Théramène, the text suggests that the speech should be delivered as an attempt at self-defence by the governor who has just seen his charge come to grief. Thésée's opening questions provide the clue:

> Théramène, est-ce toi? Qu'as-tu fait de mon fils?
> Je te l'ai confié dès l'âge le plus tendre.
>
> (*Phèdre* 1488–9)

This anticipatory accusation requires a defence. The details of Théramène's narration seem to emphasize that it would have been impossible for any human being, let alone him, to prevent the catastrophe.

La Mesnardière found all the details in Seneca's version of this *récit* unacceptable. He took the messenger's account of Hippolytus' death as an example of a 'Narration extrémement vicieuse'[15] and explained (p. 358):

Là on verra un Personnage extrémement interessé en la perte de ce Prince, décrire si pompeusement la manière de sa mort, & dire de si belles choses sur l'orage furieux, & sur le monstre épouvantable qui tua ce chaste Garçon, qu'on jugera facilememt que ce brave Déclamateur a fait une haute imposture, quand il a dit que la douleur lui étouffait le discours, & l'empeschoit de raconter un trépas si déplorable.

The detail is so eloquent that the *récit* becomes implausible and the messenger appears to be no more than a declaimer. Yet d'Aubignac takes Seneca's *récit* as one of his examples of verbal action. Why? It could be that d'Aubignac is being unusually gener-

---

[15] *La Poétique* (Paris, 1640), 358.

ous in not pointing out those deficiencies in this *récit* that La Mesnardière noted. But when d'Aubignac gives this narration as an example of verbal action it is sufficient for his purposes at the time to draw attention, as La Mesnardière does, to the fact that the messenger must be motivated to deliver his narration. D'Aubignac leaves for his chapter specifically on narrations detailed discussion about what can make a narration an acceptable dramatic action, and in this chapter he criticizes Seneca for writing excessively long narrations (p. 294).

It is no doubt the detail in Théramène's *récit* which caused some seventeenth- and eighteenth-century spectators to express reservations.[16] Fénelon thinks that Théramène says far too much: 'Théramène, qui vient pour apprendre à Thésée la mort funeste de son fils, devrait ne dire que ces deux mots, et manquer même de force pour les prononcer distinctement: "Hippolyte est mort. Un monstre envoyé du fond de la mer par la colère des Dieux l'a fait périr. Je l'ai vu".'[17] Marmontel makes a similar criticism: 'Théramène raconte à Thésée tout le détail de la mort d'Hippolyte: la personne et le lieu sont bien choisis; mais ce n'est point dans le premier accès de sa douleur qu'un père qui se reproche la mort de son fils peut entendre la description du prodige qui l'a causée.'[18] It is significant that it is this particular death *récit* which caused such controversy. For Racine seems to want to include a detailed account of Hippolyte's death that had by the seventeenth century become a traditional feature of the dramatic treatment of the Phaedra and Hippolytus legend. His other death *récits* did not raise problems, precisely because he presented them as verbal, or persuasive, action in the way described. Yet the judicial connotations of Théramène's account seem to be Racine's invention. They are not found in Euripides', Seneca's, Garnier's, or Pradon's versions of the legend. Indeed the narrator in the first three of these versions is only a faceless messenger, who has no established relationship with either Hippolytus or Theseus, as Théramène has in Racine's version. Racine tries to have his cake and eat it: to include all the details of the death, but to justify them by the

---

[16] For a history of the *querelle du récit de Théramène* see Mesnard's edn. of Racine's *Œuvres* (Paris, 1865–73), iii. 271–2, 274–8.
[17] *Lettre à M. Dacier sur les occupations de l'Académie* (1714), quoted by Mesnard, in Racine, *Œuvres*, iii. 276.
[18] *Éléments de littérature* (Paris, 1879), ii, 412.

judicial context, in which Théramène is required to give the details in order to exculpate himself from the charge of negligence.[19]

Racine's use of the death *récit* might seem especially surprising after d'Aubignac's warning that terminal *récits* can be particularly tedious and undramatic. Racine seeks to ensure the dramatic impact of his *récits* by building on d'Aubignac's suggestions for the engagement of the narrator and the listener in the events being narrated. Racine's tendency is to introduce into his presentation of the *récit* an element of persuasive interaction.

The critic will search the later plays of Pierre Corneille in vain for any similar persuasive elements in his terminal *récits*. Corneille takes steps to ensure a degree of plausibility in the way in which he presents narrations. But in his plays these passages do not have the momentum generated in Racine's narrations by the interaction of the narrator and his interlocutor. In *Œdipe* v. 8 Nérine narrates to Jocaste's daughter Dircé and to her suitor Thésée the suicides of Phorbas, who was instrumental in bringing Œdipe back to Thebes, and of Jocaste. And in v. 9 Dymas tells them how Œdipe has blinded himself. All that is happening between narrator and interlocutor is the transmission of information. Nor is it the case that the listeners are able to use the information to reach an important decision affecting the plot. For the narrations themselves reveal the resolution of the plot. The same comments can be made about Lépide's narration of the death of Sophonisbe in

---

[19] Louis Racine attempts to defend the *récit* in his *Comparaison de l'"Hippolyte' d'Euripide avec la tragédie de Racine sur le même sujet*, which he read to the Académie des inscriptions et belles-lettres in 1728. It is interesting that his defence rests upon the notion of interaction between narrator and listener, albeit from a slightly different perspective from the one which I have discussed: '[Théramène] parle à un père qu'il croit encore irrité et plongé dans l'erreur; qu'il doit tâcher de l'attendrir par un récit touchant' (quoted by Mesnard, in Racine, *Œuvres*, iii. 276–7). J. Scherer in *La Dramaturgie classique* draws attention to the defensive nature of Théramène's *récit*, but does not point out Racine's peculiarity in this respect (pp. 241–2). It might be added that the defensive element in Ulysse's *récit* at the end of *Iphigénie* is also peculiar to Racine's version. The most famous modern study of Théramène's speech is L. Spitzer's 'The "Récit de Théramène" in Racine's *Phèdre*', in *Essays on Seventeenth-Century French Literature* (Cambridge, 1983). Spitzer considers the speech to be intended especially for Thésée and to have 'the function of driving home at last the truth of divine perfidy and human helplessness' (p. 214). The speech would then be an accusation against the gods, for which there is evidence, albeit slight: 'Par un triste regard elle [Aricie] accuse les dieux' (*Phèdre* 1584). Most recently R. Day has defended the speech on poetic grounds as one which demonstrates a symbolic and musical coherence ('La Poétique du récit de Théramène', *PFSCL* 17 (1990), 465–80).

Sophonisbe v. 7. His listeners simply imbibe the information. This death *récit* can be said to be one of the few which really do resemble a funeral oration and are examples of demonstrative oratory. For the *récit* is followed by comments from the other characters expressing admiration for Sophonisbe's pride and courage. In *Attila* v. 6 the Hun's death is recounted by Valamir to Honorie, both of whom are immensely relieved by the loss of the threatening tyrant. But, yet again, news of the death itself is the resolution of the plot. There is nothing uncertain or unexpected about the reaction of the characters to the news.

In the light of these few examples, it is possible to appreciate what lies at the heart of d'Aubignac's warning about terminal *récits*. As soon as the messenger has come on and announced the fate of the character in question the spectators know all that they need and want to know. Racine's use of the persuasive element prevents the audience from feeling satisfied too soon, for it provokes curiosity about the persuasive strategies being used and the response of the interlocutor. Racine's death *récits*, except in *Iphigénie*, never come so close to the end of the play as Corneille's, for Racine has found a way of introducing into them a new dramatic interest, which requires further interaction between the characters before the plot can finally be resolved.[20]

While I believe that the notion of persuasion contributes to the theatricality of Racine's death *récits*, I do not wish to convey the impression that a death *récit* which is not persuasive in the way that Racine's tend to be is of necessity inferior theatrically. In the first place, the degree of persuasion differs considerably between Racine's own death *récits*. Oreste's involves a good deal of persuasive manipulation by the narrator, while the persuasive element is less immediately noticeable in Théramène's *récit*. Moreover, there are many other ways in which a death *récit* might be successful in the theatre. It might tell a story which is gripping in its own right, like Taxile's last stand against Porus or Mithridate's against the Romans (though Arbate's account is not strictly a death *récit* as Mithridate is not yet dead). Alternatively the content might be such as would allow the narrator almost to act out the events that he is narrating. The audience could find this enthralling, as is

---

[20] Barnwell also notes Racine's extension of the action beyond the death *récit* in *Andromaque* and *Britannicus* (*The Tragic Drama of Corneille and Racine* (Oxford, 1982), 157–8).

suggested by the eighteenth-century critic Claude-Joseph Dorat with respect to the *récit* of Cinna in *Cinna* I. 3. Though not a death *récit*, it is, like some death *récits*, potentially monotonous unless acted with special skill. Dorat notes how in 1720 the actor Baron won over a partly hostile audience when he came to the lines:

> Vous eussiez vu leurs yeux s'enflammer de fureur;
> Et dans le même instant, par un effet contraire,
> Leurs fronts pâlir d'horreur et rougir de colère.
>
> (*Cinna* 160–2)

There had apparently been some members of the audience ready to express their displeasure with Baron's relatively subdued style of acting: 'mais lorsque, dans le tableau de la Conjuration, il vint à ces beaux vers: *vous eussiez vu*...On le vit pâlir et rougir successivement. Ce passage si rapide fut senti par tous les Spectateurs. La cabale frémit et se tût.'[21] Grimarest in his *Traité du récitatif* suggests how dramatic *récits* might be read aloud. He lays great emphasis on performing direct speech in the appropriate tone (pp. 98–9): 'La Prosopopée, qui consiste à introduire une personne parlante, veut être prononcée différemment, suivant les personnes qui parlent, selon les personnes qui écoutent, & selon les raisons, & les sentimens que l'on exprime.' He gives examples of the different tones that the narrator might assume and illustrates the tone of regal nobility from Créon's account of the deaths of Étéocle and Polynice at the end of *La Thébaïde* (p. 99). He concludes that 'dans toutes ces occasions on observe avec soin de marquer la passion de celui que l'on fait parler' (ibid.). It is perhaps reasonable to suppose that the recommendations of Grimarest, although destined for the general reader, are related to the practice of actors on the stage. Actors could do much to make a *récit* exciting. It is easy to imagine the scope offered by the account of Attila's death to a resourceful actor. Attila is stopped in his tracks by a haemorrhage. The actor can imitate the threatening tones with which Attila warns those around him:

[21] *La Déclamation théâtrale* (Paris, 1771), pp. 82–3, quoted by A. Capatti in *Teatro et 'imaginaire'*, (Rome, 1975), 180 n. 172. The same anecdote is also told by the abbé de La Porte in his *Anecdotes dramatiques*, 3 vols. (Paris, 1775), i. 204, referred to by M. Descotes in *Les Grands Rôles du théâtre de Corneille* (Paris, 1962), 173.

> 'S'il [le sang] ne veut s'arrêter,
> Dit-il, on me paiera ce qu'il m'en va coûter'.
>   (*Attila* 1735–6)

The narrator might convey by gesture the implied physical activity of Attila as he hallucinates and imagines himself faced by the shades of some of those whom he has murdered (1743–8):

> Et déjà de son front la funeste pâleur
> N'opposait à la mort qu'un reste de chaleur,
> Lorsqu'une illusion lui présente son frère,
> Et lui rend tout d'un coup la vie et la colère,
> Il croit le voir suivi des Ombres de six Rois,
> Qu'il se veut immoler une seconde fois.

The actor might also suggest the horror of the haemorrhage, graphically described by Corneille (1755–64), as well as Attila's last faltering steps (1765). For all that this passage does not permit of persuasive interaction between the narrator and his listener, it none the less has much theatrical potential in the hands of an imaginative actor.

What Racine has to offer, that Corneille generally does not, is an extension into the death *récit* of the verbal battles which characters have been waging throughout the play. This adds an extra theatrical dimension to narrations, which seventeenth-century dramatic theorists agreed needed to be shored up by special efforts on the part of the dramatist. The death *récit* in Racine is not that stately funeral oration, set apart from the surrounding action, which critical tradition so readily assumes it to be. Racine's death *récits* are most often persuasive actions, which, like the monologues and the major confrontations between characters in conflict, invite the spectators to take an interest in the persuasive strategies of the characters and in the way in which these very strategies bring about a new state of affairs.

Conclusion

Ce poète qui a déclaré vouloir ne mettre en paroles dans ses
tragédies que ce qui ne pouvait s'y passer en action semble
préférer à l'action le discours: et il aime mieux, en effet, dire
l'action que la montrer. Car l'action de Racine est dans la
confrontation des êtres, dans les disputes, dans les délibéra-
tions intérieures.

(T. Maulnier, *Racine*, 76)

1. ARGUMENTS

The importance to Racine's dramatic technique of showing characters engaged in acts of persuasion has long been recognized by
modern critics.[1] In reiterating the importance of persuasion in
Racine's tragedies, does this book offer anything new?

Previous commentary on the persuasion undertaken by characters in Racine's plays, like that of Maulnier and Vinaver and
W. G. Moore, has, on the whole, been restricted to a few im-
pressionistic and generalized sentences or paragraphs, useful none
the less for their stimulating observations: '[The themes of French
classical drama] all seem to point to dramatic confrontations with
the impossible. Such confrontation is bound to be dramatic in the
highest degree. Since mortals can only accomplish the possible,
any challenge by the impossible must reduce them to absurdity or
ruin.'[2] While recognizing the dramatic importance of confrontation, Moore does not explore its practical implementation in plays.
The more substantial contribution of P. France in *Racine's Rhetoric*
(chapter 6) gives an account of some types of argument commonly
used by Racine's characters and describes the structure of some of
their more formally organized speeches. Nobody, as far as I am
aware, has attempted to analyse in detail their verbal means of

---

[1] In addition to Maulnier, *Racine* (Paris, 1947), see E. Vinaver, *L'Action
poétique dans le théâtre de Racine* (Oxford, 1960), 9.
[2] W. G. Moore, *The Classical Drama of France* (London, 1971), 131–2.

persuasion and to relate such an analysis to the theatrical impact of Racine's plays.

In insisting that speech constituted action in tragedies of their time, the seventeenth-century theorists pointed to the qualities needed in dramatic speech to make it theatrically successful. The quality most needed seems to be persuasiveness. Speeches are interesting in the theatre if characters are arguing with each other for and against different courses of action. The audience observes how characters set about their persuasive tasks and is keen to find out what the outcome of the persuasion will be. The best means available to the critic of analysing characters' persuasive strategies is to use the recommendations of rhetoricians about how to speak persuasively. These recommendations, although designed as tools for the construction of discourse, lend themselves to use as tools of analysis. I have examined characters' use of *inventio* and *dispositio*, for it is principally *what* characters say and, though perhaps to a lesser extent, the order in which they say it that contribute to the ability of their speeches to grip an audience. It must be admitted, however, that this approach could usefully be extended to an analysis of characters' persuasive use of *elocutio*[3] and *actio*. Analysis of *actio* would open up the question of how visual effects and tone of voice relate to the concept of verbal action.[4]

The notion of persuasion can readily be applied to scenes of confrontation between protagonists whether they adopt the role of formal orators or not. But the same notion is useful in demonstrating the theatricality of discourse in scenes involving confidants, in monologues, and in narrations. Indeed the resulting analyses suggest a modification of some critical commonplaces. Racine's confidants, often thought, with a few notable exceptions, to be dramatically uninteresting characters, can be brought alive when they are considered from the perspective of their persuasive interaction with the protagonists; Racine's monologues, usually seen as poetic interludes, often show characters arguing vigorously with themselves; and narrations, generally seen as long descriptive passages, informing the audience of something forced by dramatic

[3] P. France comments on the persuasive use of *elocutio* in *Racine's Rhetoric* (Oxford, 1965), ch. 6. But his main interest is in the dramatist's, as opposed to the characters', use of *elocutio*.

[4] On this see D. Maskell, *Racine* (Oxford, 1991), chs. 4–5.

convention to take place off stage and rendered palatable by poetic elaboration, can also, on closer inspection, be seen to be woven into the persuasive texture of Racine's plays. And, more generally, the view promoted by Vinaver that Racine's tragedies are essentially about discovery and the depiction of souls can yield some ground to the rather different view that they turn on the making of decisions and on the means by which decisions are made.[5]

From comparisons with other dramatists of the period it seems to emerge that Racine is distinctively successful at introducing relentless persuasion into his drama. Others, and particularly P. Corneille in his later plays, do not make their characters work so single-mindedly and incisively in pursuit of their persuasive aims; sometimes, and especially earlier in the century, dramatists preferred a more lyrical drama. Racine also seems more careful to present his characters and their aims in a way which allows the audience to savour their deployment of rhetorical strategies. Such conclusions are inevitably tentative until more detailed comparative analyses have been done. But rhetorical analysis would seem to be a promising means of discussing similarities and differences in the theatrical discourse of Racine and his contemporaries.

II. PROBLEMS

The method deployed in this book raises two major problems: the first relates to my assessment of the impact of scenes of persuasion on a theatre audience; the second, to the amount of text in any given play which lends itself to analysis in terms of verbal action, *inventio*, and *dispositio*.

Communication in the theatre takes place along two axes. Characters communicate with each other and, in some elusive way, the dramatist uses his characters' communication to communicate with the audience. Whatever special aims individual dramatists may have in communicating with an audience, the fundamental aim of every dramatist must be to keep the

---

[5] e.g. Vinaver sums up Racine's achievement thus: 'La poésie de l'égarement et de la reconnaissance se donna une tâche plus noble encore, et plus ardue: celle de déterminer [des états d'âme], de recréer . . . le principe même de la douleur, de l'illusion et des brusques réveils' (*Racine et la poésie tragique* (Paris, 1963), 175).

audience interested in what is happening on stage. Characteristically, what happens on stage in a seventeenth-century French tragedy is verbal action, or persuasion. This is quite different from much other drama, where persuasion can be of lesser importance and other things of interest can happen on stage. In Shakespeare's plays, for instance, where characters often seem to step outside their roles to deliver poetic reflections on the human predicament, much of the discourse could not be described as verbal action. Similarly, in modern television drama and in film the appeal to the viewers' eyes can often be made independently of any appeal to their ears. So, although verbal conflict is generally assumed to be vital to all drama,[6] its importance to the seventeenth-century French tragedian is particularly acute. This means that rhetorical theory can provide especially useful tools for analysing what is happening on the stage axis.

A problem arises, however, from my theatrical perspective. This perspective has required me to relate my analysis of what is happening on stage to the theatrical impact of these happenings, that is to the communication between the dramatist and the audience. In this respect my analysis is often subjective, and for two reasons. First, the theatrical context is too complex for traditional *inventio* and *dispositio* to be able to offer a framework for analysing the twin axes of communication. Secondly, theatre audiences were various in the seventeenth century and have been various since, varying both in their composition and in their response to plays which themselves, over the years, have been performed in many different ways.

When I attempt to assess the theatricality of instances of persuasion by stating that the audience reacts in this or that way, that the audience is interested in this or that strategy, or that the audience looks forward to such and such an outcome, I am inevitably being subjective. What evidence do I have for such reactions? And what audience do I have in mind?

I base my assessment on the evidence, albeit slight, of seventeenth-century reactions specifically to the persuasive activity represented

---

[6] e.g. E. Ionesco in *Notes et contre-notes* (Paris, 1966) twice makes this point: 'Le théâtre a une façon propre d'utiliser la parole, c'est le dialogue, c'est la parole de combat, de conflit' (p. 63); 'Le conflit existerait, autrement il n'y aurait pas de théâtre' (p. 298).

on stage.[7] It might be objected that this evidence of the audience's engagement in the acts of persuasion on stage comes from writers with a special interest in dramatic theory and practice, and that it is therefore not necessarily typical of most theatre-goers in the mid- and later seventeenth century. Racine's audiences were heterogeneous. It may be the case that the first performance of *Iphigénie* in the Orangerie at Versailles interested the courtly spectators in different ways from the play's more mixed audience on the occasion of its first performance in the Hôtel de Bourgogne. It may even be the case, if some observers of seventeenth-century theatre conditions are to be believed, that on some occasions the audience would have had difficulty not only in following but even in hearing the arguments of the characters on stage, because of the rowdiness of some spectators who, as well as talking, might have been robbing or even murdering those around them.[8] The variables are so great and the evidence so slight as to prevent any accurate reconstruction of the potentially different reactions to persuasive activity by a mixed audience of the seventeenth century. But scrutiny of d'Aubignac's *Pratique du théâtre* and the contemporary evidence in Picard's *Nouveau Corpus Racinianum* makes it abundantly clear that what audiences especially appreciated in tragedies were 'passions' and 'sentiments', and both these features are closely related to characters' attempts at persuasion. 'Passions' prompt a character to undertake persuasion, and 'sentiments' are expressed in the course of persuasion.

Bearing the contemporary evidence in mind, I have tried to give a plausible account of the reactions of an intelligent spectator who could hear what the actors were saying. There is no reason to suppose that such reactions might not also be those of a modern spectator.

An accurate account of the characters' attempts at persuasion is especially possible and necessary, because what is happening on stage in a Racinian tragedy is almost constant persuasion. This observation raises a second problem. What is the force of the

---

[7] Three essential pieces of evidence are quoted in Chs. 1, 2, and 3: d'Aubignac, *La Pratique du théâtre*, ed. P. Martino (Algiers, 1927), 310–11, and *Dissertation sur 'Sophonisbe'*, in Granet, *Recueil*, i. 143–4; Villars, *La Critique de 'Bérénice'*, in G. Michaut, *La 'Bérénice' de Racine* (Paris, 1907), 246.

[8] See d'Aubignac, *Projet pour le rétablissement du théâtre françois*, in *La Pratique*, 394.

word 'almost' in the phrase 'almost constant persuasion'? In fact, some scenes are not scenes of verbal action, as I have defined it, and do not therefore necessarily invite the sort of analysis that I have so readily accorded to most scenes. There are two sorts of scene which are exceptions.

The first exception is the chorus scenes in *Esther* and *Athalie*, exceptional because of the musical accompaniment to the words, and because the words are not the persuasive words of important characters contributing to the progress of the overall dramatic action. The words can of course be analysed rhetorically, and such analysis highlights their exceptional nature. Often there are instances of deliberative oratory, prayers to God, as in this stanza from *Esther* 1. 5:

> Tu vois nos pressants dangers:
> Donne à ton nom la victoire;
> Ne souffre point que ta gloire
> Passe à des dieux étrangers.
> *(Esther* 359–62)

Or there may be lamentations of a judicial nature addressed by individual members of the chorus to others, as in this example from the same scene (325–9):

> Hélas! si jeune encore,
> Par quel crime ai-je pu mériter mon malheur?
> Ma vie à peine a commencé d'éclore.
> Je tomberai comme une fleur
> Qui n'a vu qu'une aurore.

The young girl in this example is in fact addressing the audience as much as the other Israelites; what is prominent in performance is not so much the girl's own communication as that of Racine and the composer Moreau, who are using the girl to appeal, by a combination of words and music, to the pity of the spectators.[9] The choruses in Racine's last two plays are a departure from the normal functioning of verbal action, because, although they may be attempting to persuade God, the members of the chorus are rarely interacting persuasively with each other.

---

[9] The evidence for this reaction is in Mme de Sévigné's letter to her daughter of 21 Feb. 1689. See her *Correspondance*, ed. R. Duchêne (Pléiade edn.; Paris, 1978), iii. 508–9. She remarks that 'tous les chants convenables aux paroles... sont d'une beauté qu'on ne soutient pas sans larmes' (p. 508).

What of the second sort of departure from verbal action? This occurs in those scenes which P. France calls ' "utility" scenes or scenes of action'.[10] These are scenes which 'contrast agreeably with the tirades and *récits* surrounding them' (p. 150). In the light of my elucidation of the concept of verbal action, it has become clear that tirades and *récits* do in fact constitute scenes of action, and are, quantitatively, the most important scenes of action in Racine's plays. So the exceptional scenes to which P. France alludes might best be described as utility scenes.[11] These are usually short scenes, which may serve to make a liaison between two longer scenes, allowing one character to leave and another to enter. Or they may serve to inform the characters on stage and the audience of a piece of news, which the dramatist does not wish to develop into a long narration. Dramatically, these scenes are very important. Not only do they help to hold together the structure of the play; they can also supply some striking effects in their own right. *Britannicus* II. 4 is such a scene. Néron has explained to Junie how he intends to be secretly present at her interview with Britannicus in order to make sure that she coldly dismisses the young man whom she loves (II. 3). Junie begs to be spared this interview (685–6). At this very moment Narcisse arrives to announce that Britannicus wishes to speak to Junie, and Néron asks that he be sent in. Narcisse's announcement and Néron's response serve the function of engineering Britannicus's arrival. They are not part of any persuasive action. Yet their words are intensely dramatic because of the horror that they prompt in Junie.

Some scenes, however, which may appear to be purely functional utility scenes, are actually integrated into the persuasive action. The short scene at the end of Act III of *Bajazet* can strike fear into the spectators' hearts. Roxane has, in a monologue, been assessing her evidence in the case against Bajazet and Atalide. Zatime's sudden appearance in III. 8 and her announcement of the presence of the dreadful Orcan are like the arrival of an unexpected witness bringing new evidence for Roxane to assess. The sultana now realizes that she must reach a quick decision about

[10] *Racine's Rhetoric*, 150.
[11] Even this designation is problematic, as it seems to imply (wrongly) that these scenes are useful and that other scenes are not.

Bajazet's future. The presence of Orcan requires either the immediate death of Bajazet or the immediate accomplishment of the conspiracy against the sultan. This sudden injection of evidence ensures that, as the act closes, the audience's worries for Bajazet and Atalide are increased.

Utility scenes, then, may sometimes defy the sort of analysis which I have been promoting. But while utility scenes can be used to striking effect, together they account for only a tiny proportion of the lines in any given play. The small number of lines accorded to choruses and utility scenes, and the realization that even some utility scenes are integrated into persuasive activity, throws into relief the vast amount of text governed by the notion of verbal action. Purposeful acts of persuasion executed by characters battling with each other over important issues are the single most important source of theatrical pleasure in the plays of Racine.

III. RHETORIC AND TRAGEDY

'Sur cette scène transformée en champ de bataille, comment la muse tragique saura-t-elle élever la voix?'[12] Racine wanted to do more than simply hold the attention of his audience. He certainly congratulates himself in his prefaces on the degree of attention with which his audiences and even his critics listened to his tragedies, noting for instance that the thirtieth performance of *Bérénice* was as keenly heard as the first (p. 325). It is equally clear from the prefaces, however, that Racine wanted above all to make his plays work specifically as tragedies. By the late twentieth century the constituents of tragedy and the tragic have been variously identified.[13] But for Racine the tragic pertained to a particular kind of effect that a play might have on a theatre audience. In order to be tragic a play had to stir the emotions of the spectators, and especially to touch them, to move them to pity. The pleasure of a tragedy is closely related to the spectators' being touched by what they see and hear. All the recommendations of the theorists,

---

[12] Vinaver, *L'Action poétique*, 9–10. Vinaver's answer to the question lies in what he calls the poetic elements of Racine's writing. My own answer relates the tragic to the theatrical.

[13] For a useful summary of the various identifications of the tragic see J. Truchet, *La Tragédie classique en France* (Paris, 1975), 173–85.

according to Racine, are designed to facilitate the emotional impact of the play on the audience:

La principale règle est de plaire et de toucher. Toutes les autres ne sont
faites que pour parvenir à cette première. Mais toutes ces règles sont d'un
long détail, dont je ne leur conseille pas [à mes critiques] de s'embarrasser
... Qu'ils se réservent le plaisir de pleurer et d'être attendris (*Bérénice*,
preface, 325).

Pity is the chief tragic emotion and it manifests itself in tears. On
several occasions Racine happily recalls the tears provoked by his
plays. Henriette d'Angleterre wept when he first read *Andromaque*
to her (dedicatory epistle, 129). He implies that the spectators
too were moved deeply, if not to tears, by the sight and sound of
Andromaque's own tears (second preface, 132). It is because he
has written a play which makes them cry that Racine thinks
spectators of *Bérénice* should be especially grateful to him
(p. 325). According to Barbier d'Aucour's witty suggestion,
Iphigénie provoked such floods of tears that it caused a rise in
the price of handkerchiefs.[14] Racine, in his preface to the play
(p. 511), specifically equates its emotional effect with its tragic
nature:

Mes spectateurs ont été émus des mêmes choses qui ont mis autrefois en
larmes le plus savant peuple de la Grèce et qui ont fait dire qu'entre les
poètes, Euripide était extrêmement tragique ... c'est-à-dire qu'il avait
merveilleusement excité la compassion et la terreur, qui sont les véritables
effets de la tragédie.

To pity is added, in the Aristotelian tradition, the emotion of fear.

Given the importance to Racine of arousing emotion in his
spectators, is it not perverse to write at length about his means of
merely interesting an audience? In fact, when it is recognized that
for Racine the tragic is a theatrical phenomenon, the way is
opened to seeing how verbal action is manipulated by Racine to
produce tragic effects. For persuasion itself often plays on the
emotions. Verbal action is an almost constant feature of his
tragedies; making the audience cry and feel afraid is a spasmodic
feature. Spectators were surely not meant to cry from the opening

---

[14] '[La pièce] fait chaque jour par des torrents de larmes | Renchérir les
mouchoirs aux dépens des pleureurs', quoted by Picard in *Nouveau Corpus
Racinianum* (Paris, 1976), 87.

of Act I to the end of Act V. Other commentators, following Aristotle's lead, have examined the general conditions necessary for the arousal of the tragic emotions.[15] But is it possible to say what specific parts of a text will trigger the emotions of the audience?

It could be that rhetorical analysis will suggest an answer to this question. When protagonists appear, they are most often engaged in discussions of issues which are of considerable importance to them, if not matters of life or death. Sometimes they engage in desperate pleading in the hope of preventing catastrophe and ensuring their happiness. One of the three basic means of persuasion which they may use is of course *affectus*. Characters can, at given points in their speech or speeches, deliberately play upon their opponent's emotions. This is also surely something which makes a considerable emotional impact in the theatre. For when characters try to arouse one another's pity or when they try to frighten one another, the emotions are transferred from the stage axis to the spectator axis and the spectators too find themselves being moved to pity or becoming afraid.

The ultimate appeal to pity and fear comes in the form of the threat of suicide or murder. How often this threat, especially the threat of suicide, occurs in the tragedies of Racine! Jocaste's final persuasive card as she faces the two *frères ennemis* is based on *affectus*:

> Je ne condamne plus la fureur qui vous presse;
> Je n'ai plus pour mon sang ni pitié ni tendresse:
> Votre exemple m'apprend à ne le plus chérir
> Et moi je vais, cruels, vous apprendre à mourir.
> (*La Thébaïde* 1187–90)

As Jocaste leaves the stage, Antigone shows with her exclamations that her mother's use of *affectus* has touched her, but it has not touched those whom it was designed to persuade (1191):

> Madame . . . O ciel! que vois-je? Hélas! rien ne les touche!

---

[15] e.g. J. C. Lapp, *Aspects of Racinian Tragedy* (Toronto, 1955), ch. 6, on 'The Essence of Racinian Tragedy'; O. de Mourgues, *Racine* (Cambridge, 1967), chs. 3 and 4, on passion and the *héros moyen*; and H. T. Barnwell, *The Tragic Drama of Corneille and Racine* (Oxford, 1982), ch. 8, on 'Tragic Quality'.

It is surely not too fanciful to suppose that the spectators too are supposed to be affected by Jocaste's threat, and that this emotional effect is compounded by their seeing the evident insensitivity of the two brothers.

The first act of *Andromaque* ends with an emotional climax as both Pyrrhus and Andromaque use the ultimate appeal to *affectus*, one threatening murder, the other suicide. Once again the emotions work on the spectator axis as well as on the stage axis. The audience is afraid for Andromaque lest her son be killed, and pities her, as her distress drives her to contemplate suicide.

Even in that least bloody of tragedies, *Bérénice*, suicide is often on the cards. Each of the three protagonists threatens or hints at suicide as part of a persuasive strategy. Bérénice threatens suicide after she thinks that she has been rejected by Titus (1188–94); in v. 6 Titus threatens suicide in order to prevent that of Bérénice (1417–22); and finally Antiochus threatens suicide (1458–60), a threat which persuades Bérénice to offer the unhappy compromise with which the play ends.

These are just a few examples of the many exploitations of *affectus* by Racine's characters. It is the verbal action or the persuasive activity of the characters which, as well as constantly maintaining the interest of the audience in what is happening on stage, also serves as a medium through which a play produces its tragic effects. Spectators can be gripped by scenes of persuasion; they can also be moved by them to feel pity and fear. Rhetorical analysis illuminates the tragic effect; it also permits a truly theatrical exploration of Racinian discourse.

Appendix
Scheme of *Inventio* and *Dispositio*

This appendix lists those terms of *inventio* and *dispositio* important for my analyses. The meaning of each is explained and illustrated in Chapter 1.

Three kinds of oratory: judicial, deliberative, demonstrative.

Inventio
(*a*) Finding things to say:
  mores, affectus, probationes (*inartificiales* and *artificiales*)

Probationes artificiales include the following *loci*:
  1. *definitio*
  2. *partium enumeratio*
  3. *notatio*
  4. *coniugata*
  5. *genus*
  6. *species*
  7. *similitudo*
  8. *dissimilitudo*
  9. *contraria*
  10. *adiuncta*
  11. *consequentia*
  12. *antecedentia*
  13. *repugnantia*
  14. *causae*
  15. *effecta*
  16. *comparatio minorum, parium, maiorum*

(*b*) Forming arguments:
  ratiocinatio (syllogism, enthymeme)
  inductio and *exemplum*

Dispositio
(*a*) *exordium*
(*b*) *narratio*
(*c*) *confirmatio* (with *refutatio*)
(*d*) *peroratio*

Bibliography

The bibliography distinguishes manuscript from printed material. The section on printed material is divided into three parts. The first lists works originally published before 1800 (including, therefore, ancient works and modern editions); the second lists works published since 1800 (excluding modern editions of earlier works); and the third lists unpublished theses.

I. MANUSCRIPTS

CICERO, *Opera* (Lyons, 1540): Bibliothèque Nationale: Rés. X. 2293 (contains Racine's marginal annotations relating to *De Inventione, De Oratore,* and *Orator*).

RACINE, J., 'Extraits ecrits par Jean Racine des auteurs Latins qu'il lisoit à Port Royal en 1656', Bibliothèque Nationale: Fonds Français 12888 (contains extracts from Quintilian, pp. 239–493).

II. PRINTED MATERIAL

(a) Works Published before 1800

ARISTOTLE, *The Works of Aristotle,* ed. J. A. Smith and W. D. Ross, 12 vols. (Oxford, 1908–52); vol. xi contains Anaximenes, *Rhetorica ad Alexandrum.*

—— *Poetics,* in *Ancient Literary Criticism,* ed. D. A. Russell and M. Winterbottom (Oxford, 1972), 90–132.

—— *The Art of Rhetoric,* trans. J. H. Freese (Loeb edn.; London, 1926).

ARNAULD, A., and NICOLE, P., *La Logique ou l'art de penser,* ed. P. Clair and F. Girbal (Paris, 1965).

AUBIGNAC, F. HÉDELIN, ABBÉ D', *La Pratique du théâtre,* ed. P. Martino (Algiers, 1927).

—— *Dissertation sur 'Sophonisbe',* in Granet, *Recueil* (*q.v.*), i. 134–53.

BARY, R., *La Rhetorique françoise* (Paris, 1673).

CAUSSIN, N., *Tragoediae sacrae* (Paris, 1629).

—— *De Eloquentia Sacra et Humana libri xvi* (Lyons, 1643).

CHAPPUZEAU, S., *Le Théâtre français,* ed. G. Monval (Paris, 1876).

CICERO, *Brutus, Orator,* trans. G. L. Hendrickson and H. M. Hubbell (Loeb edn.; London, 1962).

—— *De Inventione, De Optimo Genere Oratorum, Topica,* trans. H. M. Hubbell (Loeb edn.; London, 1949).

—— *De Oratore*, trans. E. W. Sutton and H. Rackham, 2 vols. (Loeb edn.; London, 1942).

—— *Pro Publio Quinctio, Pro Sexto Roscio Amerino, Pro Quinto Roscio Comoedo, De Lege agraria*, trans. J. H. Freese (Loeb edn.; London, 1930).

CORNEILLE, P., *Œuvres complètes*, ed. G. Couton, 3 vols. (Pléiade edn.; Paris, 1980–7).

—— *Cinna*, ed. D. A. Watts (London, 1964).

—— *Pompée*, ed. H. T. Barnwell (Oxford, 1971).

—— *Writings on the Theatre*, ed. H. T. Barnwell (Oxford, 1965)

CORNEILLE, T., *Stilicon*, ed. C. J. Gossip (Geneva, 1974).

CYRANO DE BERGERAC, S., *La Mort d'Agrippine*, ed. C. J. Gossip (Exeter, 1982).

Dictionnaire de l'Académie Françoise, 2 vols. (Paris, 1694).

DU RYER, P., *Esther*, ed. P. Gethner and E. J. Campion (Exeter, 1982).

—— *Thémistocle*, ed. P. E. Chaplin (Exeter, 1972).

EURIPIDES, *Works*, trans. A. S. Way, 4 vols. (Loeb edn.; London, 1912).

FURETIÈRE, A., *Dictionaire universel* [*sic*], 3 vols. (The Hague and Rotterdam, 1690).

—— *Dictionnaire universel*, 3 vols. (The Hague, 1727).

GARNIER, R., *Two Tragedies: 'Hippolyte' and 'Marc Antoine'*, ed. C. M. Hill and M. G. Morrison (London, 1975).

GRANET, F., *Recueil de dissertations sur plusieurs tragédies de Corneille et de Racine*, 2 vols. (Paris, 1739).

GRIMAREST, J. L. LE GALLOIS DE, *Traité du récitatif dans la lecture, dans l'action publique, dans la déclamation, et dans le chant* (Rotterdam, 1740).

—— *La Vie de M. de Molière*, ed. G. Mongrédien ([Paris], 1955).

HARDY, A., *Coriolan*, ed. T. Allott (Exeter, 1978).

HORACE, *Ars Poetica*, trans. H. R. Fairclough (Loeb edn.; London, 1929).

LA MESNARDIÈRE, J.-H. PILET DE, *La Poétique* (Paris, 1640: Slatkine Reprints; Geneva, 1972).

LAMY, B., *L'Art de parler, avec un discours dans lequel on donne une idée de l'art de persuader* (2nd edn.; Paris, 1676).

LECLERC, M., *Iphigénie* (Paris, 1676).

LE GRAS, *La Réthorique* [*sic*] *française ou les préceptes de l'ancienne et vraye eloquence* (Paris, 1671).

LONGEPIERRE, H.-B. DE R. DE, *Parallèle de Monsieur. Corneille et de Monsieur Racine*, in Granet, Recueil (*q.v.*), i. 47–69.

MARMONTEL, J.-F., *Éléments de littérature*, 3 vols. (Paris, 1879).

Mémoire de Mahelot, Laurent, et d'autres décorateurs de l'Hôtel de

Bourgogne et de la Comédie Française au XVIIᵉ siècle (Le), ed. H. C. Lancaster (Paris, 1920).

MONET, D., *Invantaire des deus langues, françoise, et latine* (Lyons, 1636).

MONTCHRESTIEN, A. DE, *Two Tragedies: 'Hector', 'La Reine d'Escosse'*, ed. C. N. Smith (London, 1972).

NADAL, A., *Dissertation sur la tragédie de 'Mithridate'*, in F. and C. Parfaict, *Histoire* (*q.v.*), xi. 253–67; followed by remarks from the preface to the 1741 edn. of Racine's plays (pp. 267–71).

NICOT, J., and P. DE BROSSES, *Le Grand Dictionaire* [*sic*] *françois-latin* (Lyons, 1625).

PARFAICT, F. and C., *Histoire du théâtre françois*, 15 vols. (Amsterdam and Paris, 1735–49).

POMEY, F., *Le Dictionaire royal* (Lyons, 1687).

PRADON, J., *Phèdre et Hippolyte*, ed. O. Classe (Exeter, 1987).

QUINAULT, P., *Astrate*, ed. E. J. Campion (Exeter, 1980).

QUINTILIAN, *Institutio Oratoria*, trans. H. E. Butler, 4 vols. (Loeb edn.; London, 1920–2).

—— *De Institutione oratoria liber primus*, ed. C. Fierville (Paris, 1890).

RACINE, J., *Œuvres*, ed. P. Mesnard, 8 vols. (Paris, 1865–73).

—— *Œuvres complètes*, ed. R. Picard, 2 vols. (Pléiade edn.; vol. i, Paris, 1980; vol. ii, Paris, 1966).

—— *Théâtre complet*, ed. J. Morel and A. Viala (Paris, 1980).

—— *Alexandre*, ed. M. Hawcroft and V. Worth (Exeter, 1990).

—— *Andromaque*, ed. R. C. Knight and H. T. Barnwell (Geneva, 1977).

—— *Athalie*, ed. P. France, (Oxford, 1966).

—— *Bajazet*, ed. X. de Courville (Paris, 1947).

—— *Bajazet*, ed. M. M. McGowan (London, 1968).

—— *Bérénice*, ed. C. L. Walton (Oxford, 1965).

—— *Bérénice*, ed. J. Scherer et al. (Paris, 1973).

—— *Britannicus*, ed. P. Butler (Cambridge, 1967).

—— *Iphigénie*, ed. D. Achach (Paris, 1970).

—— *Mithridate*, ed. G. Rudler (Oxford, 1960).

—— *Phèdre*, ed. J. L. Barrault (Paris, 1946).

—— *Phèdre*, ed. R. C. Knight (Manchester, 1955).

—— *La Thébaïde*, ed. M. Edwards (Paris, 1965).

RAPIN, R., *Les Réflexions sur la poétique de ce temps et sur les ouvrages des poètes anciens et modernes*, ed. E. T. Dubois (Geneva, 1970).

Ratio atque institutio studiorum societatis Iesu (Rome, 1606).

Rhetorica ad Herennium, trans. H. Caplan (London, 1954.)

RICHELET, P., *Dictionnaire françois* (Geneva, 1680).

ROTROU, J., *Œuvres*, ed. Viollet-le-Duc, 5 vols. (Paris, 1820).

—— *Iphygenie* (Paris, 1641).

—— *Hercule Mourant*, ed. D. A. Watts (Exeter, 1971).

ROUSSEAU, J.-J., *Julie ou la Nouvelle Héloïse*, ed. R. Pomeau (Paris, 1960).

SAINT-ÉVREMOND, C. DE MARGUETEL DE, *Œuvres en prose*, ed. R. Ternois, 4 vols. (Paris, 1962–9).

SENECA, *Tragedies*, trans. F. J. Miller, 2 vols. (Loeb edn.; London, 1917).

SÉVIGNÉ, M., MARQUISE DE, *Correspondance*, ed. R. Duchêne, 3 vols. (Pléiade edn.; Paris, 1972–8).

SOAREZ, C., *De Arte Rhetorica libri tres* (Paris, 1612).

VILLARS, N.-P.-H. DE MONTFAUCON, ABBÉ DE, *La Critique de Bérénice*, in Michaut, *La 'Bérénice' de Racine* (*q.v.*), 241–59.

VOLTAIRE, F.-M. AROUET DE, *Œuvres complètes*, ed. L. Moland, 52 vols. (Paris, 1877–85).

—— *Commentaires sur Corneille*, ed. D. Williams, 3 vols. (Banbury, 1974–5).

(b) Works Published since 1800

ABRAHAM, C., *Racine* (Boston, Mass., 1977).

ADAM, A., *Histoire de la littérature française au XVIIe siècle*, 5 vols. (Paris, 1948–56).

—— *Le Théâtre classique* (Paris, 1970).

ARAGON, C. E., 'Étude de quelques actes de langage dans *Bajazet*', *Cahiers de littérature du XVIIe siècle*, 5 (1983), 75–106.

ARNAUD, C., *Étude sur la vie et les œuvres de l'abbé d'Aubignac* (Paris, 1887).

AUSTIN, J. L., *How to Do Things with Words*, ed. J. O. Urmson and M. Sbisà (Oxford, 1975).

BACKÈS, J.-L., *Racine* (Paris, 1981).

BARKO, I., 'Le Récit de Thésée', *AJFS* 2 (1965), 171–82.

BARNETT, D., 'La Vitesse de la déclamation au théâtre (XVIIe et XVIIIe siècles)', *DSS* 128 (1980), 319–26.

BARNETT, R. L., 'Sur une scène de *Bérénice* (v. 6): Étude générative', *Les Lettres romanes*, 31 (1977), 144–67.

—— 'Le Travestissement de la parole racinienne', *Studi di letteratura francese*, 5 (1979), 157–81.

—— (ed.), *Re-lectures raciniennes: Nouvelles approches du discours tragique* (Paris, 1986).

BARNWELL, H. T., *The Tragic in French Tragedy* (Belfast, 1966).

—— 'Seventeenth-Century Tragedy: A Question of Disposition', in J. C. Ireson *et al.* (eds.), *Studies in French Literature Presented to H. W. Lawton by his Colleagues, Pupils, and Friends* (Manchester, 1968), 13–28.

—— *The Tragic Drama of Corneille and Racine: An Old Parallel Revisited* (Oxford, 1982).

—— '"They have their exits and their entrances": Stage and Speech in Corneille's Drama', *MLR* 81 (1986), 51–63.

BARTHES, R., *Sur Racine* (Paris, 1963).

BAYLEY, P., *French Pulpit Oratory 1598–1650: A Study in Themes and Styles with a Descriptive Catalogue of Printed Texts* (Cambridge, 1980).

BÉNICHOU, P., *Morales du grand siècle* (Paris, 1948).

BENTLEY, E., *The Life of the Drama* (London, 1965).

BIARD, J. D., 'Le Ton élégiaque dans *Bérénice*', *FS* 19 (1965), 1–15.

BONNEFON, P., 'La Bibliothèque de Racine', *RHLF* 5 (1898), 169–219.

BOYSSE, E., *Le Théâtre des Jésuites* (Paris, 1880: Slatkine Reprints; Geneva, 1970).

BRAY, R., *La Formation de la doctrine classique en France* (Paris, 1927).

BRERETON, G., *French Tragic Drama in the Sixteenth and Seventeenth Centuries* (London, 1973).

BROCKLISS, L. W. B., *French Higher Education in the Seventeenth and Eighteenth Centuries: A Cultural History* (Oxford, 1987).

BRODY, J., '*Bajazet*, or the Tragedy of Roxane', *The Romanic Review*, 60 (1969), 273–90.

BROOKS, C., and WARREN, R. P., *Modern Rhetoric* (New York, 1970).

BROOKS, W., 'Chappuzeau and the *Orateur*: A Question of Accuracy', *MLR* 81 (1986), 305–17.

—— '*Harangue* or Dialogue? The Publicity of the *Orateurs* on the French Stage, 1634–1673', *SCFS* 8 (1986), 166–76.

BUSSOM, T. W., *A Rival of Racine: Pradon, His Life and Dramatic Works* (Paris, 1922).

BUTLER, P., *Classicisme et baroque dans l'œuvre de Racine* (Paris, 1959).

CAMPBELL, J., 'The Tragedy of *Britannicus*', *FS* 37 (1983), 391–403.

CAMPION, E. J., '"Inventio" and "Amplificatio" in Louis Bourdaloue's "Sermon sur le jugement téméraire"', *Newsletter of the Society for Seventeenth-Century French Studies*, 4 (1982), 88–95.

CAPATTI, A., *Teatro e 'imaginaire': Pubblico e attori in Racine* (Rome, 1975).

CAVE, T., *Recognitions: A Study in Poetics* (Oxford, 1988).

CLARKE, M. L., *Rhetoric at Rome* (London, 1953).

COENEN, H. G., *Elemente der Racineschen Dialogtechnik* (Münster, 1961).

COLLINS, D. A., *Thomas Corneille: Protean Dramatist* (The Hague, 1966).

CONESA, G., *Le Dialogue molièresque: Étude stylistique et dramatique* (Paris, n.d.).

COUSIN, J., 'Rhétorique latine et classicisme français', *Revue des cours et conférences*, 1932–3 (7 articles on rhetoric; iii and iv on tragedy, pp. 159–68, 234–43).

COUTON, G., *La Vieillesse de Corneille (1658–84)* (Paris, 1949).

—— *Corneille et la tragédie politique* (Paris, 1984).

CURTIUS, E. R., *European Literature and the Latin Middle Ages*, trans. W. R. Trask (London, 1953).

DAINVILLE, F. DE, *Naissance de l'humanisme moderne* (Paris, 1940).

—— 'L'Évolution de l'enseignement de la rhétorique au XVIIe siècle', *DSS* 80–1 (1968), 19–43.

DAVIDSON, H. M., *Audience, Words and Art: Studies in Seventeenth-Century Rhetoric* ([Columbus], OH, 1965).

—— 'Pratique et rhétorique du théâtre: Étude sur le vocabulaire et la méthode de d'Aubignac', in M. Fumaroli (ed.), *Critique et création littéraires en France au XVIIe siècle* (Paris, 1977), 169–75.

DAWSON, S. W., *Drama and the Dramatic* (London, 1970).

DAY, R., 'La Poétique du récit de Théramène', *PFSCL* 17 (1990), 465–80.

DECLERCQ, G., 'L'Énonciation et la personne de l'orateur dans le texte dramatique', in G. Maurand (ed.), *Pouvoir et dire: Actes du colloque d'Albi: Langages et significations, 1982* (Toulouse, n.d.), 268–94.

—— 'Crime et argument: La persuasion dans *Britannicus* acte IV, scène 4', in *Lalies: Actes des sessions de linguistique et de littérature (Aussois, 1er–6 septembre 1981)* (Paris, 1984), 165–75.

—— 'La Ruse oratoire dans les tragédies de Racine', *Cahiers de littérature du XVIIe siècle*, 6 (1984), 115–23.

—— 'Le Lieu commun dans les tragédies de Racine: Topique, poétique et mémoire à l'âge classique', *DSS* 150 (1986), 43–60.

—— 'Stylistique et rhétorique au XVIIe siècle: L'analyse du texte littéraire classique', *DSS* 152 (1986), 207–22.

DEFRENNE, M., 'Récits et architecture dramatique dans *Bajazet* de Racine', *Travaux de linguistique et de littérature*, 19 (1981), 53–70.

DELCROIX, M., *Le Sacré dans les tragédies profanes de Racine* (Paris, 1970).

DELMAS, C., *Mythologie et mythe dans le théâtre français (1650–76)* (Geneva, 1985).

DESCOTES, M., *Les Grands Rôles du théâtre de Jean Racine* (Paris, 1957).

—— *Les Grands Rôles du théâtre de Corneille* (Paris, 1962).

DICKSON, W. J., 'Corneille's Use of Judicial Rhetoric: The Last Act of *Horace*', *SCFS* 10 (1988), 23–39.

DIXON, P., *Rhetoric* (London, 1971).

DU PASQUIER, C., '*Les Plaideurs* de Racine et l'éloquence judiciaire *sous Louis XIV*, leçon d'ouverture du cours d'histoire de l'éloquence judiciaire prononcée à l'université de Neuchâtel (Paris, 1919).

DUPONT-FERRIER, G., *Du Collège de Clermont au Lycée Louis-le-Grand (1563–1920)*, 3 vols. (Paris, 1921–5).

EDWARDS, M., 'Créon, homme de théâtre' *JR* (1963), 67–81.

EKSTEIN, N. C., *Dramatic Narrative: Racine's 'Récits'* (New York, 1986).

ELAM, K., *The Semiotics of Theatre and Drama* (London, 1980).

FLOWERS, M. L., *Sentence Structure and Characterization in the Tragedies of Jean Racine* (Rutherford, NJ, 1979).

FORD, P. J., 'Neo-Latin Literature in Seventeenth-Century France', *Newsletter of the Society for Seventeenth-Century French Studies*, 3 (1981), 60–70.

FORESTIER, G., *Le Théâtre dans le théâtre sur la scène française du XVIIe siècle* (Geneva, 1981).

FRANCE, P., *Racine's Rhetoric* (Oxford, 1965).

—— 'Racine', in J. Cruickshank (ed.), *French Literature and its Background*, ii. *The Seventeenth Century* (Oxford, 1969), 168–86.

—— *Rhetoric and Truth in France: Descartes to Diderot* (Oxford, 1972).

—— *Racine: 'Andromaque'* (London, 1977).

—— 'Rhetoric and Modern Literary Analysis', *Essays in Poetics*, 5 (1980), 1–14.

—— 'The Uses of Rhetoric', *History of European Ideas*, 1 (1981), 133–41.

FREEMAN, B. C., and BATSON, A., *Concordance du théâtre et des poésies de Jean Racine*, 2 vols. (Ithaca, NY, 1968).

FUMAROLI, M., 'Rhétorique et dramaturgie dans l'*Illusion comique* de Corneille', *DSS* 80–1 (1968), 107–32.

—— 'Rhétorique et dramaturgie: Le Statut du personnage dans la tragédie classique', *Revue d'histoire du théâtre*, 24 (1972), 223–50.

—— (ed.), *Critique et création littéraire en France au XVIIe siècle* (Paris, 1977).

—— *L'Age de l'éloquence: Rhétorique et 'res litteraria' de la Renaissance au seuil de l'époque classique* (Geneva, 1980).

GENETTE, G., 'Rhétorique et enseignement', in *Figures*, 3 vols. (Paris, 1966–72), ii. 23–42.

GOLDMANN, L., *Racine: Essai* (Paris, 1970).

—— *Le Dieu caché: Étude sur la vision tragique dans les 'Pensées' de Pascal et dans le théâtre de Racine* (Paris, 1959).

GOODDEN, A., *'Actio' and Persuasion: Dramatic Performance in Eighteenth-Century France* (Oxford, 1986).

GOODKIN, R. E., 'The Performed Letter, or, How Words Do Things in Racine', *PFSCL* 17 (1990), 85–102.

GORDON, A. L., *Ronsard et la rhétorique* (Geneva, 1970).

GOSSIP, C. J., *An Introduction to French Classical Tragedy* (London, 1981).

GREAR, A., 'A Background to Diderot's *Paradoxe sur le comédien*: The Role of the Imagination in Spoken Expression of Emotion, 1600–1750', *Forum for Modern Language Studies*, 21 (1985), 225–38.

GRIFFITHS, R., 'The Influence of Formulary Rhetoric upon French Renaissance Tragedy', *MLR* 59 (1964), 201–8.

—— *The Dramatic Technique of Antoine de Montchrestien: Rhetoric and Style in French Renaissance Tragedy* (Oxford, 1970).

HARWOOD, S., 'Logic and Emotion: The Structure of Orations and the Uses of Rhetorical Figures in Corneille', *PFSCL* 3 (1975), 23–32.

—— *Rhetoric in the Tragedies of Corneille* (New Orleans, 1977).

HAWCROFT, M., 'Racine, Rhetoric, and the Death *Récit*', *MLR* 84 (1989), 26–36.

HERRICK, M. T., *Comic Theory in the Sixteenth Century* (Urbana, Ill., 1964).

HEYNDELS, I., *Le Conflit racinien: Esquisse d'un système tragique* (Brussels, 1985).

HIGMAN, F. M., *The Style of John Calvin in his French Polemical Treatises* (Oxford, 1967).

HOUSTON, J. P., *The Rhetoric of Poetry in the Renaissance and Seventeenth Century* (Baton Rouge, La., 1983).

HOWE, A., 'The Dilemma Monologue in Pre-Cornelian French Tragedy (1550–1610)', in A. Howe and R. Waller (eds.), *'En marge du classicisme': Essays on the French Theatre from the Renaissance to the Enlightenment* (Liverpool, 1987), 27–63.

HUGO, V., *Théâtre complet*, ed. J. Thierry and J. Mélèze, 2 vols. (Pléiade edn.; [Paris], 1963–4).

IONESCO, E., *Notes et contre-notes* (Paris, 1966).

JASINSKI, R., *Vers le vrai Racine*, 2 vols. (Paris, 1958).

JONDORF, G., '"An Aimless Rhetoric"? Theme and Structure in Jacques de la Taille's *Alexandre*', *FS* 41 (1987), 267–82.

JOSEPH, B., *Elizabethan Acting* (Oxford, 1964).

JOSEPH, (SISTER) M., *Shakespeare's Use of the Arts of Language* (New York, 1966).

KENNEDY, G., *The Art of Persuasion in Greece* (London, 1963).

—— *The Art of Rhetoric in the Roman World* (Princeton, NJ, 1972).

—— *Classical Rhetoric and its Christian and Secular Tradition from Ancient to Modern Times* (Chapel Hill, NC, 1980).

KIBÉDI-VARGA, A., *Rhétorique et littérature: Étude de structures classiques* (Paris, 1970).

—— 'Analyses d'une tragédie [*Sertorius*]', *Het Franse Boek*, 40 (1970), 55–63.

—— 'La Perspective tragique: Éléments pour une analyse formelle de la tragédie classique', *RHLF* 70 (1970), 918–30.

—— 'L'Invention', in *Mélanges de langues et de littératures romanes offerts à Lein Geschiere par ses amis, collègues et élèves* (Amsterdam, 1975), 145–51.

—— 'Analyse textuelle: Relire *Le Cid*', *Het Franse Boek*, 47 (1977), 14–18.

—— 'Rhetoric, a Story or a System? A Challenge to Historians of Renaissance Rhetoric', in J. J. Murphy (ed.), *Renaissance Eloquence: Studies in the Theory and Practice of Renaissance Rhetoric* (Berkeley, Calif., 1983), 84–91.

—— 'L'Histoire de la rhétorique et la rhétorique des genres', *Rhetorica*, 3 (1985), 201–21.

KNIGHT, R. C., *Racine et la Grèce* (Paris, 1951).

—— (ed.), *Racine: Modern Judgements* (London, 1969).

KÜNTZ, P., 'Esquisse d'un inventaire des ouvrages de langue française traitant de la rhétorique entre 1610 et 1715', *DSS* 80–1 (1968), 133–42.

LACROIX, P., 'Le Langage de l'amour dans *Alexandre le Grand* de Racine', *DSS* 146 (1985), 57–67.

LANCASTER, H. C., *Pierre Du Ryer Dramatist* (Washington, DC, 1912).

—— *A History of French Dramatic Literature in the Seventeenth Century*, 9 vols. (Baltimore, 1929–42).

LANHAM, R. A., *A Handlist of Rhetorical Terms: A Guide for Students of Literature* (Berkeley, Calif., 1968).

LANTOINE, H. E., *Histoire de l'enseignement secondaire en France au XVIIe siècle* (Paris, 1874).

LAPP, J. C., *Aspects of Racinian Tragedy* (Toronto, 1955).

LARTHOMAS, P., *Le Langage dramatique: Sa nature, ses procédés* (Paris, 1972).

LAUSBERG, H., *Handbuch der literarischen Rhetorik*, 2 vols. (Munich, 1960).

LEBEGUE, R., *La Tragédie religieuse en France* (Paris, 1929).

LE BIDOIS, G., *De l'action dans la tragédie de Racine* (Paris, 1900: subsequent edns. are entitled *La Vie dans la tragédie de Racine* and have the same pagination as the 1st edn.).

LOCKWOOD, R., 'Subject and Ceremony: Racine's Royalist Rhetoric', *Modern Language Notes*, 100 (1985), 789–802.

LOUGH, J., *Paris Theatre Audiences in the Seventeenth and Eighteenth Centuries* (London, 1957).

—— *Seventeenth-Century French Drama: The Background* (Oxford, 1979).

LYONNET, H., *Les 'Premières' de Racine* (Paris, 1924).

MCFARLANE, I. D., 'Notes on the Rhetoric of *Horace*', in T. G. S.

Combe and P. Rickard (eds.), *The French Language: Studies Presented to L. C. Harmer* (London, 1970), 182–210.

—— 'Reflections on the Variants in *Andromaque*', in W. D. Howarth et al. (eds.), *Form and Meaning: Aesthetic Coherence in Seventeenth-Century French Drama: Studies Presented to Harry Barnwell* (Avebury, 1982), 99–114.

McGowan, M. M., *Montaigne's Deceits: The Art of Persuasion in the 'Essais'* (London, 1974).

Masefield, J., 'The Joy of Story-Telling', *Atlantic Monthly*, 187 (Mar. 1951), 21–30; (Apr. 1951), 61–70.

Maskell, D., 'La Précision du lieu dans les tragédies de Racine', in the forthcoming volume of Vinaver Studies in French devoted to Racine.

—— *Racine: A Theatrical Reading* (Oxford, 1991).

Maulnier, T., *Racine* (Paris, 1947).

Mauron, C., *L'Inconscient dans l'œuvre et la vie de Racine*, Aix-en-Provence (1957).

May, G., *Tragédie cornélienne, tragédie racinienne* (Urbana, Ill., 1948).

Michaut, G., *La 'Bérénice' de Racine* (Paris, 1907).

Moore, W. G., *The Classical Drama of France* (London, 1971).

Moravcevich, J. A. McF., 'Racine and the Rhetoric of Naming', *PFSCL* 3 (1975), 11–22.

Morel, J., *Jean Rotrou: Dramaturge de l'ambiguïté* (Paris, 1968).

—— 'Rhétorique et tragédie au XVIIᵉ siècle', *DSS* 80–1 (1968), 89–105.

—— 'La Poétique de Racine', in P. Ronzeaud (ed.), *Racine: La Romaine, la Turque, et la Juive (regards sur 'Bérénice', 'Bajazet', 'Athalie')* (n.pl., 1986), 11–21 (followed by discussion, pp. 23–6).

Morello, J., *Jean Rotrou* (Boston, Mass., 1980).

Mornet, D., *Histoire de la clarté française* (Paris, 1929).

—— *Histoire de la littérature française classique* (Paris, 1940).

—— *Jean Racine* (Paris, 1944).

Morrissey, R., '*La Pratique du théâtre* et le langage de l'illusion', *DSS* 146 (1985), 17–27.

Mourgues, O. de, *Racine or the Triumph of Relevance* (Cambridge, 1967).

Munteano, B., *Constantes dialectiques en littérature et en histoire* (Paris, 1967).

Muratore, M. J., 'Aphorism as Discursive Weaponry: Corneille's Language of Ammunition', *L'Esprit créateur*, 22/3 (1982), 19–27.

—— 'Racinian Stasis', in R. L. Barnett (ed.), *Re-lectures raciniennes* (Paris, 1986), 113–25.

Murphy, J. J. (ed.), *Renaissance Eloquence: Studies in the Theory and Practice of Renaissance Rhetoric* (Berkeley, Calif., 1983).

Murray, T., 'Non-Representation in *La Pratique du théâtre*', *PFSCL* 9

(1982), 57–74.

NADAL, O., *Le Sentiment de l'amour dans l'œuvre de Pierre Corneille* (Paris, 1948).

NELSON, R. J., *Corneille: His Heroes and their Worlds* (Philadelphia, 1963).

NIDERST, A., *Les Tragédies de Racine: Diversité et unité* (Paris, 1975).
—— *Racine et la tragédie classique* (Paris, 1978).

OLGA, M. M., 'Vers une esthétique du confident racinien', *JR* (1964), 1–12.

O'REGAN, M., *The Mannerist Aesthetic: A Study of Racine's 'Mithridate'* (Bristol, 1980).

PARISH, R., '"Un calme si funeste": Some Types of Silence in Racine', *FS* 34 (1980), 385–400.

PHILLIPS, H., 'The Theatricality of Discourse in Racinian Tragedy', *MLR* 84 (1989), 37–50.

PICARD, R., *La Carrière de Jean Racine* (Paris, 1956).
—— *Nouveau Corpus Racinianum: Recueil-inventaire des textes et documents du XVIIᵉ siècle concernant Jean Racine* (Paris, 1976).

POCOCK, G., *Corneille and Racine: Problems of Tragic Form* (Cambridge, 1973).

POMMIER, J., *Aspects de Racine* (Paris, 1954).

REBOUL, O., *La Rhétorique* (Paris, 1984).

REISS, T. J., *Toward Dramatic Illusion: Theatrical Technique and Meaning from Hardy to 'Horace'* (New Haven, Conn., 1971).

RICHARDS, I. A., *The Philosophy of Rhetoric* (Oxford, 1936).

ROMANOWSKI, S., 'The Circuits of Power and Discourse in Racine's *Bajazet*', *PFSCL* 10 (1983), 849–67.

ROUGEMONT, M. DE, 'L'Acteur et l'orateur: Étapes d'un débat', *DSS* 132 (1981), 329–33.

SARCEY, F., *Quarante ans de théâtre 1860–99*, 8 vols. (Paris, 1900–2).

SARTRE, J.-P., *Un théâtre de situations*, ed. M. Contat and M. Rybalka (Paris, 1973).

SAYCE, R. A., 'Racine's Style: Periphrasis and Direct Statement', in R. C. Knight (ed.), *Racine: Modern Judgements* (London, 1969), 132–46.

SCHERER, J., *La Dramaturgie classique en France* (Paris, 1950).
—— *Racine: 'Bajazet'* (Les Cours de Sorbonne; Paris, n.d.).

SEARLE, J. R., *Speech Acts: An Essay in the Philosophy of Language* (Cambridge, 1969).

SEGRE, C., 'A Contribution to the Semiotics of the Theater', *Poetics Today*, 1 (1980), 39–48.

SELLSTROM, A. D., 'Rhetoric and the Poetics of French Classicism', *French Review*, 34 (1961), 425–31.

SHORT, J. P., *Racine: 'Phèdre'* (London, 1983).

SNYDERS, G., *La Pédagogie en France aux XVIIe et XVIIIe siècles* (Paris, 1965).

SOTER, I., *La Doctrine stylistique des rhétoriques du XVIIe siècle* (Budapest, 1937).

SPITZER, L., *Essays on Seventeenth-Century French Literature*, trans., ed., and with an introduction by D. Bellos (Cambridge, 1983).

—— 'Racine's Classical *piano*', in *Essays*, 1–113.

—— 'The "Récit de Théramène" in Racine's *Phèdre*', in *Essays*, 209–51.

STEGMANN, A., *L'Héroïsme cornélien: Genèse et signification*, 2 vols. (Paris, 1969).

STEINER, G., *The Death of Tragedy* (London, 1961).

SUPPLE, J. J., *Racine: 'Bérénice'* (London, 1986).

STEWART, W. McC., 'L'Éducation de Racine: Le Poète et ses maîtres', *Cahiers de l'Association internationale des études françaises*, 3 (1953), 55–71.

SWEETSER, M.-O., *La Dramaturgie de Corneille* (Geneva, 1977).

TAINE, H., *Nouveaux essais de critique et d'histoire* (3rd edn.; Paris, 1880;.

TOBIN, R. W., *Racine and Seneca* (Chapel Hill, NC, 1971).

TOPLISS, P., *The Rhetoric of Pascal* (Leicester, 1966).

TRUCHET, J., *La Prédication de Bossuet: Étude des thèmes*, 2 vols. (Paris, 1960).

—— 'Pour un inventaire des problèmes posés par l'étude de la rhétorique', *DSS* 80–1 (1968), 5–17.

—— *La Tragédie classique en France* (Paris, 1975).

—— (ed.), *Recherches de thématique théâtrale: L'Exemple des conseillers des rois dans la tragédie classique* (Paris, 1981).

UBERSFELD, A., *Lire le théâtre* (Paris, 1978).

VAN DELFT, L., 'Language and Power: Eyes and Words in *Britannicus*', *Yale French Studies*, 45 (1970), 102–12.

VAN DER STARRE, E., *Racine et le théâtre de l'ambiguïté: Étude sur 'Bajazet'* (Leiden, 1966).

VENESOEN, C., 'Le Néron de Racine: Un cas curieux d'impuissance verbale', *IL* 33 (1981), 130–6.

VICKERS, B., *The Artistry of Shakespeare's Prose* (London, 1968).

—— *Classical Rhetoric in English Poetry* (London, 1970).

—— 'Shakespeare's Use of Rhetoric', in K. Muir and S. Schoenbaum (eds.), *A New Companion to Shakespeare Studies* (Cambridge, 1970).

—— *In Defence of Rhetoric* (Oxford, 1988).

VINAVER, E., *L'Action poétique dans le théâtre de Racine* (Oxford, 1960).

—— *Racine et la poésie tragique* (Paris, 1963).

—— *Entretiens sur Racine* (Paris, 1984).

WEINBERG, B., *The Art of Jean Racine* (Chicago, 1963).

YARROW, P. J., *Corneille* (London, 1963).

—— *Racine* (Oxford, 1978).

(c) Unpublished Theses

GREAR, A., 'Rhetoric and the Art of the French Tragic Actor (1620–1750): The Place of *Pronuntiatio* in the Stage Tradition', Ph.D. thesis, Univ. of St Andrews, 1982.

MORAVCEVICH, J. A. McF., 'Monologue et action dans les trois premières tragédies de Racine et dans le théâtre de son temps', Ph.D. thesis, Univ. of Wisconsin, 1970.

SLAMOVITZ, H., 'The Impact of Juridical Eloquence on the Dramaturgy of Corneille', Ph.D. thesis, Indiana Univ., 1984.

Index of Rhetorical Terms

Italicized page numbers refer to an explanation of the term.

Index of Racine's Works

Italicized page numbers refer to detailed analysis of scenes.

Index of Names